Governance in South Asia

Thank you for choosing a SAGE product! If you have any comment, observation or feedback, I would like to personally hear from you. Please write to me at <u>contactceo@sagepub.in</u>

—Vivek Mehra, Managing Director and CEO,
SAGE Publications India Pvt Ltd, New Delhi

Bulk Sales

SAGE India offers special discounts for purchase of books in bulk. We also make available special imprints and excerpts from our books on demand.

For orders and enquiries, write to us at

Marketing Department
SAGE Publications India Pvt Ltd
B1/I-1, Mohan Cooperative Industrial Area
Mathura Road, Post Bag 7
New Delhi 110044, India
E-mail us at <u>marketing@sagepub.in</u>

Get to know more about SAGE, be invited to SAGE events, get on our mailing list. Write today to <u>marketing@sagepub.in</u>

This book is also available as an e-book.

————————ಬಿ☙❧ಬಿ————————

Governance in South Asia

State of the Civil Services

Edited by
K.S. Chalam

 www.sagepublications.com
Los Angeles • London • New Delhi • Singapore • Washington DC

First published in 2014 by

SAGE Publications India Pvt Ltd
B1/I-1 Mohan Cooperative Industrial Area
Mathura Road, New Delhi 110 044, India
www.sagepub.in

SAGE Publications Inc
2455 Teller Road
Thousand Oaks, California 91320, USA

SAGE Publications Ltd
1 Oliver's Yard, 55 City Road
London EC1Y 1SP, United Kingdom

SAGE Publications Asia-Pacific Pte Ltd
3 Church Street
#10-04 Samsung Hub
Singapore 049483

Published by Vivek Mehra for SAGE Publications India Pvt Ltd, Phototypeset in 10.5/13 Adobe Garamond Pro by RECTO Graphics, Delhi, and printed at Saurabh Printers Pvt Ltd, New Delhi.

Library of Congress Cataloging-in-Publication Data

Governance in South Asia : state of the civil services / edited by K.S. Chalam.
   pages cm
Includes bibliographical references and index.
 1. Civil service—South Asia. I. Chalam, K.S. (Kurmana Simha), 1948–
JQ98.A67G68   352.6'30954—dc23   2014   2014004949

ISBN: 978-81-321-1365-2 (HB)

The SAGE Team: Shambhu Sahu, Shreya Chakraborti, Rajib Chatterjee and Rajinder Kaur

Contents

PART I
Governance and Civil Service

CHAPTER 1
Governance and Public Service   27
Mohammad Hamid Ansari

CHAPTER 2
Constitutional Status of Civil Service in India   31
K.S. Chalam

CHAPTER 3
Civil Service Values and Neutrality   39
Bhure Lal

CHAPTER 4
Importance of Social Security in Good Governance   59
T.S.N. Sastry

PART II
Civil Service Reform in India

CHAPTER 5
Accountability in Public Service   79
N. Vittal

List of Illustrations

Tables

Figures

List of Abbreviations

ACC	Anti-Corruption Commission
ACC	Appointments Committee of the Cabinet
ACES	Automation in Central Excise and Service Tax
ACR	Annual Confidential Report
AEP	Afghan Expatriate Programme
AIS	All India Services
ANDS	Afghanistan National Development Strategy
ARC	Administrative Reforms Commission
ARMC	Administrative Reform Monitoring Commission
ASER	Annual Status of Education Report
ASI	Assistant Sub-inspector
BC	Backward Classes
BCS	Bangladesh Civil Service
BCSR	Bhutan Civil Service Rules and Regulations
BJP	Bhartiya Janata Party
BoP	Balance of Payment
BPL	Below Poverty Line
BPS	Basic Pay Scale
BSC	Bangladesh Public Service Commission
CAG	Comptroller and Auditor General
CAP	Capacity for Afghan Public service
CAS	Ceylon Administrative Service
CAT	Central Administrative Tribunal
CAT	Common Admission Tests
CBDT	Central Board of Direct Taxes
CBEC	Central Board of Excise and Customs
CBI	Central Bureau of Investigation
CBN	Central Bureau of Narcotics
CD	Capacity Development

CDS	Capacity Development Secretariat
CGST	Central GST
CIA	Central Investigating Agency
CIAA	Commission for Investigation of Abuse of Authority
CM	Chief Minister
CPMG	Chief Post Master General
CrPC	Code of Criminal Procedure
CSAT	Civil Service Aptitude Test
CSB	Central Silk Board
CSC	Civil Service Commission
CSP	Civil Service of Pakistan
CSS	Central Secretariat Service
CVC	Central Vigilance Commission
DA	Disproportionate Assets
DAC	Development Assistance Committee
DANICS	Delhi, Andaman Nicobar Island Civil Services
DDG	Decentralised Distributed Generation
DG	Director General
DGP	Director General of Police
DGRI	Directorate General of Intelligence
DGTD	Directorate of Technical Development
DM	District Magistrate
DoPT	Department of Personnel and Training
DPC	Departmental Promotion Committee
DPMD	Development Policy Management Division
DRI	Directorate of Revenue Intelligence
DSPE Act	Delhi Special Police Establishment Act
ECB	Election commission of Bhutan
ED	Enforcement Directorate
EDI	Electronic Data Interface
EG	Entrepreneurial Government
ESP	Educational Service Index
FARC	First Administrative Reforms Commission
FDI	Foreign Direct Investment
FERA	Foreign Exchange Regulation Act
FPSC	Federal Public Service Commission
GAR	General Administrative Reserve

GATT	General Agreement on Tariffs and Trade
GDP	Gross Domestic Product
GDS	Gram Dak Sevak
GNH	Gross National Happiness
GRP	Gross Rating Point
GST	Goods and Services Tax
HAG	Higher Administrative Grade
HDI	Human Development Index
HIS	Health Service Index
HR	Human Resource
HRA	House Rent Allowance
HRD	Human Resource Development
HRM	Human Resource Management
HSN	Harmonised Systems of Nomenclature
IARCSC	Independent Administrative Reform and Civil Service Commission
IAS	Indian Administrative Service
IB	Intelligence Bureau
ICS	Indian Civil Service
ICS	Imperial Custom Service
ICT	Information and Communication Technologies
IDLG	Independent Directorate of Local Governance
IFoS	Indian Forest Service
IFS	Indian Foreign Service
IGP	Inspector General of Police
IIM	Indian Institute of Management
IIPA	International Intellectual Property Alliance
ILO	International Labour Organization
IMF	International Monetary Fund
IMR	Infant Mortality Rate
IPoS	Indian Postal Service
IPS	Indian Police Service
IPSC	Indian Public Service Commission
IRS	Indian Revenue Service
IRTS	Indian Railway Traffic Service
IT	Income Tax
J&K	Jammu and Kashmir

JRY	Jawahar Rozgar Yojana
LBSNAA	Lal Bahadur Shastri National Academy of Administration
LEP	Lateral Entry Programme
LIC	Life Insurance Corporation
MBPA	Market Based Public Administration
MCA	Ministry of Company Affairs
MCP	Management Capacity Program
MCQ	Multiple Choice Questions
MGEP	Mainstreaming Gender Equity Programme
MLA	Member of Legislative Assembly
MNC	Multinational Company
MGNREGS	Mahatma Gandhi National Rural Employment Guarantee Scheme
MoE	Ministry of Establishment
MoGA	Ministry of General Administration
MoU	Memorandum of Understanding
MoWCSW	Ministry of Women, Children and Social Welfare
MSY	Mahila Samrudhi Yojana
NABARD	National Bank for Agriculture and Rural Development
NACEN	National Academy of Customs, Central Excise and Narcotics
NATO	North Atlantic Treaty Organization
NCERT	National Council of Educational Research and Training
NCP–M	Nepal Communist Party–Maoist
NGO	Non-government Organization
NPA	New Public Administration
NPM	New Public Management
NREP	National Rural Employment Programme
OBCs	Other Backward Classes
ODA	Official Development Assistance
OECD	Organisation for Economic Co-operation and Development
PAR	Public Administration Reform
PAS	Pakistan Administrative Service

PC Act	Prevention of Corruption Act
PDS	Public Distribution System
PFS	Pakistan Foreign Service
PIL	Public Interest Litigation
PLA	Personal Ledger Account
PM	Prime Minister
PPS	Pakistan Police Service
PPSC	Pakistan Public Service Commission
PSC	Public Service Commission
PSD	Public Service Division
PSEs	Public Sector Enterprises
PT	Personality Test
RAA	Royal audit authority
RAW	Research and Analysis Wing
RCSC	Royal Civil Service Commission
RGoB	Royal Government of Bhutan
RTI	Right to Information Act
SAARC	South Asian Association for Regional Cooperation
SAFEMFOPA	Smugglers and Foreign Exchange Manipulators Forfeiture of Property Act
SAG	Senior Administrative Grade
SAP	Structural Adjustment Program
SARC	Second Administrative Reforms Commission
SC	Scheduled Caste
SEBI	Securities and Exchange Board of India
SGST	State GST
SLAS	Sri Lanka Administrative Service
SP	Superintendent of Police
SVPNPA	Sardar Vallabhbhai Patel National Police Academy
SRB	Special Recruitment Board
SRO	Self-Regulatory Organisation
SRP	Self-Removal Procedure
ST	Scheduled Tribe
TFC	Thirteenth Finance Commission
UGC	University Grants Commission
UNCTAD	United Nations Conference on Trade and Development

UNDP	United Nations Development Programme
UNICEF	United Nations Children's Fund
UPSC	Union Public Service Commission
VAT	Value Added Tax
VPP	Value Payable Post
WTO	World Trade Organization

Preface

Bureaucracy in India has slowly attained the status of a Civil Service System like any other structure in an organised state. It has acquired and developed several institutions to replace the old structure of bureaucracy with modern institutions to make it more functional in a changing economy and society. There were many studies describing the character, structure and the progress of the system in India. There are also some autobiographical accounts about the system by retired bureaucrats. But, there seems to be limited literature on the system in the present context of numerous reforms both in administration and in economy connecting with the present status and exigencies of the civil service in India to meet the objectives of accountability, neutrality etc.

The Indian subcontinent was once under the umbrella of British administration. There are now about half a dozen independent sovereign states in the region after 1947. Each one of the countries has adapted the system to its changing ethos and vision. We do not have a comprehensive study on the region's present civil service systems. Therefore, a need was felt when the delegates of the national service commissions of South Asian Association for Regional Cooperation (SAARC) region met for the first time at the Union Public Service Commission (UPSC), New Delhi, in 2010. I had the opportunity to officially represent India in the conference and interact with my colleagues. I have mooted the idea of bringing out an edited volume incorporating the present status of Indian Civil Service (ICS) along with the status of service commissions in the region. I have received a very good response to my proposal.

I have entered the UPSC, New Delhi, as Member, from an academic background after serving as a professor of Economics and vice chancellor. I was studying the system as an academic ever since I joined the Commission and collected material from the Commission's library, including the articles published in reports and souvenirs of the

Commission. I sent a letter in my personal capacity to all our former and serving colleagues, including the chairman, UPSC, and some identified senior civil servants and academics to contribute to the volume. I received very encouraging support from every one of them. Similarly, most of the chairmen of the national service commissions of SAARC responded to my request and contributed papers. I thank Dr Mohammad Hamid Ansari, Vice President of India, who has permitted me to make use of his UPSC lecture to be part of this volume (on the dais that I shared with him on the occasion). I take this opportunity to thank Justice Rana Bhagwandas of Pakistan, Dr Pirthiman Pradhan, Commissioner of Royal Bhutan Civil Service Commission, for specially contributing to the volume. Dr B.K. Chaturvedi, Dr Bhure Lal, Dr N. Vittal, Ms Parveen Talha, Ms Humera Ahmed, Professor P.K. Saxena, Professor T.S.N.N. Sastry and Dr D. Francis were requested to make special contributions to the volume; Dr Madhav Godbole has permitted me to make use of his published paper. I express my sincere thanks to all of them for obliging to my request. I am grateful to Professor D.P. Aggarwal, Chairman, UPSC, and all the members of the Commission during 2005–11 for providing me with excellent cooperation, inputs and encouragement in the completion of this volume. I have tried to avoid as far as possible the recurrence of ideas in the contributions as they are written by senior officers at different points of time.

I take this opportunity to express my gratitude to the authors for their contributions. I acknowledge the help received from my friend Professor I. Ramabrhmam in identifying the topics for the volume. Mr Rajkumar, my personal staff, and Anil, my younger son, have typed the manuscript for publication. I convey my sincere thanks to all of them.

K.S. Chalam
New Delhi

Introduction

K.S. Chalam*

The Indian bureaucracy or state administration is as old as the Mauryan Empire. *Arthashastra* of Chanakya is credited to be one of the earliest treatises on state craft in human history. The *Arthashastra* tells us that a single wheel cannot turn and so governance is only possible with assistance. Therefore, a king should appoint councillors and listen to their advice. Kautilya, or Chanakya, had specified seven elements to create an administrative apparatus with different grades and salary structure. Thus, the Indian bureaucracy is one of the ancient systems that dates back to around 400 BC and seems to have no parallel (except China). The socio-historical studies explaining the emergence of a bureaucracy to maintain public works in all hydraulic societies in Asia further supports the argument that India had an ancient civil service system. The modern bureaucracy imported into the country through colonial rule of the British is of very recent origin in the long history of the country. The administration introduced by the colonial masters was again based on the French model developed after 1789 to provide democratic principles to bring forth a rule of law. It was not, however, based purely on the cultural milieu of the West and there were many indigenous ideas and practices that were incorporated in the British India administration.

The company rule in India had several problems in dealing with the native Indians due to multiple systems of the so-called 'dharma' enunciated in *Shruti*s, *Smriti*s and compilations such as *Dayabhaga, Mitakshari,* etc.

---

*Ex-member, UPSC.

They got perplexed and summoned Macaulay to study and recommend a system and structure of law for British India. The Macaulay Committee recommended that it is 'undoubtedly desirable that the civil servants of the company should have received the best, the most liberal, the most finished education that the native country affords' (Government of India, 2008a). The cadre of ICS was developed as trusted agents of the British in India. The ICS officers were recruited and trained in London and sent to India. The induction into the civil service after the Macaulay Committee Report was based on merit replacing the hitherto some kind of a spoil system.

The British system of revenue collection was not altogether their innovation as it was based on the system of Mughal emperor Akbar, the contemporary of Queen Elizabeth I. The Munsabdari system along with the reforms in land revenue had required a civil service which Akbar nurtured during the mediaeval period. The British India administration that came into operation in the 19th century after the company was formally made a part of the empire was confined to law and order and land revenue collection. It became an elite system as the recruits were drawn from Oxford and Cambridge. The nascent independence movement made the British government to recruit Indians as ICS officers with the establishment of Civil Service Commission. It had facilitated the privileged few to enter the system under the 50 per cent quota for the natives and the remaining 50 per cent came from the UK.

After Independence, the Constitution of the republic made elaborate provisions for a permanent civil service for the country. In fact, the basic structure of the Constitution is made on the principle of separation of powers wherein the executive consisting of the civil service is made autonomous and accountable to the legislature through the political executive under whose control they function. It has also facilitated a permanent tenure with pension and a career. Articles 310–20 empowered the government to create All India Services (AIS) and service commissions for the centre and states to recruit civil servants on the basis of merit established through examinations with a minimum educational qualification of undergraduate degree. At the lower level, single task based jobs, such as steno-typist, clerk, dispatch clerk, etc., were created and recruited through local agencies. They are now being slowly replaced with multiple task-oriented careers designed with the support of Information and Communications Technology (ICT) now.

Civil Service as Elite Service

Though the Constitution and the provisions in it relate to the broad principles of democracy and equal opportunity, the legacy of the British haunted the service for a long time, as majority of the recruits used to come from the privileged few, and from select social groups which included only a few families. At one stage, the service has become the prerogative of particular kind of attitudes, modes and methods that broadly fit into the character of an elite class (Goyal, 1989). The bureaucracy has realised the limitations and started tinkering with it in a piecemeal manner so as to tune in with the system of governance of the day, since approval of the ruling political class is essential for any reform. It is broadly agreed by many scholars now that the service is slowly shedding its past and trying to emerge as a universal civil service system.

The structure of civil service consists of three layers: the AIS, the central service and the state service. The AIS officers are recruited and trained by the Government of India and allotted to the state governments and the central service officers are employed as officers of various departments of the central government to run administration and to coordinate activities with the state governments. The Foreign Service officers are employed in the diplomatic missions and internal organisational set-up. The state service officers are responsible for the functions listed in the state list of the Constitution. They have a quota to get inducted into the union civil services through UPSC. It is very interesting to find that the civil servants are the real workers at the grass roots to maintain the national integration of the country. It is noticed, for instance, that a sub postmaster in a village represents the Government of India and connects the whole country as one unit. The AIS officers carry the tasks of collection of revenue, developmental programmes etc. of the state as well as the central government at the district level. The unit of administration throughout the country is the district. The civil servants are also required to implement the laws of the land made by the Parliament and the state legislatures. The public sector employees are not generally considered as civil servants as they have their own structures and code of conduct. But some of the employees, mostly the management cadre, are drawn from the civil servants on deputation. The central or union civil service consists of group A officers who are recruited through UPSC and the B, C, D and Central Secretariat Service (CSS) are drafted by the Staff Selection Commission. (Some of the functions of UPSC were transferred due to work load.)

The Character of the Service

The civil service system is described by scholars as 'mediating institutions that mobilise human resources in the service of the affairs of the state in a territory' (Bekke and Meer, 2000). This is different from the concept of bureaucracy that is used in a pejorative sense. It is just not an organisation that implements rules and regulations formulated by an authority but it is much more than that. Civil service systems in most of the modern states have grown in stature and strength that can sustain a state in the absence of a political government by following the mandate of a constitution. It has even circumvented the critiques, who termed the civil servants as selfish as politicians, working for a career and/or for rent seeking. The public choice theorists who were critical about the bureaucrats have advocated for the withdrawal of the state or for a minimalist role for the state so that the influence of the public servants can be minimised and market be given predominant role in their place. The theories of public choice developed around 1980s were responsible for the advancement of the New Public Management (NPM). However, it is found in recent years that international agencies, such as the World Bank, have changed the tone and are now emphasising on the effective state so that it can take up developmental programmes. On the other hand, philosophers and scholars such as Rawls, Amartya Sen and others have argued for a people friendly democratic state to achieve equity and justice in the society, particularly in the developing countries. In fact, influenced by the advocates of minimalist state, countries, such as India, have downsized the civil service. There is no doubt that there was a glut in public services in the aftermath of independence and the development agenda of Jawaharlal Nehru government. It is also found that some civil servants coming from the elite classes have made use of it for their self-development by abusing power. But there are equally sound facts to show that it was due to the imagination and vision of some of the so-called bureaucrats that India could achieve self-sufficiency and the critical minimum to achieve a sustained growth later due to the fundamentals developed by them (Frankel, 2006).

Civil service as a universal class in India is internally differentiated. The ICS was a privileged service during the British rule and continued to be the same even after Independence. Though the recruitment into the civil service was based on merit and educational qualifications, it was not made universal as the foundation itself was uneven. The educational facilities, particularly higher education, were confined to urban areas and those who had obtained a minimum qualification of a degree and were in the age group of 21–24; such individuals were only eligible to sit for the civil services examination that was conducted in English. This had restricted the entry of common people with limited means and rural background. It was in 1976 that the government appointed the Kothari Committee to recommend proposals for reform. The reforms implemented by the government through UPSC have facilitated the entry of both rural and urban aspirants into the system. But the social background of the entrants has not undergone a substantial change except in the case of the Scheduled Castes (SCs) and Scheduled Tribes (STs).

The most preferred and privileged service is Indian Administrative Service known as IAS. There is a perceptible change in the attitude of aspirants after the 2008 economic crisis. The AIS and central services are considered by everyone now as a premier service and competition for the services are increasing manifold after the Sixth Pay Commission. It is observed that the salary and perks received by a group A officer is comparable if not better than corporate executives. Therefore, the number of aspiring candidates for civil services has crossed the million mark for around 1,000 vacancies per year.

The *Varna* System

The civil services in India are supposed to be reflecting the Indian society, not in the positive sense but in a discrepant reference to the unique social system. The IAS officers are considered as arrogant and appear to be always in league with their own clan. This needs to be empirically studied and proved, but as of now the behaviour pattern of all the civil servants can be categorised into the traditional *varna* system. There seem to be some influence of the ethos of *varna* on the structure of the system as the IAS is placed on top based on the merit in the UPSC examination, followed by the Indian Police Service (IPS) and so on, though there would be little difference once they enter active service. But the initial thrust given to each service is considered as its worth and carried as a birth right. In fact, the authority and power of the officers selected by UPSC come from the provisions in the Constitution (which many disregard). The IAS officer, it is alleged, behaves as if he/she is a superior human being with all the knowledge and power at his/her command and expects others should respect him/her like that of a traditional Brahmin. Of course, there are gradations within depending upon the caste of the officer and seniority in service like the subcastes within a caste. The IPS or police service officers behave as if they are the Kshatriyas and are ordained to discipline the society. The Indian Revenue Service (IRS) officers are found to be collectors or receivers of revenue from people and all the time absorbed with money matters like a Vaishya. The three important services resemble our traditional *dvija varna* (twice born) which later became castes with all the privileges and prerogatives. The rest of the services including forest service, engineering, medical, etc. are considered as Shudras whose job is to serve rest of the society and are at the lower end of the society. The so-called class IV or group D employees can be considered as the Panchama. The 50 odd civil services of the union government can fit into some of the castes that had emerged and have multiplied after the post-Vedic period. In other words, the character and attitude of the civil servants, including those who have occupied the positions due to caste-based reservations, reflect the *varna* system with few exceptions here and there. This may be considered as one of the contributing factors for the recreation of the caste system in India. One may muse that the static nature of the civil service in India may be due to this attribute.

The social background of the civil servants has been studied by scholars to indicate how it is not skewed. Women officers were very few before 1960; to be precise there were only 17 in the IAS. The proportion has slowly increased, exceeding 10 per cent of the total after the year 1981. A study conducted by Santosh Goyal on the Indian Administrative Officers has indicated that Brahmins constituted around 40 per cent of the service, followed by Kayasthas at 13 per cent, Kshatriyas at 9 per cent and Vaishyas at 8 per cent. As there was caste-based reservation, the proportion of SCs, STs and Backward Classes (BCs) was limited to 28 per cent (Goyal, 1989).

1. Though the data relates to 1985, the proportions remain the same with minor changes due to the introduction of Other Backward Classes (OBCs) reservations from 1995. It is interesting to find that in all southern states, Bengal and Assam, Brahmins dominated the service with more than 42 per cent representation and Shudras even in Tamil Nadu were confined only to 7.5 per cent. Yet, in another study organised on the civil service trainees at the Academy in Mussoorie in 2008, it was noticed that the social background of the trainees played a predominant role in their informal gatherings and socialising process at the Academy.

2. It was mentioned in the study that there were very few from other communities to have gathered when Ambedkar Jayanthi (Dalit leader and chairman of the Constitution drafting committee) was celebrated in the Academy, indicating the reality that caste prejudices haunt the officers even after being selected for secular jobs. The above facts confirm the formulation of the incidence of *varna* system in the civil services in India.

The ICS has been the patrimony of the upper classes and elite belonging to the urban area. The proportion of entrants into the system from urban areas constitute around 70 per cent, as late as in 2007. There are allegations that the reforms introduced in 2011 in the form of Civil Service Aptitude Test (CSAT) or preliminary examination to filter the aspirants will further increase the number as it is biased against the rural and social sciences. The academic background of the recruits is specious as those who are qualified for the civil services opt out of subjects in which they did not get their academic qualifications. The civil administration was dominated by humanities and social science graduates till 1980s. Now more number of graduates from engineering, medical, agriculture and others are qualified in subjects other than their academic disciplines (mostly in social sciences), making the teaching of the social sciences in universities problematic as a majority of them are qualified through informal training.

Social Justice as a Legacy

The British India government had the opportunity to encourage universal values with Indian characters by encouraging individuals and movements that came under their contact. In fact, the social reform movements in India are generally attributed to the British officers or civil servants, such as Macaulay, Bentinck and several others at different layers of admin- istration. English education led to the natives accessing developments outside the country, whereby they imbibed some of the liberal outlook. This had a bearing on the social movements that have asserted social justice and equality of treatment in public affairs of the state. The Mandal Commission recommendations and the subsequent judicial overreach have codified the reservation of posts in civil service to the extent of 50 per cent at various services and categories. There are, however, very few studies to relate the performance of an officer and his academic achievements to confirm or reject meritocracy in civil service in India.

Alienation of Civil Service

The British India government had developed academic disciplines, such as anthropology, to learn about the people of India and to reach out to the unreachable. There were many civil servants who have throughout their career remained humble servants of the people. Some of them used to mentor the younger recruits into the system. But today we have stories narrated by officers and colleagues how the superior service officers treat their juniors and officers from other services with sunken outlook. In fact, most of the officers get their routine time-scale promotions without much contribution to offer. The kind of experience that they claim in dealing with subjects is really preposterous as it is humanly impossible for a person to claim expertise in agriculture today and a year after in nuclear energy and so on. Even if we concede that they deal only with administrative matters, common sense tells us that an expert in the field is more appropriate to deal with policy than a mere pen-pusher. In fact, the power and privileges enjoyed by some of them are derived from the constitutional provisions and not necessarily from their competencies.

In one of the constitutional bodies, it was reported that an IAS officer did not turn up at an official meeting of the boss as he happened to be an officer from another service. There are also reports that some of the senior IAS officers or those who are in plum postings do not care to attend or respond to the calls of the same cadre or superiors who have come from other services, such as academics, engineering, etc., to show that they are superior humans. The kind of arrogance and depraved relations with the colleagues are not found to be mediated with the illiterate political bosses. Sometimes they are seen carrying out orders and belongings like that of a personal staff of the minister. This attitude and unawareness of some of the officers is responsible for the decadence of the esteem of the service as reflected in the contempt that they suffer once they superannuate. It is also reported that some astute officers cultivate power brokers who are close to the political power and get desired postings, awards and rewards. In this process majority of them are alienated from the common man. But there are always exemplary characters in the service whose names are carried as legacy in the service and people keep on respecting them whether they are alive or dead. The findings of some empirical studies have categorised these personalities into different taxonomies.

The understanding or the so-called domain knowledge of some of the civil servants is so poor that they try to trounce the other party with their position and power rather than with the wisdom. This may be one of the reasons why these cohorts do not shuffle with others and those who are committed do not have time to mend such characters. Some of these officers get into distress due to this deficiency. In a recent media account, it is noticed that a respected senior civil servant was reported to have indicted that the central or union government should never interfere with agriculture and leave it to the states to make policies. This shows the ignorance of the officer as agriculture comes under the state list and there are provisions in the Constitution that the union is empowered to give directions on any matter and can cause to make laws that will be binding on the states. There are many civil servants, particularly the younger ones, whose knowledge about the Constitution is very poor and some even have contempt for the Constitution. When a person or expert other than the colleague excels in domain knowledge in an interaction, some bureaucrats show their intolerance by trying to pick up some acronyms and show off that they know everything about the subject. This is partly due to the deviation of the subjects in which they are qualified for the civil services and the subjects of their academic degrees. It is also noticed that there are some very intelligent and fast-grasping learners who get on to their job very quickly by picking up the threads through their training and common sense and outshine others. Some of the delinquent officers are becoming corrupt and are becoming a great threat to the system and governance.

The power enjoyed by the general service officers or IAS compared to others has been a subject of disdain for others in the civil service system. Some of those who have failed to make it to IAS would struggle for it till he/she exhausts the mandatory attempts and finally settles in a service which is allotted to him as per his/her merit. The general complaint of those who couldn't make it to IAS is that the difference between them and the IAS qualified is about five marks at the time of recruitment. But the positions of power and privileges enjoyed by them are very wide. It is also found that most of the policies made by the government are ultimately passed through or scrutinised by the IAS officers and, therefore, it is alleged that service conditions are always biased in favour of them. Much worse, a system of bureaucratic technique of a committee of secretaries innovated to vet policies is alleged to be used to circumvent any order that goes against their service. The quarrel between IAS and other services including IPS, IRS, defence, etc., after the recommendations of the Sixth Pay Commission is well-known. It is noticed that they are so powerful that even cabinet decisions, resolutions made by the constitutional bodies, reports of the expert committees too are scrutinised by them. Unless this process of usurping power by manoeuvring in the name of political decision goes through a watchful eye (who can spare time), it has the greatest potential for misuse. The recent corruption and conspiracy cases against senior civil servants in Delhi, Hyderabad and other places convey the turpitude in the higher bureaucracy. However, it seems to be a priority area of empirical research to study how they make use of their power in getting their things done, including postings, empanelment, post-retirement assignments, etc., in a parliamentary democracy.

IPS officers are considered disciplined and well-organised civil servants who also manage other paramilitary services in the country. They are regarded in recent times as the most loyal servants of politically strong individuals and some of them are alleged to be involved in corruption along with the political bosses. The serious indictment against the service is that they violate human rights and twist issues in favour of the accused for consideration. Some clever officers are known to have taken powerful postings because of their fundamentalist leanings and are facing enquiries while some laugh at it once they retire. The major complaint against the uniformed service from a section of the minority community is that they do not behave as if they are in a secular service and take emotional decisions in times of emergencies. However, there are some upright officers who stand for service values and face serious consequences because of the power politics. The data on the crime records bureau maintained by the government and managed by service officers indicate the status of the law and order situation in the country. In fact, there is also a public perception that most of the IPS officers who are directly selected by the UPSC are honest and upright, but it is only the state service lower-level officers with the connivance of criminal elements in the department who make the upright vulnerable. There is also a predicament of dearth of officers in different parts of the country. The absence of a proper method in maintaining some scientific ratio in creating posts for the service is considered as a serious problem in the department.

The central services officers are by and large believed to be hard working in carrying the mandate of the departments. However, it is found that the officers from IRS, Indian Railway Traffic Service (IRTS), Railways and other lucrative services are quite often booked under disproportionate assets (DA) cases. The Foreign Service officers are the least publicly exposed cadre, except when they are posted as passport officers in small towns where they sometimes pick up quarrels with clients. The Foreign Service has been considered as very prestigious and privileged service due to its overseas exposure. The officers are very competent and diplomatic in getting some crucial positions in government. The state service is to be treated as a part of civil service. But majority of the people in the service have lost their esteem due to the indifference to people's needs and also due to rampant corruption in some departments. In fact, most citizens directly interface with the lower-level officialdom consisting of petty officials and due to the age-old practices expect reward for everything that they do forgetting that the state pays salary for their services. It appears that no government is serious about the need to reorganise and reform the system at the state level and scientifically link it with the AIS.

Corruption and Ethics in Civil Service

It seems the Hegelian prescription of the 'universal interest of the society' was reflected in the actions of the civil servant in the past (Government of India, 2008a). This seems to be missing now due to the overall change in the vision of the state. If there were any seeds of fortuitous elements in the system, they were blown out of proportion when the primacy of individual interests was given importance in place of the society. It appears that majority of the civil servants who entered the system around 1970s succumbed or were co-opted into the grand design of hedonism. The past civil service ethics and code of conduct were given a decent burial. The government noticed the seeds of corruption in the early 1960s and appointed the Santhanam Committee to make recommendations to deal with corruption. An executive decision was taken to establish a vigilance wing in the government and later a Prevention of Corruption (PC) Act was brought in 1988 to deal with public servants whose assets are found to be disproportionate to their known sources of income.

The illiterate and ignorant people in the third world countries expect that the educated and well-recognised civil servants should be exemplary in character. There is also some kind of a comparison with the British civil servants and the elite officers by the old timers to point out their integrity. Theoretically, the evaluation of values in society is to be mediated through deontological considerations or teleological concerns with ethical ideas. But the philosophical extractions are given tepid treatment and religious orientation is given predominance in the prescription of values of public behaviour in India. The same trend is carried into the civil service administration. Rather, the policy makers should have relied upon the constitutional morality in the fait accompli of civil service codes or values to guide the incumbent. The second Administrative Reforms Commission (ARC) under the chairmanship of Veerappa Moily has pointed out the lacunae in Civil Service Ethics and drafted the Ethics in Governance as its fourth report to the government (Government of India, 2008b). The depressing part of the story is that the government has taken up the report for consideration but failed to accept important recommendations. The civil servant is now functioning under several constraints. Further, the transition of the economy from mixed to purely private orientation with attendant institutional arrangements, such as citizen's charter, Right to Information Act (RTI), PC Act, etc., make the life of a sincere civil servant complicated and he/she has a propensity to commit mistakes.

The Indian Judiciary is known for its ideological orientation and alleged to be atavistic in some of their pronouncements. It is also known for its procrastinating judicial process, particularly in civil matters and further prone to this in service litigation. There are also allegations of corruption in the judiciary that jeopardise the progressive implementation of programmes of the government. The realisation of the objectives of social legislation is considered to be very tardy due to the attitude of the police and judiciary in the country that needs reform and training for proactive orientation.

The issue of rampant corruption at the local level is attributed to the state service officials who in general directly function under the political leaders. The frequent explanation given by such people is that they were compelled to take bribe or do certain jobs under consideration due to the political pressure of sharing it with them. This is not correct. There are honest people even among the political leaders who care less for considerations and help people. The vital element in the issue appears to be the fact that most of the things are done against the rules and regulations framed or laws in operation in the department. There are too many regulations that give scope for interpretation and discretionary powers that are abused to favour some for a consideration. The inherent human weakness of retribution through religious payback to the deity or to a place of worship to satisfy the inherent feeling of guilt is causing moral damage. Interestingly, the intensity of this drift is increasing in proportion to the acquisition of the so-called attributes of modernisation or westernisation in a traditional society. Unlike in the Japanese society where public shame is a value and the corrupt once branded do not seem to reappear while such characters become an idol.

The concept of *binami*, a typical Indian category to conceal the original owner, is being used by the public servants, including the civil servants. The judiciary and the legislature are aware of it and on many occasions are becoming part of this evil. However, the need to maintain honesty and public demeanour among the civil servants in a developing country is hardly emphasised. The social and economic inequalities are so grave in India that the common man is prone to accept simple corruption as a part of life or treat this as ordained by God due to karma and believes that the corrupt will eventfully meet *karmafala* (fruit of vile behaviour). This attitude of the people in India has resulted in what Amartya Sen has called in his latest book, *The Idea of Justice,* as *niti* (ethical conduct) and *nyaya* (instrumental justice) dichotomy (Sen, 2011). In other words, the issue of accepting a corrupt officer or corrupt government in India is ingrained as part of the pragmatic approach of the people. They were never told that the simple shady dealings would ruin the developmental projects implemented by the government. Unfortunately, the kind of orientation and training given to the civil servants now seem to be not so comprehensive to equip the incumbents to understand and tackle some of the issues raised here.

Training and Orientation

The training for the civil servants, particularly the AIS officers, had been continued based on the colonial system for some time even after Independence. One of the vestiges of the policy is that of training the officers in riding a horse. We are told that horse riding was essential for the officers, particularly for those who were entrusted with the district administration as they were supposed to meet the people in inaccessible areas and geographically isolated places. Horse riding was the only way through which the officers used to go to places when infrastructure was very poor. Now it is still imparted to the trainees so as to provide the necessary ruggedness and to resolve authority. The credit for revamping the training for all civil servants and the expansion of facilities at different levels goes to Prime Minister Rajiv Gandhi. A national training policy was formulated on the basis of principles of responsiveness, commitment, awareness and accountability to be inculcated among the civil servants. A structured two-year training programme is designed for the group A service officers, including IAS, IPS, Indian Foreign Service (IFS), IRS, etc., cadres starting with a combined foundation course at Lal Bahadur Shastri National Academy of Administration (LBSNAA) at Mussoorie, Uttarakhand. LBSNAA has been specialising in the training of IAS; Sardar Vallabhbhai Patel National Police Academy (SVPNPA), Hyderabad, specialises in training IPS and other specialised training institutes for each service are located at different parts of the country. The individual states have also developed their state institutes of administration for state service officers. In addition to the induction training, there are opportunities of training at mid career and in different phases through the Department of Personnel and Training (DoPT). Similar training programmes are also designed for group B and lower-level civil servants but it is left to the individual departments to design courses as per need.

The course structure includes the usual academic subjects in Public Administration, Economics, Law, Social Institutions, Maintenance of Records and department-specific laws, accounting norms, topics and others. The practical training and on-the-job training facilities are also included in the courses, apart from optional courses at Indian Institute of Management (IIM), Ahmedabad, International Intellectual Property Alliance (IIPA), etc. There are several committees nominated by the government and the two administrative reforms commissions that have recommended policies for training in American universities and at international institutes. Some of the committees have also pointed out the weaknesses of the existing training, indicating that the domain expertise and knowledge of various sectors are not adequately taken into account and are found to be outdated to cope with the developments in the world. It is also noticed that overemphasis is given to management orientation rather than the administrative functions of civil servants particularly after economic reforms. It is instructive to bring here what P.C. Alexander, a senior bureaucrat and former governor, has noted in an article in the *Asian Age* (Alexander, 2007). He said:

> [M]id-career training planned for 2007, is training in India jointly by Indian institutions like the IIMs and certain US institutions like Kennedy School of Government in Harvard, the Duke centre in Duke University etc. A question that naturally arises is whether through such involvement of US institutions in the training courses and by sending large numbers of officers to the US on training visits, the authorities organizing these programmes are giving too much of a role to the US in the training of senior IAS officers … In fact, training by senior officers through close supervision of the work of their juniors and constructive advice and guidance to them is as much important as any number of training courses by experts from outside the system.

The criticism against such sponsored training and courses is alleged to be due to lobbies that are working behind to promote business interests and to orient the system towards a particular direction.

The orientation of the service has undergone a change after liberalisation. The professional qualities of honesty, integrity, accountability, responsiveness and transparency are replaced with business like values of a commercial manager. Further, the state's role is redefined as that of a facilitator rather than a provider of a service. Therefore, policies and rules are formulated by the officers in such a way that business or economic interests or outcomes are reflected in such activities of the civil servant. The larger good and welfare of the citizen for whom the state exists is replaced by interests of the market. In other words, the theories of public choice that accused civil servants as selfish are replaced with larger interests of the economy measured in terms of efficiency and rates of growth. The shift in accent to advanced countries' values in a pluralistic third world country like India has created several contradictions. The civil servants are neither trained nor are able to understand to resolve the emerging quandary.

The Challenges

The civil service system in India has evolved over a period of thousands of years of state craft. It has a legacy that is more ingrained in the Indian ethos and life. It is now subjected to various kinds of reforms and experiments based on the developments that are taking place in the advanced countries. There is a need to have a reappraisal of the system with the idea to retain those practices that are valid and discard those that are redundant for a modern state. For instance, no one should object to the introduction of ICT to provide effective services to the people instead of depending upon the old norms of the quagmire of bureaucracy. It is also necessary to transfer some of the routine functions such as testing, measuring, and certification of the government departments to accredited private sector operators. There are many functions which the state undertook when the country was in the process of development as a model employer and as a facilitator to develop certain sectors that were crucial. Now there are competent and even advanced enterprises in the private sector that can be entrusted with some of the commercial services by sufficient safeguards and regulations. It is possible to downsize the system to that extent.

The idea of transferring some of the functions of the state to the private sector on the basis of the arguments of public choice theorists that civil servants are rent seekers, and NPM is the better alternative, is fraught with several limitations. Indian bureaucracy or civil service system is not a replica of the West. It has its own identity with checks and balances drawn from the traditional laws of the land with elaborate rules and regulations to monitor the conduct of the civil servant. The civil servant is a fulltime employee of the state to exercise sovereign authority on behalf of the state. This cannot be delegated to a private party. It is evolved on the foundation of depersonalisation, that is, the power is not vested with a particular individual servant but, delegated to him/her on certain terms and conditions as per the constitution. This may not be true in other systems and therefore cannot be compared. To that extent Indian civil service is unique.

India as a country has evolved out of several small provinces and princely states with a civil service system to maintain integrity and security to everyone unlike the US or small countries in Europe. It is strange that the administrative reforms commissions and several expert groups have never attempted to examine what is happening in our immediate neighbourhood, such as Japan and Thailand, or similar systems elsewhere like the Swedes or Dutch, but cite a city state Singapore equivalent in size to that of a municipal corporation in India to be emulated. Further, the private sector working on the principle of profit always has the option to close down the operations without assigning any reasons. But the state apparatus, like the civil service system, would under no circumstances resort to declare an end to its operations, lest the cessation of the state is imminent. In fact, the executive power of the union according to the Constitution 'shall be exercised by him (President) either directly or through officers subordinate to him in accordance with this constitution' (Article 538). The constitutional power vested with the executive as a subordinate to the elected government makes the system to function in a political environment. It is here several grey areas are emerging that may need reform.

The principle of internal labour market operates in civil service as it has its own career path with no external competition for positions and, therefore, is obliged to select candidates as per its requirements on merit. The civil service neutrality as a principle and value is the distinctive character that separates the political executive from the career-based government servants. The civil servant is rule bound and supposed to uphold the constitutional provisions in all his activities. This will ensure impartiality as eulogised by Clement Attlee in 1954. It is reported that he has said that

> when I succeeded Mr. Churchill as prime minister and returned to the conference at Potsdam, I took with me precisely the same team of civil servants, including even the principle private secretary, as had served my predecessor. This occasioned a lively surprise among our American friends who were accustomed to the American system whereby the leading official advisers of the president and of the members of his cabinet are usually politically of his and their own political colour. The incident brought out very forcibly the very special position of the British civil service, a position which has developed during the past hundred years as the result of the Northcote-Trevelyan reforms. I don't think that this remarkable attribute of impartiality in the British civil service is sufficiently widely known nor adequately recognizes for what it is- one of the strongest bulwarks of democracy. (Lord Fulton, 1968)

This indicates the contrasting values of civil service in a democracy in the UK and the USA that has remained intact despite the Thatcher administrative reforms (except the tenure arrangements). In fact, India has also followed the earlier reforms suggested by the Fulton report (1968) of the UK. It is reported that the system of administration in some of the

European countries, including the UK, are influenced by the agendas of the European Commission rather their own. India has no obligations nor is connected with any such formation in the region except that it is in a leadership role to guide other members in the SAARC region.

One of the challenges that the system encounters today is the transition from a classical British system to that of a market-based American system. It appears that India can resolve most of its contradictions if it confines to its original bearings with constitutional values. The problem of political interference as some senior civil servants have remarked in the following papers is due to the vicious and selfish attitude of a few bureaucrats, who are more interested in their careers than defending the system and have developed nexus with politicians and their sponsored contractors. There is an allegation that some of the senior officers are not different from their political bosses in treating the subordinates. If the rules are made in such a way that they are based on sound principles of public policy such as efficiency, equal opportunity, internal and external productivity of the system rather than based on whimsies and fancies of arrogant and self-centred bureaucrats and politicians, the system can sustain even in a new environment. The Chinese system of administration is applauded as one of the efficient structures even after its move towards a market economy. The recent innovations in China include frequent change of officers dealing with sensitive matters like permits, regulations, economic issues, etc., and a constant vigil with severe penalty that might include death sentence.

Rule making is the prerogative of the higher bureaucracy. Rules are drafted after an Act is passed in the legislature and in certain routine matters on the basis of the powers delegated to the executive. There seem to be no theoretical frame under which rules are framed in the government by the officers. In most of the cases they are made on ad hoc basis and are known to be *show me the person I will tell you the rule* kind of formulations. It is also alleged that the rules that generally originate at the lower level may be at the level of a section officer in the department who is the memory keeper of the department and not the boss who comes there as head from outside. The so-called note is processed through several layers of administration to see the accuracy of the subject and to bring in the so-called precedent and practices in the department. The officer who comes from outside would ascertain (what is the practice in the department rather than going through the origin and the substantive matter of the subject) certain details and finally approves it. He is also sometimes burdened with too much of routine work and finds little time to go through the issue in detail and puts his seal of approval. The political executive is generally dependent on the civil servant as he/she is supposed to know the rules and advise him on the policy direction and the rule that directs to achieve the policy. It needs lot of hard work and understanding of the subject or domain knowledge. There are very few who can come up to the expectations and many need orientation in the subjects before taking up the responsibility. As we have already seen that the training of the higher bureaucracy is lukewarm and lopsided and, therefore, administration has become routine without any creative ideas getting into the policies and the rules that are made. Some of the officers are victimised if he/she fail to push the blame any further downwards in the system. The argument that political pressures are responsible for committing certain mistakes is not only an excuse but it is a blatant supplant of the constitutional protection provided to them to remain neutral.

It is discussed time and again the idea of lateral entry of officers based on domain experience at the level of joint secretary and above (even across civil services) is somehow scuttled. It is strange to note that some of the Western practices such as NPM, privatisation, etc., are implemented with sincerity but this particular idea is given a tepid treatment. In other words, the challenge is how to democratise and secularise the civil service operations as per the Constitution of India and not to be led away by external pressures for inapt reforms.

Reforms in Recruitment Agencies

Some of the predicaments voiced by the reformers of civil services arise due to the weak recruitment policies followed in some of the countries. But India, like its neighbour China, had inherited a system based on merit and time-tested procedures. The Public Service Commissions (PSCs) in India and in SAARC countries have been following scientific methods of recruitment based on different layers of competitive examinations and tests without any political or external influence. Most of the commissions are given constitutional status to safeguard their autonomy. The durability of the recruitment policy depends upon its ability to adapt itself to the changes brought in through technology and innovations in testing. There is not even a single incident of alleged abuse of authority in the recruitment by the UPSC in its 80 years long history, shows the endurance of the system in India. However, the recent initiative to introduce reforms in the examination system became controversial, accusing UPSC as partisan and elitist in the Parliament debates.

The service commissions need to maintain international standards by adopting the best practices in place both in the private and public sectors' human resource and manpower planning policies. Though the commissions are protected under the Constitution and, therefore, insulated from any criticism, they are supposed to come out of the stereotypes particularly in the state service commissions. They should concentrate on research and development as to how to capture the young with the necessary attributes for civil services rather than allowing them to slip into the private sector. The temptation to follow the West in assigning the responsibility to recruit (small number) candidates for civil service is to be introverted in India and SAARC countries as the number is very large. The quality and efficiency of the system depends upon the service commissions in capturing the most suitable, sustainable and trainable candidates for the civil service.

Keeping the above issues of civil service system in India and SAARC countries in mind, an attempt is made here to review the functioning of the structure in relation to its utility or obsolescence to the present conditions. The method adapted here to get the review is made in the form of reflections of the civil servants who have given their life for the system. There are around 100 departments or agencies in the union government. Most of the civil servants who have expressed their views here have either worked in some of them or have interactions with other departments. The authors of these chapters are all senior officers who have served at the level of cabinet secretary and secretary of a department in the Government of India and are known for their integrity in the system. An attempt is also made to cover important departments and different services such as IAS, IRS, IPoS, etc. We have not made any attempt to bring in all services and categories at one place, which would be a huge multi-volume exercise; it is beyond the scope of the present volume.

Keeping this in mind, we have selected some representative views of civil servants mostly from group A services.

The volume has four sections. Each section of the volume has a brief introduction.

References

Alexander, P.C. 2007. 'How to Train Civil Servants and Legislators', *The Asian Age*, 14 June.

Bekke, Hans A.G.M. and Frits M. van der Meer (eds). 2000. *Civil Service Systems in Western Europe*. UK: Edward Elgar.

Frankel, Francine. 2006. *India's Political Economy 1947–2004*. New Delhi: Oxford University Press.

Lord Fulton. 1968. *The Civil Service Vol I Report of the Committee*. London: Her Majesty's Stationery Office.

Government of India. 2008a. *Tenth Report*. Second Administrative Reforms Commission, Government of India, New Delhi.

———. 2008b. *Fourth Report: Ethics in Governance*. Second Administrative Reforms Commission, New Delhi.

Goyal, Santhosh. 1989. 'Social Background of Officers in the Administrative Service', in F. Frankel and M.S.A. Rao (eds), *Dominance and State Power in India*. New Delhi: Oxford University Press.

Sen, Amartya. 2011. *The Idea of Justice*. New Delhi: Oxford University Press.

I

Governance and Civil Service

The chapters that follow are selected to reflect on the governance and civil service in India. The notion of civil service is broadly understood as class I service in India, though class II officers also do come under the title. Most of the provincial services are recruited and maintained by the state governments and the few central secretariat services are entrusted to the Staff Selection Commission for recruitment. Some of them enter class I service through internal quotas and, therefore, a separate analysis of the state and other services that come under the broad caption is not undertaken here in view of the huge size and scope. It is assumed that the analyses made in these chapters related to the class I services are broadly applicable to other segments of civil service in India.

In most developed countries, civil service is given a statutory status through legislation, such as the Australian Public Service Act 1999. But the civil service in India is created through constitutional provision and is broadly obliged to implement the constitutional provisions and values. The incumbent civil servants both at the higher level and at the lower administration are hardly aware of this fact that the power and authority that they enjoy in discharging their duties emanate from the Constitution. The drift from this realisation is gone to such an extent that even senior officers hardly know the provisions under which a particular activity is undertaken and are overwhelmed by the concepts that are alien to our democratic republic. There is also some confusion as to the difference between the supply of service and provision of public good or utility and the governance principles that oversee the accomplishment. The business principles and models that are quite often used in developed countries are blindly applied in all public service activities without judicious application of public reasoning. The idea of rule of law is given tepid treatment and, thus, political pressures and personal weaknesses enable some of the civil servants to bend and twist rules as per the requirements. Thus the rule of law in such a context becomes complex. The kind of civil service culture that is cultivated in the country for the last several decades makes the service elite-oriented rather than mass based. Given the advancements in technology, education, legal literacy of the common man, the civil servant is obliged to be more knowledgeable, compassionate and accountable and should stand for certain values as an exemplary citizen.

The record of events in the recent past in the area of civil service in India is not very cheerful. There are officers who jump into political fray after cultivating a particular political party or even a community without minding the values and traditions of the civil service. The age old civil service value of service neutrality is given a decent burial at the peril of making it extinct. The principle of public accountability administered through parliamentary processes and through administrative instruments is not given the treatment it deserves. In fact, neutrality and account-ability would always protect the sincere civil servant in testing times. The notion of good governance, which is narrowly understood by many as producing tangible outcomes, have created problems as the civil servant in a constitutionally elected government must also think about the security and welfare of the people. The idea of developing administration is replaced by service orientation to facilitate private sector players to settle and exploit resources for the overall development of the country. But all the departments of the government are not amenable to this and there are sectors, such as irrigation, agriculture, welfare, culture, etc., which really enrich the identity of a nation and are actually dependent on the ingenuity and creativity of the bureaucrats. There are instances where such dedicated civil servants are remembered by the common man even after their demise, and this should work as an inspiring experience for an incumbent civil servant. At the same time the turnaround brought in by civil servants in sectors that are crucial for the economy are always rewarded with recognition and post-retirement jobs in India. But main-taining a balance between the two seems to be the need of the hour.

The civil servant has become a scapegoat in the recent past in the dozens of scams unearthed by the investing agencies. It is not only the civil servant, as an executive, but even the political executive, as a public servant, who are deeply involved in some of the popular scams that speak about the nexus. Corruption as defined by the World Bank, the use of public service for private gains, is a narrow definition that may not incorporate institutions and actions of people that go against the objectives of the collective will of the people. It is noted by some of the scholars that good governance as the traditional dharma as enunciated by Bhishma is given a pass even by those who stood for traditional values. Yet, the constitutional provisions and the intervention of the apex court in interpreting the right to life that incorporates education, health, shelter and social security would remind the civil servant to be vigilant and proactive.

The outcry and the public discourse on corruption due to jaundiced media support and promotion of certain individuals or movements did not allow a dispassionate debate on the issue. It is commonly believed that the civil servant in connivance with the politician is responsible for corruption in India, particularly after liberalisation. There is no doubt that some dishonest and morally corrupt officers from the IAS, IPS, IRS in the ranks of secretary, chief secretary, director general of police (DGP), etc., are booked under DA cases. But why is it that incidence of dishonesty and swindle has increased in the post-reform period than during the immediate phase of our independence? Though there are cases such as Life Insurance Corporation (LIC), Mundra, Bofors, etc., they are very rare and the involvement of the civil servant is minimal. There is rarely any reflection of the impact of policy regimes on the administration—few chapters are included in the volume. The chapters incorporated here reflect the popular opinion of the senior cadres, who have at different stages either formulated the policies or implemented them without qualms.

We may reflect here on the dichotomy between public administration and new public management that suffer from looking at the constitutional structure of administration in India. As vehemently argued by John A. Rohr (2000), a scholar on public service: '[M]anagerial innovations cannot change the fact that administration is governance ... public service ethics in a country's constitutional tradition is that the connection between ethics and governance is immediate.' It is instructive for Indian commentators to look at the irrelevance of the USA principles of administration, which we sheepishly barrow, to note that it would make no sense in a parliamentary regime. Rohr has reproduced from his study carried at Woodrow Wilson Center in Washington to show that constitutional foundations of administrative practices are different from others. He has narrated the case of Baron Haussman, the 19th century mayor of Paris, a close associate of Emperor Napoleon III, who transformed the city as a case study. The author has explained the virtues, vices, financial irregularities, political meddling, etc., of Haussman to expose the soft underbelly of a constitutional approach to public administration. It is instructive for Indian policy makers to read John A. Rohr's (2000) conclusions to see the analogous nature of ethical traditions of the administration.

> [P]ublic service ethics presupposes that one has made, or at least should have made, a prior judgment on the moral legitimacy of the regime in which one serves. Recall Aristotle's distinction between a good man and a good citizen but may also be a bad human being, for example a good Nazi is by definition a bad person. Consequently, the question of public service ethics cannot arise in thoroughly unjust regime because an unfavorable answer to the fundamental question on the moral legitimacy of the regime itself precludes further inquiry.

Reference

Rohr, John A. 2000. 'Ethics, Governance, and Constitutions: The Case of Baron Haussmann', in Richard A. Chapman (ed.), *Ethics in Public Service for the New Millenium*, pp. 203–16. Aldershot, United Kingdom: Ashgate Publishing Ltd.

1

Governance and Public Service

Mohammad Hamid Ansari*

It is a truism that an overwhelming majority of human beings live in politically organised societies that require for their normal functioning a set of persons entrusted with the implementation of laws and rules made by the polity for its welfare. The concept of civil services, as of judiciary and of defence forces, is inextricably linked to this requirement.

It is for this reason that every state in history has utilised the instrumentality of civil services, tailored to its requirements. These needs have changed with times, with the nature of the state, and with its end purposes. Some essential traits have nevertheless persisted down the ages. We can, therefore, read with benefit to this day Kautilya's short chapter on 'Service with a King' and its emphasis on the need to give advice at all times in accordance with *dharma* and *artha*.

The relevance of the civil servant to the ruler (individual or a collective) was perhaps best described by the medieval historian Ibn Khaldun: 'you are', he wrote, 'the ears through which they hear, the eyes through which they see, the tongues through which they speak, and the hands through which they touch'.

This need to seek the best available talent, and condition it appropriately for the requirement of society and the state, was practiced at all

---

* Vice President of India. This chapter is a reproduction of his speech at UPSC Annual Lecture Series. Original of the same is available online at http://www.upsc. gov.in/lectures/vicepresident_speech.pdf (accessed 4 March 2014).

times in our own history. Modern India thus inherited an established tradition. It's imperative necessity was appreciated by the Founding Fathers of our Republic. The end product was incorporated in Part XIV of the Constitution.

In the past six decades, the Union Public Service Commission (UPSC) has ably discharged its constitutional function in the recruitment of the higher civil services. The civil services, in turn, have responded in varying measure to their core mandate of dispensing social, economic and political justice. The framework of the political and bureaucratic Executive has made a significant effort at ameliorating the quality of life of citizens and in doing public good. In the same time span, however, the socio-economic and political context has evolved in good measure and substantive notions of justice and equality have filled the interstices of the constitutional principles and fundamental rights.

This has brought about a virtual revolution in expectations.

It is therefore essential to comprehend the impulses at work. Together, they pose a set of six challenges:

First, government interventions are now viewed by citizens through the prism and framework of rights. The days of the so-called *mai-baap sarkar* are over. Today, and particularly in matters relating to education, health, roads or good governance, the operative expression is right and entitlement. Increasing levels of literacy and economic success has contributed to this conceptual shift in some measure.

Second, advances in technology, means of communication and interaction, and changes in civil society perceptions have multiplied manifolds the instrumentalities available to a common citizen to engage with the government, assert entitlements and rights, and challenge decisions of the government that impact adversely.

Third, given the unsatisfactory record of dispensation of justice through the court process, the burden of dispensing it has shifted in considerable measure to the government, civil society and the public in general. Enhanced legal literacy, establishment of regulatory frameworks in various sectors, and reliance on administrative facilitation have enabled citizens to assert their rights without the need for interventions of courts. The role of civil servants and public service delivery has become critical in this effort.

Fourth, as an economy and as a society, we are in the process of transition from the use of controls and regulations to bring about desired public policies to harnessing of incentives and markets for the same. The market looms large in all spheres of personal and public life. It affects our choices of profession, ways of life, modes of living and entertainment, education, health care, and even, ideologies and belief systems.

Fifth, the broad framework of our social and political contract that sustains the legitimacy of the government and its interventions for public and social good is increasingly facing erosion. This has come about principally on account of the actual and perceived inequities of the growth process, marginalisation and impoverishment of segments of citizenry and also perhaps, a balkanisation of the mind. It has wider, perhaps disturbing, implications for our democracy and the rule of law.

Sixth, we have a young generation that is exposed to global standards of living and service, is impatient with the pace of change, and demands equal opportunity in sharing the fruits of development. This is more pronounced in urban areas, but equally true for rural India. Their despondency finds reflection in hostility towards elites in polity, business and industry and society; at times, it takes violent forms of protest targeted against the state, its structures and agencies. These manifestations retard growth, erode democracy and legitimise anarchy.

Emanating from the above, a set of questions come up for consideration:

How should we deal with the huge asymmetries of power, and the socio-cultural propensity of tolerating its misuse through dilution of systemic and institutional safeguards?

How can public policy bring the citizen to the centre stage of service delivery and governance, and not put him/her at the mercy of the State and its agencies, or of the market and its mechanisms?

What role can the civil service play in this regard?

I venture to think a good starting point is recognition that the civil services in our country represent the societal elite and that elite behaviour represents a significant challenge to the supremacy of Rule of Law.

We do not need to go far to substantiate this. The national and international media is full of reports of how the elite are able to subvert the Rule of Law with money or influence. Sections of society and polity even accept this as a way of life. As a result, Rule of Law norms are being sidelined or subverted through systemic discrimination and exclusion based on community, gender, class and other limiting and distorting considerations. Its impact on the quality of governance is all too evident.

The higher civil services in the country, therefore, must be role models of elite behaviour upholding the Rule of Law. This is not a homily; it is part of our constitutional scheme of things and a professional and moral obligation of a civil servant to the nation and to the citizens.

This necessitates an element of out-of-the-box thinking on quality and content issues pertaining to our higher civil services.

The UPSC, I understand, is already implementing some reforms in the recruitment pattern, especially in the syllabus and examinations. The issue of life-long cadres for All India Services, reluctance or inability to serve adequate period of careers outside the cadres whether at the Centre or other States, equitable access to posts covered under the Central Staffing Scheme, and possibility of lateral access into and out of the civil service are issues that could benefit from such out-of-the-box thinking.

A review of the performance of the civil service since independence would show that in terms of Sardar Patel's parameters, while the polity has delivered by giving constitutional safeguards to civil servants and implementing sound recruitment procedures, the political leadership has at times faltered on discipline and control and the civil servants themselves have often enough succumbed to the temptation of tailoring professionally sound advice to subjective considerations.

The need for introspection and correction is compelling; inaction is no longer an option, nor is reticence in the face of evident wrong. The need is also for a moral imperative that is comprehensive, not selective, and which emanates from and encapsulates constitutional morality.

We do need reiteration that Civil servants are functionaries of the state and not of the government alone, that they are paid to render *honest* professional advice however unpalatable, and that they should be guided in their work by the principles and objectives, and the charter of rights and duties, enshrined in our Constitution.

Systemic improvement in governance and service delivery to citizens is an ongoing process and effort of the UPSC in this regard deserves our appreciation. It is time to remember, and remind, that the objective in the final analysis is indeed—'Public Service'.

2

Constitutional Status of Civil Service in India

K.S. Chalam

The founding fathers of the Constitution have deliberated on the future of the country and have created several institutions for a democratic deliverance. It is well recognised and accepted in jurisprudence that there is a basic structure for the Constitution that cannot be altered through the existing parliamentary practices. What is not known to the common man is that the founding fathers had wisely devised a structure that takes care of the separation of powers. Thus, it w as deliberated to create a Supreme Court to take care of judiciary, an Election Commission for the legislature and the UPSC to create the executive. They are indispensable constitutional organs with autonomous powers. The executive is made independent. The civil servants are protected under Article 311 to avail the freedom, status and term of office. The Constitution has laid down procedures to deal with delinquent officers and the service rules are formulated both for the ordinary civil servants and for the AIS officers.

The UPSC and state service commissions are created through constitutional provision under Articles 315–23. The functions of the UPSC are clearly laid down in Article 320 without any ambiguity. The Commission is entrusted with the function to conduct examinations for appointment to the services of the union. In addition to the recruitment, the Commission is mandated to formulate policies to make appointments to the civil services, disciplinary matters, methods of recruitment and consults the president of India on any matter referred to them. The chairman and members of the Commission are appointed by the president and enjoy the status equivalent to the Supreme Court judge and cannot be removed without referring to the apex court by the president.

The civil service in India consists of all those who are holding civil posts other than defence and judicial. Article 310 says that

> not withstanding that a person holding a civil post under the union or a state holds office during the pleasure of the President or, as the case may be, of the Governor of the state, any contract under which a person, not being a member of a defense service or of an all-India service or the union or a state, is appointed under this Constitution to hold such a post may, if the President or the Governor as the case may be, deems it necessary in order to secure the services of a person having special qualifications, provide for the payment to him of compensation. If before the expiration of an agreed period that post is abolished or he is, for reasons not connected with any misconduct on his part, requires to vacate that post.

The civil service is broadly divided into different ranks as classes I, II, III and IV. There are two categories of services at the federal or central government which are called Central Services and the AIS; these consist of the IAS, IPS and Indian Forest Service (IFoS). The AIS officers are posted in the states and their conditions of service are regulated by the respective departments with the consultation of the UPSC. There is state-level civil service for each state and the AIS are common both for the union and states. There are around 58 central group A services. All of them are protected under Article 311 as mentioned elsewhere. They can also be divided into technical and non-technical, functional and general services depending upon the job entrusted to them. The highest position in the government is cabinet secretary and only IAS cadre officers occupy this position by convention.

There are two commissions to recruit officers into the civil service. As mentioned above, the UPSC is mandated to conduct examinations to recruit civil servants. Later, a separate Staff Selection Commission was created through an executive order to transfer the recruitment of some of the subordinates and group B and central secretariat services from UPSC. The UPSC conducts annual examinations for civil services including IAS, IPS, IFoS and IRS. The examination has three stages.

First, the preliminary test to filter about a million candidates—with a basic undergraduate degree—is conducted. About 12,000 candidates are made eligible to appear for the main examination to sort out 3,000 candidates for personality test. Finally, around 1,000 candidates are selected on the basis of the combined merit list prepared based on the performance in the written and personality test. The written examination is for 1,800 marks and the personality test carries 275 marks. The scheme of examination is reorganised with more weightage to General Studies. There is also a state quota for the three AIS where the respective state governments prepare lists of candidates from the state service to be evaluated by the UPSC on the basis of records to confer the status of IAS, IPS and IFoS. The second Administrative Reforms Commission has made recommendations to change the structure of the examination and other suggestions that are being examined by the government.

The constitutional status of a civil servant needs to be understood in the context of the increasing public perception that they are protected without any trial. This is not correct. What is clear in the Constitution is the provision of natural justice to a public servant and he should not be denied it simply because he happened to be recruited by the government. It is on the basis of these provisions that the administrative wings of the departments have prepared disciplinary rules for the cadre overseen by the Department of Personnel and Training. The cases may appear to be in limbo for a long time. But the fact of the matter is that the judiciary is also involved in resolving some of the cases before a final advice is given to the president/governor by the service commissions on disciplinary matters. Further, disciplinary matters does not confine to corruption alone, there are other norms and values of administration that need to be observed by the civil servant in discharge of his duties.

There is a public debate on the question of discipline among the civil servants and it is generally perceived that the system has failed to contain corruption. The government has enacted the Central Vigilance Commission (CVC) Act in 2003 to deal with those who come under the PC Act 1988. By now CVC has created a huge structure to deal with such officials who are in the government and with public sector organisations. The issue of bringing an Act to create a Lokpal or ombudsman by a section of the civil society activists seems to have not considered the existing provisions to deal with corruption and inclined to create a God or demon like institution. For instance, the UPSC, a constitutional authority, is entrusted with the function of advising the president on all disciplinary matters that come under Article 311, including the AIS officers. One of the greatest traditions established by the UPSC in matters of disciplinary cases is its democratic method of arriving at final decisions in the Commission (about the charges against the officers and the penalties recommended). It is well-established in administrative law that the disciplinary authority consults the CVC twice before it finally arrives at a penalty and before sending the file to UPSC for its advice. The decisions of the Commission are always respected and upheld by the apex court.

The allegation that so far no public servant was punished in India is not borne out of facts. The annual report of the UPSC is kept on the table of the Parliament every year as per constitutional mandate. It provides data on the number of disciplinary cases reported and penalties awarded to each group of officials. Similarly, the CVC website presents information on the number of cases reported and the penalty wise advice rendered to departments. The latest annual report 2009–10 of the UPSC in its appendix table 36 gives data on 797 cases disposed of by it during the year. It is found that the Commission has rendered advice on 252 group A officers, 60 group B officers, 73 group C officials and only three group D staff during the year. Contrary to the allegations of the civil society functionaries, the UPSC has recommended dismissal of 42 officials, 10 removals, 15 compulsory retirements and rest have been awarded penalties ranging from pecuniary punishment to censure, cut in pension, etc. (some 402 cases are returned to departments for incomplete information). It is only in 26 cases that it has recommended dropping of proceedings due to several infirmities in the process. There is a stringent condition in the disciplinary rules that if the concerned department doesn't agree with the penalty recommended by the commission, it has to go through a process before it is reported to the parliament in the annual report.

There seem to be some cases of corruption that are reported in the media but finally do not reach the logical end because of litigations and other reasons. If the culprits are not brought to book, it is not due to lack of provisions in the Act or weak legislation; more than anyone in the society the legal professionals who are part of the present civil society group know it very well and hesitate in addressing these. In fact the civil society activism in the recent period due to the kick up it gets from elsewhere has given an impression, due to the overzealous media, that it is only a government servant who is corrupt and all the corruption in the government originates from them. We know how the private sectors with the connivance of the so-called civil society activists (some) are manipulating policies. Is it not a fact that the consistent activity of some individuals on trivial issues is diverting the attention of the public, mostly the urban middle classes, from the real manipulators who have become billionaires overnight through corruption, frauds and all kinds of mafia activities? What kind of laws are needed to control the mining mafia? Are there not sufficient legal provisions to deal with these elements? Why is it that the civil society has not paid its attention to the private sector frauds where billions are said to be involved? Why is the civil society is concentrating on the pliable public servant who is now at the receiving end or at the mercy of the forces that sponsor all kinds of activities to divert the attention of people from the real issues? Why are they not scrutinising the liberalisation policies that are the root cause, according to some, for all these ills?

There are, however, some weaknesses in the existing procedures where the victims are quite often drawn from those who do not have any godfathers in the system. The UPSC is respected by all government servants in the country for the last several decades because it is the last resort of such persons. The perception among the people is that justice is done to majority of the victims without knowing, unlike in the judiciary, who is dealing with their cases. It would be a travesty of justice to create a body to punish the guilty without first providing opportunities of natural justice to the accused (now opportunities are given to the charged officer in the existing system).

The whole debate on corruption in the public domain as carried out by the civil society activists is again mostly directed at the civil servant in the federal and the state services. Interestingly, the debate which was originally aimed at the public servant that included the political executive now has ended up with the civil servant. Everyone, including some of the cynical civil servants, is willing to sacrifice the consecrated beast. But one may look at the evolution of the civil service to judge the place of the maligned civil servant. The record of economic and social progress achieved during the first three decades after Independence is the real bequest accomplished by them. Most of the civil servants of that time or the so-called bureaucrats have carried the legacy of utilitarianism and built the independent country with dedication, integrity and commitment. If India was a grand destination for Western investments in the 1990s, it was due to the infrastructure, the human resources, the sighting of natural resources, etc., developed by them. Then what went wrong with the system?

The iron frame as a part of the constitutional structure, in which they were shaped, was strong enough to protect them from political abuse of power. Though there were occasional incidents of corruption, the political establishment seemed to be morally upright in initiating action against such incidents. It was found that both the categories of the executive were guided by the inspissation feeling for the country rather than the individual. This moral code was perhaps devolved of the expectations of the society. The ethos of the country was not disturbed and its explicit influence in shaping the values of various functionaries was undamaged. In other words, the ethics in public service was shaped by the overall culture of the so-called Indianness. It seems the universal interest of the society was reflected in the actions of the civil servant in the past. This seems to be missing now due to the overall change in the vision of the state. If there were any seeds of fortuitous elements in the system, they were blown out of proportion when the primacy of individual interests was given importance in place of the society. There seem to be decadence in the system around 1970s and the moral authority of the system started crumbling. It may be due to the fact that some of the officers have started giving importance to their careers rather than the welfare of the people whom they are supposed to serve.

It is quite often seen that people talk about the character and countenance of public servants and expect that they should remain exemplary. The discourse on ethics takes the religious route to prescribing values in public life in India. The philosophical extractions are given tepid treatment. The same trend is carried into the civil service administration in India. Rather the policy makers should have relied upon the constitutional morality in the fait accompli of civil service codes or values to guide the incumbent. There seem to be some confusion and lack of clarity in the civil service till the second Administrative Reforms Commission under the chairmanship of Veerappa Moily pointed out the lacunae and drafted the Ethics in Governance as its fourth report to the government. There is no dearth of reports or recommendations as we have around 600 reports on the functioning of the civil service system in India!

The issue before the government now is how to penalise the corrupt and protect the honest with the Whistle Blowers Protection Act and other laws. The present Conduct Rules of the civil servants provide for broad contours of expected public behaviour. At the same time, the civil servant is subordinate to the political executive. As the recommendations of the Moily Commission on Ethics in Governance have not seen the light of the day and the Parliament has passed bills to regulate the behaviour of the civil servant, there is grey area where conflict of propriety arises. The tenure and status of civil servant is protected under the Constitution. He/she is expected to declare allegiance to democratic, secular and socialist values, while the government keeps on changing its policy as per its vision that may sometime go against the inherent principles. It is also found that there is a move towards the principles of New Public Management where output and outcomes are counted as evidence of performance rather than the inputs and processes. How this shift in emphasis is translated into administrative practice so that the civil servants' commitment to ethics is evaluated.

The ethical standing of the serving officer is shaped by his personal, professional, organisational and public interest. He/she has to balance the values in the context of the legal framework or laws of the land. Further, the transition of the economy from mixed to purely private orientation with attendant institutional arrangements, such as citizen's charter, RTI, PC Act, etc., makes the life of a civil servant complicated and has a propensity to commit mistakes. It is here the civil society can come to the rescue of the ethically committed civil servant in the interests of the society at large. Now we have a Whistle Blowers Protection Act in place, the civil society team can devote their time to identify and list out in each department of the government the interface between the public or stake holders and the expected outcome of public goods. This will help all the stakeholders.

The Constitution of India has thus protected the civil servant from unnecessary political interference and at the same time created institutions to monitor the functioning of the system with immunity. It all depends how effectively the system would make use of the provisions in the Constitution. As one of the ancient civilisations in the world, India has no dearth of laws, rules, values and sermons and these have all been sufficiently taken care of by the Constitution. It is not the Constitution that failed the system; it is the vile in people who did that.

3

Civil Service Values and Neutrality

Bhure Lal*

Civil servants render service to governments of various political hues with equal dedication and efficiency. They may disagree strongly with the government's policy but should not let this affect their behaviour. The Westminster system has framed certain conventions for maintaining neutrality of civil servants, such as anonymity, loyalty, permanence, restricted political rights of public servants, secrecy and ministerial responsibility. Parliament is supreme and must control all branches of administration. Ministers are part of administration and must be accountable to Parliament; civil servants are their subordinates. In the words of Clark, 'If Minister is put responsible for what happens then neither the opinion nor the actions nor words of civil servants, who are not responsible, must embarrass him or force his decisions' (Elliott and Thomas, 2011).

An enlightened civil service signifies the values of integrity, impartiality and merits, and provides the framework for efficient administration ensuring good governance. The civil servants should be service-oriented and citizen centric. They need to be insulated against undue political interference. There is a need to constantly improve the skills of the civil servants so that they can grapple with the explosion of knowledge and mange the dynamic changes effectively.

---

* Ex-Member, UPSC.

Public Service Values

The Constitution lays down certain values and protects the civil servant who sincerely follows the rules and traditions of the system. However, the system is so complex and restrictive today that it easily serves the goals of corrupt. The weakness of the system provides opportunities to the corrupt in amassing huge wealth. The lack of protection to honest officers and values is another area which discourages them to stand and fight corruption. If officers follow their superiors blindly there is bound to be bad governance and integrity of the government system might collapse. Therefore, there is need to devise a system which provides firm protection to whistle-blowers so that they may not be victimised. This will introduce transparency in the system and will discourage the corrupt superiors. Bureaucracy must play an instrumental role rather than become a rent-seeking institution. Politicians must also be subjected to accountability; this will ensure that illegal and inappropriate interferences are not done. Based on empirical findings the following values can be enumerated:

1. Allegiance to Constitution and law
2. Function to serve as instruments of good governance
3. Political neutrality
4. Objectivity, honesty, integrity, courtesy and responsiveness
5. Uphold highest ethical standards and establish high standards of quality in services
6. Merit in employment, promotion and placements
7. Prudent use of public money
8. Accountability in decision making
9. The officials must not promote their own interest by misusing power and authority
10. Government to notify Code of Ethics to keep morale of the employees high
11. Code of Ethics to ensure compliance of public service values
12. Breach of the code will be punishable under law
13. Directions in violation of values to be invalid

Management code is developed by the government after consultations with stakeholders and is based on the following principles:

1. Public service as a highly professional, merit-based institution for promoting good governance
2. Mechanisms and incentives to maintain high levels of productivity, efficiency and excellence
3. Policies and structures for ensuring viability and sustainability of public services
4. Establishing interface between political executive and public servants
5. Government to ensure implementation of code within 12 months and submit annual report to Parliament on compliance of code
6. Setting up of separate tribunals for dowry and property cases as they have a great scope for illegal gratification, and revenue/police officials involve themselves in such cases neglecting their normal duties and in the process raising the level of graft in the civil services
7. Information on all cases of procurement of stores and award of tenders beyond a particular ceiling should be put on the public domain automatically
8. People with criminal records should not be allowed to contest election and the elections must be funded through a bank account and any expenditure not booked to this account should be treated as unauthorised expenditure and, hence, a corrupt practice.

Civil Service Neutrality

The neutrality principle may be equated with silence, and works largely to protect ministers against public expression of views contrary to their own by people whose views they cannot dismiss on the grounds of ignorance. The doctrine is that civil servants must not express their own philosophy on any issue of public importance. He is to analyse the issue in a neutral and an impartial manner. This applies not only to active party politics but also includes controversial policy issues. According to the traditions of the British Constitution, a civil servant is a faceless entity operating through official rules. Nevertheless, he is an important part of the administrative culture. The principle of neutrality implies this sort of facelessness; otherwise civil servants would not command the confidence and trust of successive governments. Some civil servants are bound to have private views different from their minister's views and expression of these views by the civil servants in public would jeopardise and destabilise the position of the minister. The civil servants would acquaint themselves well by presenting the ministers with various possible solutions to a policy issue and leaving it to the minister to make the choice in the light of the political programme of the party. Thus the civil servant would provide non-partisan expert advice on controversial issues upholding the principle of professional neutrality. The top civil servants are the close collaborators of the ministers and advise them about the likely fallout and consequences of their policy. Elsewhere, political neutrality is thought to mean taking no side on political issues and render advice to the political boss in an objective manner. In some countries ministers may appoint politically or personally sympathetic officials to key posts. In India, there are no such designated posts. Appointments should be made on the basis of professional competence alone and once appointed a civil servant should not be removed on political grounds. He should serve successive governments with equal commitment and dedication. The guiding principle of service in this regard is that a civil servant must serve, whatever master comes along, with equal loyalty.

The doctrine of administrative neutrality has restricted public employees participating in political activities. The Hatch Acts framed during 1930s put barriers on political activities by government workers with a view to establish a National Political Machine. Despite their popularity, a national controversy has surrounded these Acts since the beginning. The protagonists considered the Hatch Acts necessary for an efficient, professional and non-partisan public service enjoying wide spread public confidence. The opponents asserted that Hatch Acts restricted the freedom unconstitutionally, created job dissatisfaction leading to moral problems for government servants.

The civil servants retain their position regardless of the Civil Service Neutrality and Civil Service Values and the fortunes of politicians.

The politicians may create situations in which the civil service may demand some form of political rights to organise, defend and vindicate it. In the words of political scientist Frederic C. Mosher (1982)[1] the modern state is 'the provisional state in which the policy formulation and particularly policy implementation, calls for highly specialized knowledge and sophisticated administration. No political leadership can govern without a great deal of technical and managerial assistance'. The civil service provides this expertise. Disputes between hungry politicians and civil servants cannot be ruled out and one of them, mostly the civil servant, is made a scapegoat. The possibility of there being a wide gap in the perception of a political party and the civil servants on national issues cannot be ruled out. This gap takes a critical turn when the former comes to power. The relationship changes because of protocol and powers of the ministers. Politicians, particularly the younger generation, view the civil service with scant respect. They have little faith in the civil service and regard bureaucrats as impediments in achieving their objectives. Every change in the political set-up necessitates a change in the administrative structure. Under such circumstances some officers succumb to pressure or patronage creating a crack in service morale and make the politician's job easy. The senior becomes scared to stand up for harassed, honest and independent officers. The feeling of *esprit de corps* is adversely affected among the rank and file of the civil service. The sense of professional awareness and oneness goes for a toss. Some officers acquire a servile attitude and believe in carrying out the legal as well as the illegal orders of their political masters. The primary objective of such officers is to provide cover to illegal activities of their political bosses and friends in industry and trade. They become instruments of misuse of power. The code of conduct and constitutional obligations are thrown to winds. Civil servants act as active politicians and they do not hesitate if their names are associated with organisations which perpetuate casteism and communalism; rather they regard such an association to be the stepping stone in the direction of promotions to reach the top. Such civil servants can never remain neutral in an emergency. The official machinery becomes incapable to accept the challenge created by political, communal and caste groups. It will be the most unfortunate day for all of us when private armies will collect protection money from innocent people and the writ of mafia–politician alliance will be aided and abetted by administration. The civil service must effectively counter the nefarious design of mafia dons enjoying political patronage. The job of civil servants is very difficult under the present circumstances. The problem is not whether the civil service can meet the challenge or not but whether correct instructions are being issued to civil servants or not. The protectors of law must not themselves become breakers of law. If the civil service is to retain whatever credibility it has, it must not allow itself to be politicised because a politicised civil service is the greatest danger to a parliamentary democracy.

The ex-chief election commissioner, T.N. Seshan, while lambasting the country's bureaucracy, said most bureaucrats are 'morally corrupt since they did not stand up against politicians and ministers' (Lal, 2009). Apart from financial dishonesty the intellectual dishonesty is widespread among bureaucrats.

Civil servants carry out good deal of exercise to ascertain the views of their ministers before recording any note and the note is always tailored to meet the requirements of the political boss even if it is against rationality, justice and the interest of the country. 'When the political boss sneezes the civil servants catch cold.' Without going into merits and demerits of what Seshan said, it is time for civil servants to introspect and confront their weaknesses. Under the prevailing circumstances, it will be difficult to credit the civil service with neutrality and integrity. Incompetent and corrupt officers have been favoured by the central and the state governments for their partisan role in the discharge of their duties. The civil servants are swayed by avarice, tempted by plum postings and lucrative desks in return for the services rendered to the political bosses. Merit, intelligence and competence are discounted and an independent minded civil servant takes the back seat.

Civil servants became agents to carry out all illegal and unconstitutional orders during the Indian Emergency. The press was gagged and people were detained illegally. Arbitrary actions were carried out with impunity. Most of the officers were acting for self-aggrandisement. 'If the officers act at the instance of politicians to foster their political interest then the national interest is thrown to winds', observes Justice Shah in the Shah Commission Report Vol. II (Lal, 2009). Officers acting in collusion with politicians to carry out their evil designs are a greater danger to the democracy than the politicians because the politicians have to face the electorate but not the officers.

A civil servant will cease to be neutral if he plays party politics or imposes his own policies on the country. A civil servant will also not be neutral if he uses the patronage of politicians to boost his own career prospects. The civil servants are found not only paying obeisance to the politicians but also to the businessmen and industrialists to secure postretirement prospects.

During imposition of the President's Rule, bureaucrats are used as puppets by politicians to achieve by proxy what they had been denied by ballot. The rejected politicians are appointed in large numbers to occupy the posts of chairman of cooperative societies, State Public Enterprises, Mandi Parishads, Sahitya Academy and so on. The bureaucrats comply with the orders in anticipation of favours at the hands of politicians once popular government is installed.

Interference by the politicians can be checked if the civil servants exhibit a little courage to stand up to defend what is just and right. If the civil servants muster courage to tell the politicians about their unconstitutional designs, the politicians would develop cold feet and dare not ask them for wrong favours. The performance of civil administration depends on the quality and character of the political executive. The errant officials must be punished and the innocent should not be made scapegoats for the sins of their political masters.

Nothing should be done to demoralise the service as a demoralised bureaucracy may prove to be the last straw on the back of the tired camel. The essence of a true government is the people-oriented administration having public welfare at heart. Public must be treated as subject of a democratic state. Their grievances should attract prompt attention and remedial measures must be initiated ensuring no harassment to innocent people. It is an unfortunate situation in which people feel that dealing with government departments is a great curse. Administration must be responsive to the needs of the people forging good will and harmony. A procedure-oriented bureaucracy will fail to deliver goods in independent India as it cripples the initiative of people. Bureaucracy must be free from blemish of inertia, ineffectiveness, red-tapism, bribery and self-defeating controls. Only then it can win the admiration of the people.

The ICS of the British days was one of the finest services in the world. It was the *steel frame* of British rule in India. After the advent of Independence, the steel frame was given the name of Indian Administrative Service (IAS). It was anticipated that the IAS would represent the true spirit of public service and be fully responsive to the needs of Indian people striving to establish a new socioeconomic system in independent India. Sardar Patel, the great protagonist of AIS, remarked, 'Do not quarrel with instruments with which you want to work. It is a bad workman who quarrels with the instruments. I have worked with them during the difficult times. Remove them and see nothing but a picture of chaos all over the country' (Kumar, 1991). Pandit Nehru remarked that 'the old distinctions and differences are gone. In the difficult days ahead our services and experts have a vital role to play and we invite them to do so as comrades in the service of India' (Nehru, 2007, p. 14). It was expected that the ICS who once governed the country would become dedicated servants of free India.

After independence, the politicians and the administrators had to tackle the problems of national integration, legitimisation of the political regime, democratic sharing of political power and economic development. Masses of the people were politically ill aware and structurally different. They were required to be brought in the mainstream of not only national life but also were to be made effective partners in the running of government. The objective of the decisions of the government, the policies and their implementation, was to alleviate the difficulties of the people of the country without any distinction. Describing the prevailing situation at that time Rienhhard Bendix observed,

> In Indian history there is no comparable legacy of an abstract principle of justice or of a sovereign political order in which the several states and local communities could be integrated through a system of representation. In the absence of such legacies modern India faces difficult problems of integration, that, of establishing orderly relationship between the constituent units of the society and the centres of governmental authorities. (Tummala, 1996)

Government is elected on the basis of universal adult franchise in India. An elected government is keenly concerned with the need to motivate the work force to implement its objectives and programmes. Politicians should realise that executives respond positively towards challenging and satisfying work.

Politicians want their agenda acted upon right away to ensure that they have an impact during the limited five years term of their administration. The success of a political administrative challenges system depends on the implementation of the ideological concepts, psychological values and the social programmes at all levels. Bureaucracy and the political leadership can achieve this goal by working closely and critically. Their consensus can translate the political manifesto of the government into administrative reality. The manifesto ultimately becomes the social policy of the state. Once policy is laid down and the course of its implementation decided, it remains for the administrator to see that the policy reaches every level of society. If political leadership represents the input function the output would be achieved by the civil service. The administrative structure is an integral link between polity and society.

In our administrative culture, power is a tool of dominance and we do not view it as an opportunity to do good to people. Policy is seen by the minister only as power. It is left entirely to civil servants to provide not only policy content but also value content. The first law of politics is: *get re-elected* Politicians become unscrupulous, ideologically hollow, selfish and opportunistic. They publicly blame civil servants for the failure or non-implementation of the policy. The civil servants are not given the right of public vindication in such situations because of unconditional anonymity. *Blame the bureaucracy* has come handy to the politicians when anything goes wrong. The civil servants have been regarded as a stumbling block in the way of India's social and economic progress. Politicians have stated time and again that the present bureaucracy cannot meet the requirements of social and economic changes along socialist lines. 'The creation of administrative cadre committed to the national objectives and responsive to our social needs, is an urgent necessity' (Maheshwari, 2001).

In the absence of ideological content, politics has become a game of controlling vote banks. The vote banks become the real power behind the throne and a minister can ill afford to displease them. He has to keep them on the right side which is usually the wrong side of administration. The ministers blame that the administrative machinery has become unresponsive and inefficient. They are constructively responsible for the mistakes of civil servants but they are not ready to delegate powers to the officers because they think that ultimately they have to face the assembly/parliament and not the officers. This view is partially correct. The present-day ministers are not heavy weights having full knowledge of administration and working of the government. But they are important because they are ministers and some of them are eager to flaunt their newly acquired status and power. This creates a dichotomy between policy formulation and implementation. The dichotomy as a matter of a fact may be only theoretical and artificial. No political system can survive without public support and mobilisation of public support is the main function of a politician. He seems to be abandoning this legitimate function. This function cannot be taken over by the civil servants. The inadequate knowledge of the role of a public servant and a mistaken notion that he is no more than a direct and a voiceless subordinate have created a situation in which the ministers have ordered the civil servants *to put up and shut up or do as I say.* This tendency has curbed the initiative of not only civil servants but also of politicians because the policy initiatives arise out of hidden agendas and not out of public motives.

On the other hand, some civil servants have a feeling of self-assumed omniscience and infallibility while giving advice to the political boss. Some officers develop cynicism and frustration. Viceroy Lord Curzon had said once: 'The Government of India was mighty and miraculous machinery for doing nothing' (Murray, 1904).[2] Our Vice President (later on President), K.R. Narayanan, while addressing the probationers at LBSNAA had remarked: 'The complex developed by the officers of the Indian Administrative service that only they can deal with the real problems and are close to the people is wrong' (Lal, 2009). Civil servants are reluctant to give credit to anybody else. It will be wrong on their part to hold in contempt politicians as a class.

They are no match for a minister's practical field knowledge. They go by the stereotyped rules and responses to policy initiative from the minister. They suffer from lack of courage to communicate with people. They are ambitious and most of them resort to dishonest means and believe in political wire pulling. A civil servant must not sabotage a policy because it has emanated out of the manifesto of a political party because he considers it wrong. It will be unethical on his part to do so. Without subscribing to any political ideology or programme, a civil servant should create conditions for the proper implementation of programmes of the elected government. He should remain completely neutral in the political debates and ideological stands taken by the various political parties. Rather they should suggest techniques, ways and means to implement the policies of the ruling party without causing difficulties to the people. The concept of civil service neutrality implies that the civil servant should help the political masters to enact their political programmes within the framework of law. He is ideologically neutral and works for the success of the democratic system by simply guiding the politicians while remaining completely non-aligned to the political parties.

Almond and Powell say

> Bureaucracy dominate the output end of the political conversion process, they are indispensable in the rule making adjudication process as well as influential in the political process of interest articulation, aggregation, and communication. Other governmental structure, such as political executives, legislatures and courts must be viewed in relation to the functioning of bureaucracy. They cannot be functionally effective save through bureaucracy. (Almond and Powell, 1978)[3]

Thus the entire edifice of administration revolves around bureaucracy. The administrative structure is concerned with the achievement of given social objectives and emphasises the need of efficient means to accomplish them. The leadership structure is concerned with the task of determining social objectives. This division of functions clearly demarcates the jurisdiction of the leaders and administrators and if both of them strictly adhere to their sphere of activities, the possibilities of attaining the systematic goal will be the maximum. There are, however, ambiguities in such demarcations. At times, the civil service and the political leaders do not have a clear understanding of such a demarcation. They have a tendency towards monopolisation. The result is encroachment by one over the jurisdiction of another and this will subvert the basis of political organisation. There is a clear line of distinction between policy and administration. Best results can be achieved if both work in tandem. This is possible when there is frequent interaction between the two and the decisions are arrived at on the basis of mutual understanding and consensus. If such an interaction fails to develop, each unit will stick to its own motion because each has the pride of opinion and the conviction of being right.

Civil Service and Politicians

Experienced political leaders do not embarrass the administrators by putting unreasonable and improper demands. They do not apply pressure on them to get their demands fulfilled. It is incumbent upon the administration to evaluate the demands of political leaders rationally and legally. If the demands put up by the political leaders are illegal and irrational, they should be politely turned down. They are within their rights if they do not comply with unreasonable demands of political leaders. But it must not be forgotten, as pointed out by Peter M. Blau, 'to administer a social organisation according to technical criteria of rationality is irrational, because it ignores the non-rational aspect of social aspect of conduct' (Lal, 2009).

The civil servants and the politicians must honestly be concerned with the realisation of systematic goals. The scope of civil service activity is no longer confined to collection of revenue and maintenance of law and order. It has to play a tremendous role in economic development and social change. Without the financial backing nothing is likely to move and the civil servants as well as politicians will prove ineffective. Political leaders make promises to people to establish schools, hospitals, lay roads, provide employment to unemployed youths and so on. All these promises are not backed by adequate financial resources. These promises remain hollow and people start losing their faith in the system. The political leader conveniently blames the administrators for the lapse. The reciprocal image perception of both, administrator and political leader, reflects disaffection and unfavourable induction of each other. The political leader alleges that administrators are corrupt, rigid in their attitude and inefficient and interested mainly in their own career prospects. They are neither impartial nor mete out fair treatment. Political leaders believe that the administrators must work in the interest of the ruling groups. Much cannot be expected from very rigid procedural oriented administrators.

The administrators feel that the political leaders are not receptive and responsive to their advice and expertise. They feel that the political leaders do not appreciate their viewpoint as well as their difficulties and their proposals are often ignored. The administration feels that the political leaders give much more preference to the furtherance of narrow parochial interest. They are incapable of managing public affairs and unnecessarily create trouble for the administration. They have scant respect for administrative rules, regulations and procedures.

The struggle between the political leadership and civil servant is, as a matter of fact, a struggle for power. The administrator seeks protection under the plethora of civil service rules, regulations and procedures and tries to protect himself by greater adherence to them. He also musters the support of local leaders. At times, the administrators do not change their mindset and even regard the reformatory measures as a challenge to their own position, power and status. Thus the civil servants are suspected of being biased rather than neutral in their policy perspective. They may even try to sabotage policy proposals that political leaders want to put into effect. Therefore, neutrality of civil servant has been increasingly questioned. Even their competence in rendering valuable suggestions for enacting legislative measures has come under attack because of the increasing tendency of national policy makers to turn increasingly to specialised technical agencies for designing government programmes. The *neutral competence* provided by the administrative services did throw light on the dark corners of policy issues. But now this competence has to accept the challenge of experts who are dominating the entire gamut of economic and social activities. The new emerging activities require activism and not the passivity of neutral competence. It seems that executive bureaucracy is ceasing to be a source of neutral competence. The optimal blending of partisan responsiveness and continuity in the form of policy competence remain the most compelling methods for those committed to the improvement of governance. The political leadership will direct the state apparatus towards partisan priorities rather than completely override it.

The civil service must commit itself to the process of nation building and socio-economic development. The administrators are to guide the politicians for broad developmental ideology and cultural renaissance instead of serving as a stumbling block on the path of development. Lucian Pye says, 'The great problem today in nation building is that of relating the administrative and authoritative structure of government to the political forces within the transitional societies' (Pye, 1996).

Neutrality Improves Efficiency

Neutrality will lead to efficiency and alertness. This concept has been illustrated remarkably by Lord Attlee: 'The same men who had worked out the details of Labour Transport Act were now, at the behest of a conservative government, engaged in putting it to pieces' (Lal, 2009, p. 242). He viewed the policy makers and decision makers as a single phenomenon which can never be disentangled in practice; changes in political set-up should be of no consequence to the civil servants. When Attlee succeeded Winston Churchill as prime minister of England, he took the same team of officials, including the principal private secretary that had served under Churchill. This is the finest tradition of British Civil Service which has become a pattern for others to follow. The civil servants always like to work under an able, intelligent, sharp, alert and bold minister. A good minister listens to his staff and encourages them for discussions and a good administrator thoroughly does his home work and apprises the minister not only on policy but also on other aspects of administration. It gives immense pleasure to the administrator when the minister comes out successfully from the Parliament after dealing the Question Hour intelligently, effectively and humorously. The political leadership must make use of the neutral competence. Herbert Kaufman pointed out that

> neutral competence is a wealth of knowledge and skill available in the corridors of bureaucracy that all elected officials, no matter what their political persuasion, could call upon for both useful and disinterested advice in designing national policy. The declining faith in the neutral competence of civil servants threatens to undermine the legitimacy of bureaucratic participation in national policy making, because the courts have always regarded the professional expertise of bureaucrats as the chief justification that can be given in a democracy for allowing such unelected officials to have a major hand in shaping the country's policy decisions. (Lal, 2009, p. 242)

This neutral competence should mature into more advanced form of professionalism. The trained bureaucrats provide the knowledge and skill that will enable the government to arrive safely at its destination. The justification of the administrative system cannot be argued if the civil servant does not display qualities necessary for efficient job performance or he is held in low esteem by people. Excessive demands for unreasonable and improper gratification make the operation of legal and rational criterion of bureaucracy difficult. Appointments, writing of confidential reports, promotions, postings and transfers should be sternly and rigidly objective only then the system will work. Today, the selection and postings of officers are done on the basis of their pliability and alignment. Appointments are made on considerations other than merit. Officers are not posted on key positions on the basis of their toughness and independence or intelligence and ability. The flexible officers rule the roost and get plum postings while the independent-minded officers are sidelined. Political acceptability rather than the personal qualities of head and heart determine the postings of officers.

The civil servants do not give expert advice but only act as staff officers to implement the orders. They believe in the anticipatory compliance with the wishes of the political masters. They are keen to find out what the minister feels before they pass their orders or tender advice. The civil service goes not by convictions but by the direction of the wind. There is change of heart overnight and the bureaucrats become supporters of the policy of a political party which is likely to capture power and adapt themselves in advance to the political philosophy of the party. Thus, bureaucracy has lost sensitivity to public service and public good.

Civil service should get out of self seeking. The political masters should also realise that impartial, independent and neutral civil service is the sine qua non for an efficient administration. This is possible only when the political masters give up their narrow political objectives and the civil servants render rational advice to the political masters without any personal axe to grind. According to B.K. Nehru, 'The independence of civil services has been jeopardised by the liberty given to the State Governments in the matters of transfer, suspension and promotion. The power of transfer is very frequently used to bend an officer to the minister's will' (Nehru, 2009). There is no rule governing transfers which disturb the life of an officer. The power of suspension also affects the independence of an officer. All these factors are not congenial for a civil servant to act impartially and honestly. If the power of a politician to influence the transfer of an officer is taken away, half the administrative problems will disappear and civil service will act as a strong vibrant and independent arm of Indian democracy. When a political boss transfers his subordinate who is a part of the bureaucratic elite, his decisions may be politically motivated. In a society, where the public is educated and the mass media developed, the political boss will have to justify his decision to remove senior bureaucrat from position of power. Targeted bureaucrats, on the other hand, will try to defend themselves by proving their innocence to the public and the authorities concerned. Therefore, political boss and the bureaucratic elite are interlocked in a psychological warfare of *image building* and intense *politicking*.

In services, godfatherism is dominating today. Officers even at the junior level do not struggle to learn their jobs. They are more concerned to win the *boss* and the *madam* by resorting to all sorts of tricks. The civil service has lost respect for lack of commitment and seldom owns up responsibility in the eventuality of anything going wrong. It is the sacred duty of the civil servant to be committed to the Constitution and give advice to the minister as per his interpretation of the Constitution without fear or favour. Unfortunately, the civil servants have found it to be an uphill task during the last 60 years. There have been occasions when the civil service had to face a dilemma in India—whether to owe allegiance to the Constitution or to carry out orders of the state administration in violation of the constitutional duties. The most glaring example that can be cited here is that of the civil servants behaviour in Uttar Pradesh at the time of demolition of a disputed structure at Ayodhya.

The political boss seeks transfer of the senior bureaucrat of his ministry on account of two reasons—political or administrative accountability. The political boss perceives that high-level public servants may prove liability to him. He may dislike him because of the latter's personality and attitude, party affiliation and family background. He may have developed a personal antagonism towards the bureaucrat. Sometimes the political boss has someone else in mind to fill the position of the senior bureaucrat. The political boss prefers new men to old ones.

The other reason may be that the senior bureaucrat performs badly in his job. Such a civil servant is inefficient. The reasons for transferring a subordinate official are administrative, and not political. The senior bureaucrats may be transferred from high-level posts because of their incompetence, disobedience, malfeasance, malpractice or corruption.

Another question baffling the minds of people is the question of responsibility. The ultimate responsibility of government actions in the form of legislation, appointment, drafting of rule, and general running of the state machinery lies with the minister. The civil servant acts as the secretary of the department who guides, controls and educates the political head. But it is the minister who is the target of attack in the parliament and not his secretary or staff. The officers will feel guilty if they conceal facts and ill advise the ministers. Public policies enunciated by the political boss run the risk of implementation if cooperation from the bureaucratic elite is not forth coming. Similarly the bureaucratic elite will have Administrative Challenges a very difficult time performing their jobs if their political bosses do not support them. If the political boss and the bureaucratic elite do not get well together, the public organisation will suffer from rivalry and conflict. Michael Rush and Philip Althoff have pointed out that 'the administrative machine is such that the impact of politicians on administration and of administrator on policy is invariably profound' (Rush and Althoff, 1971). Emotions and ego are likely to dominate the interaction, at times, between the minister and the civil servants. The civil servants have to choose between unpleasantness and impropriety. The civil servants can take a stand provided they enjoy a strong reputation for honesty and efficiency. Officers with a high degree of courage, self-respect and detachment can come out unscathed. The skilful officers salvage situation without hurting minister's ego. Civil servants at lower echelon of hierarchy can give a very good account of themselves when they are supported by their superiors to take unpopular but correct decisions. In the case of an individual officer, it will depend on his personality and ideological stand to accept the challenge from his opponents in the pursuit of the policies which he deems correct. The situation, at times, becomes complex because it will not be a proper development to make administration a battleground between the officer and the minister. The causality will be public good. On the other hand, any impropriety will be like a little pregnancy which is bound to grow up. It is quite possible that if a bureaucrat yields once then there would be no end of yielding to improper demands.

The civil service should present an image of unified professionalisation so that no minister can have his way just by changing an officer. The ministers may have short-term personal stakes but the civil service has an impersonal life term perspective. Therefore, some conflict will be inevitable. These conflicts will get resolved by maintaining perpetual neutrality and rationality. The minister would appear to be decisive and benevolent in the secretariat. He will like to appear to be tough while dealing with his officers because he wants to create an image of prestige and authority in public. His behaviour may not be the same in a secretariat room. The civil service must not hesitate to apprise the minister the pros and cons of his programmes in a dispassionate manner.

Rejected politicians create strife in the society by exploiting caste/communal feelings. They keep an eye on the creation of vote banks by segregating people. No candidate for state legislature and Lok Sabha should be declared elected unless he secures a minimum of 51 per cent of the votes. This will imply an appeal by the candidate to all sections of the society irrespective of caste/community. Administrative tensions, to some extent, will get mitigated by such a move. The representation of People's Act, 1951, should be amended for the purpose. The move will also ensure that politicans do not derive strength based on factionalism. They will behave in an impartial/neutral manner among castes and communities.

Development of a performance management system covering priorities, objectives, performance indicators, strategy, plans and outcomes are to be put in place. Submission of annual Performance Report by 30 June to government comparing goals set and achieved feedback from users, standards of service delivery, quality of service, plan of action for next year well in time, etc., would play a constructive role in ensuring quality of service.

Notes

1. See also Sahni and Vayunandan (2009).
2. See also Lal (2009).
3. See also Goel and Rajneesh (2008).

Bibliography

Almond, Gabriel and G.B. Powell. 1978. *Comparative Politics.* Second edition. Boston: Little Brown and Company.

Bhattacharyya, S.K. 1984. 'Managers and Technocrats Role in the Political Administrative World: Some Current Issues', *Economic and Political Weekly*, 19 (8), 25 February.

Bhambri, C.P. 1999. *Bureaucracy and Politics in India*. New Delhi: Vikas Publications.

Dang, Satyapal. 1983. 'IAS and Politicians', *Mainstream* annual (pp. 99–101). India: Civil Service and Legislators.

Deshmukh, B.G. 1991. 'Role of Cabinet Secretary: Post Must Not Be Politicised', *Times of India*, 7 October, p. 6.

Elliott, Mark and Robert Thomas. 2011. *Public Law*. New York: Oxford University Press.

Goel, S.L. and Shalini Rajneesh. 2008. *Public Personnel Administration: Theory and Practice*. New Delhi: Deep and Deep.

Government of India. 1962. K. Santhanam Committee Report on Prevention of Corruption. New Delhi: Government of India.

Kumar, Ravindra. 1991. *Life and Work of Sardar Vallabhbhai Patel*. New Delhi: Atlantic Publishers and Distributors.

Lal, Bhure. 2009. *Administrative Challenges*. New Delhi: Siddharth Publications. Also available online at http://Fame-India.com/up47/Bhurelal_administrative_challenges.pdf (accessed 24 March 2014).

Maheshwari, S.R. 1998. *Administrative Reform in India: Past, Present and Future Prospects*. New Delhi: Centre for policy Research.

———. 2001. *Indian Administration*. Sixth edition. New Delhi: Orient Longman Private Limited.

Mosher, Frederick C. 1982. *Democracy and the Public Services*. USA: Oxford University Press.

Murray, John. 1904. Speeches of Lord Curzon. London. Available online at https://archive.org/stream/speechesonindiad00curzrich/speechesonindiad00curzrich_djvu.txt (accessed 24 March 2014).

Nehru, B.K. 1981. 'The Roots of Corruption', The G.L. Mehta Memorial Lecture. Madras.

———. 2009. 'The Civil Service in Transition', in Pratap Bhattarchya (ed.), *Readings in Bureaucracy*, pp. 3–16. Kolkata: Administrative Training Institute.

Nehru, Jawaharlal. 2007. 'Broadcast to the Nation', in *Congress Sandesh*, p. 14. Available online at http//www.congresssandesh.com (accessed 14 March 2014).

Pye, Lucian. 1996. *Aspects of Political Development*. Boston: Little Brown and Company. Available online at http://www.beyondintractability.org/essay/nationbuilding (accessed 24 March 2014).

Ridley, F.F. 1986. 'Political Neutrality: The Duty of Silence and the Right to Publish in the Civil Service', *Parliamentary Affairs*, 39 (4), October: 43–48.

Rush, Michael and Philip Althoff. 1971. *An Introduction to Political Sociology*. London: Thomson Nelson and Sons.

Sahni, Pardeep and Etakula Vayunandan. 2009. *Administrative Theory*. New Delhi: Phi Learning Pvt. Ltd.

Santhanam, K. 1964. Committee on Prevention of Corruption Report. Government of India, New Delhi.

Tummala, Krishna K. 1996. *Public Administration in India.* New Delhi: Allied Publishers.

Williams, Chris. 1985. 'The Concept of Bureaucratic Neutrality', *Australian Journal of Public Administration*, 44 (1), March: 46–58.

4

Importance of Social Security in Good Governance

T.S.N. Sastry*

Social security is a human right as well as a social and economic necessity. All successful societies and economies have employed developmental strategies where social security systems played an important role to alleviate poverty and provide economic security that helps people to cope with life's major risks or the need to quickly adapt to changing economic, political, demographic and societal circumstances (ILO, 2010).

From ancient to modern times, the administrative efficiency, economic growth, welfare policies adopted and the well-being of people of a state are assessed basing on its governance as an indicative factor (Agarwal, 2008, pp. 13–17; Sharma, 2006). But over the centuries, degeneration of moral and ethical values and self-centrist policies of rulers across the world have had an enormous upsetting the apple cart of governance, both at national and international levels (Margaret and Karen, 2005). The major changes that took place in the global arena after the Second World War, especially the end of decolonisation, redrawing of borders of many states, revolutionary affect of science and technology, expanding horizons of information technology, politico, socio-economic distress, emphatic concern for the promotion and protection of human rights and to adhere to the rule of law to the maximum extent, led the nation-states to focus

---

* Professor of Law, University of Pune, Pune.

their attention on the concept of governance once again without any inkling towards one-upmanship. The behavioural change in the mindset of the rulers and ruled around the world brought in sharp focus once again the need to rejuvenate the concept of governance with that of the concept of 'good governance' on to the international and national arena to measure the holistic effect on the governance of a state in its totality.

Definition and Concept of Good Governance

The concept of good governance is an integral part of the concept of governance.[1] Since its coinage by the World Bank in the late 1980s and early 1990s, (Chowdhury and Skarstedt, 2005; World Bank, 1992), it has occupied a prime place in the governance agenda of the world. Further, with the recognition of right to development as a human right by the United Nations in the late 1980s,[2] the focus of the whole world has once again shifted towards promotion of the concept of governance with a blend of people-centric policies to justify themselves as good governing democracies (Sabharwal, 2006). Accordingly, considering the needs and obligations that these states have in their governance, the concept of governance has been defined as:[3]

> The sum of the many ways individuals and institutions, public and private, manage their common affairs. It is a continuing process through which conflicting or diverse interests may be accommodated and cooperative action may be taken. It includes formal institutions and regimes empowered to enforce compliance, as well as informal arrangements that people and institutions either have agreed to or perceive to be in their interest.

Governance has many forms and approaches. However, in the contemporary era, the comity of nations wants to run their administrative approaches with more people-oriented policies in all sectors and to subserve the individual; this being their prime objective has led to the evolution of the concept of good governance in the modern era. In other words, the irresponsible governance, lack of respect for the basic needs of individuals, rampant corruption, relegation of human security to secondary stage, scant attention for the promotion and protection of human rights, etc., have led to the evolution of the concept of good governance. Accordingly, the concept of good governance can be defined as:

> Universal protection of human rights, non-discriminatory laws; efficient, impartial and rapid judicial processes; transparent public agencies; account-ability for decisions by public officials, devolution of resources and decision making to local levels from the capital; and meaningful partition by citizens in debating public polices and choices. (Wyman, 2011).

The principle of good governance covers a number of areas with different set of ideals for the augmentation of a better society. Hence, it has economic, political, social, cultural and legal dimensions with an aim to bring in transparent administrative process, to respect human rights of people without any legal deviation, to promote the inclusive and exclusive growth, and to promote the social security of all the people without any prejudices to the concept of equality.

Good Governance and India

The concept of governance is not new to India. A glance into the annals of ancient India clearly specifies that the concept of good governance was the prime concern of the empires of India mostly based on the notion of dharma (Kashyap, 2003).

In the words of Bhishma Pitamaha, the concept of good governance is nothing but righteousness to be strictly followed by the ruler of a state in its public affairs (Agarwal, 2008, p. 14; Ganguli, 1883–1896). This means the ruler and his ministers and public officials who have taken the oath of their offices to uphold dharma and to take care of public needs must not act unjustly or unethically because if they do so, they will not only destroy the moral basis of governance but also turn the state into a hell (Agarwal, 2008, p. 14).

Though good governance is a part of the Indian polity from ancient times, the upheaval events of frequent wars by foreign rulers, in its middle and later centuries, and the domination of the colonial masters in the modern periods had brought in a sea of change in the administrative setup and governance. Though we have achieved a tremendous economic growth, the social security region is concerned; we are still well below the 100th mark of human index in the world.[4] This brings the point to the fore that in spite a number of welfare schemes which are crafted by the legislature, the lackadaisical attitude of the administrators has brushed aside the social security infrastructure of the majority of the populace of the country. Though economic development of a country is a priority area, at the same time, social security plays a very vital role to measure the governance of a country. The Millennium Development Goals of the United Nations too categorically advocate the significance of social security in no uncertain words and request the member states to reorient their policy framework to make the populace to be self reliant.

Concept and Definition of Social Security

The concept of social security is considered as an important factor by many states. However, in the developing states to a great extent it is limited to employment and labour relations.[5] From legal perspective it is an all pervading concept; especially from the viewpoint of international law, it is recognised as a human right. The various texts on human rights have imposed obligations on the nation-states both at the national and international levels to extend state protection to every individual and provide for a sustainable environment, wherein the right to social security can be realised to its fullest extent possible by all means.[6] The United Nations bodies dealing with rights, including International Labour Organization (ILO), have enriched the scope of social security and it is defined as: encompassing the right to access and maintaining benefits, whether in cash or kind, without discrimination, in order to ensure protection, inter alia, from:

1. lack of work-related income caused by sickness, disability, maternity, employment injury, employment, old age or death of a family member
2. unaffordable access to health care
3. insufficient family support, particularly for children and adult dependants. It further emphasises the importance of

(redistributive) social security in poverty reduction and alleviation, preventing social exclusion and promoting social inclusion.

The definition makes it clear that states have an obligation to introduce schemes to help people who are unable to procure their contribution for their own protection and excluded from the social welfare schemes which mostly cover the below poverty line. It is this security that is provided to all the needy sections of a polity without any discrimination on sex, language and religion and other aspects which would be the yardsticks to decide whether the governance of a state is good or bad. In the contemporary era, apart from all other parameters, social security constitutes a most important tool and need to be augmented by all states, especially the developing world to judge their quality of governance.

Social Security in the Indian Scenario

Social security concept like that of good governance is not new to India. From ancient to modern times, the concept of social security is part and parcel of the Indian administrative system. Among all the texts of ancient India, the *Arthashastra* by Kautilya has categorically stated that it is the duty of the king to extend support to those who are in need of the state at any point of time and due to whatsoever the reason that they need the help of the state. He specially addressed the vital components of social security, such as food security, policies to protect security in natural exigencies, welfare of distressed women and children, etc. (Rao, 1958; Sastry, 1961).

The Constitution of India without any deviance of the above philosophy, in no uncertain terms, advocates through preamble and a number of other provisions, and has imposed obligations both on the Union and states to adopt broad-based social security policies to cover majority populace of the country without any deviance.[7] In order to meet the requirements of the Constitution, a number of schemes have been introduced both by the Union and states. However, in the last six decades these policies have been confined only to protect needy sections of the society, especially the BPL families and other socially backward sections and minorities and the work force of the country with a special focus in the industrial labour.[8]

In the contemporary era of globalisation and technological developments, social security needs to be a broad-based system which has to be extended to all sections of the society who are in need of the assistance of the state for one reason or the other. In the Indian context, urbanisation, extensive migrations, natural disasters, spate of diseases and changes in the joint family system, to name a few, have reinforced the need to have a relook at the social security system that is prevailing in India.[9] Though due to financial and other resource crunch, the state has limited its extension of social security to the needy, social security in the contemporary era is a comprehensive perspective which needs to prevent deprivation and assure every individual a basic minimum living income to protect himself and his family.

Interpreting the true meaning of life and liberty under Article 21 and reading with a number of other provisions, especially that of raising the standard of living as stated in Article 47 of the Constitution, the Supreme Court of India in a catena of cases, in no uncertain terms advocated that social security is one of the fundamental aspects of life and liberty and is a concept of need based depending on a number of circumstances. For instance, in P. Rathinam v. Union of India,[10] the Court defined:

> The right to live with human dignity and the same does not connote continued drudgery. It takes within its fold some of the fine graces of civilisation which makes life worth living and that the expanded concept of life would mean the tradition, culture and heritage of the person concerned.

In Olga Tellis,[11] emphasising the significance of the term life, it held that 'life is not merely restricted to animal existence of a person, it means something more and the inhibition against and deprivation to life extends to all those limits and faculties for which life is enjoyed'. In another case it articulated that 'in a welfare state the primary duty of the Government is to secure the welfare of the people'.[12]

The brief discussion amply makes it clear that social security is an integral part of the developmental process of a state and it is the duty of the state to extend protection to all sections of people, especially those who are in need of its helping hand at any point of time. It no more implies that social security is only for particular section of people or only to people below the poverty line. Accordingly, the duty of the state doesn't end by framing the policies but making its administrative units to implement the policy formulations with utmost sincerity to achieve the objectives of a welfare state as laid down in the constitution.

A Legal Perspective of Social Security

No doubt in the last six decades, the Union and the states have evolved a number of social welfare schemes to protect the needy sections of the society. However, in view of changing patterns of life cycle due to number of economic, social, cultural and other developmental perspectives, many families in India live in social insecurity. As a result, once a family considered as above poverty line may join the group either for a temporary period or on a permanent basis. In this regard, the state has to take steps to extend its social security cover to extend its realm from the below poverty line mark to extend protection to a number of people of different strata of society those who may require the extended protection mechanism of social security. In the contemporary era, this is otherwise popularly referred to as societal security (Tobias, 2010, pp. 105–23) and a growing concept especially in the regions of Europe, America and Australia and in few other parts of the developed states.

The various social welfare schemes that have been developed in India, especially, with the introduction of 20 point programme of Mrs Indira Gandhi in the mid 1970s till the 100 days rural employment scheme by Prime Minister Manmohan Singh in the recent past, almost all programmes have been targeted at a particular section of people with special focus on the BPL and to other weaker sections and minorities. Even then, they could not bring in the expected results in raising standards of these people and human index of social and security are still in a rudimentary stage. This is more so in the case of children who are the future capital of the country (*Frontline*, 2010). In reality, even the targeted sections of people, where social security measures were adopted to cover industrial workers, are also in the abysmal phase. It is evident from the statement of Krzysztof Hagemejer that the social security programmes in India, including poor health care, pensions, social assistance and unemployment benefits, are extremely limited with a large majority of the population ineligible for these benefits (Hagemejer, 2010; ILO, 2010). This brings the point to the fore; minimal social security needs to be provided as a common denominator to all the people of the society by the state through its administrative mechanism in order to achieve the human index. Then only India can tinsel in the eyes of the world as a major world power both economically and socially.

To match with the 1993 global campaign of the International Labour Conference on social security for all to improve its world ranking in the promotion of social security, apart from existing schemes to targeted group of people's welfare schemes, some of the following common standards of social security measures need to be adopted to make the people be self reliant.

Health being the most important vital basic need of all sections of the society, there is an urgent need for both the Union and the states to have a re-look at the health system of India. As suggested by the author elsewhere (Sastry, 2009), there is a need to reintegrate the existing poli-cies to evolve a national policy on the lines suggested by ILO,[13] to cover health care needs in terms of structure and volume of burden of disease, responding to demands in terms of quality expectations of people and defining level of heath care including that of preventive health care. A critical examination of the 11th Five Year Plan clearly indicates that though the per capita expenditure of the state has nominally increased compare to yester years, the GDP of the state expenditure has consider-able reduced (Planning Commission, 2008). As rightly pointed out by Ahluwalia,[14] though the expenditure of India on health sector is five to six per cent of the GDP which is equivalent to the comparable standards of other countries, the contribution of the state is mere one per cent. This in no uncertain terms calls for a relook at the health expenditure of the state which is a vital aspect to achieve social security with a number of innovative and initiating schemes.

The concept of food security and nutrition is another important area wherein the government has to shift its focus to protect and extend social security measure. According to Article 47 of the Constitution of India, it is the primary duty of the state to raise the level of nutrition and standard of living. However, in spite of a number of schemes that have been developed by the Union and the state, in the last 25 years the average height and weight of most of the Indians have not grown to the expected international standards, especially vis-à-vis women and children. The percentage of underweight children is much higher than even that of our neighbours such as Bangladesh and Pakistan. According to United Nations Children's Fund (UNICEF), India accounts for 31 per cent of the developing world's children who are stunted and 42 per cent of those who are underweight (Tobias, 2010, p. 4)[15]. The figures are highly alarming and the government has to evolve strategies that affectively redress the problems of children, the future generations of India.

In response to the judgement of the Supreme Court in Chameli Singh,[16] the Union of India has evolved a National Urban Housing and Habitat Policy to provide shelter to cover a populace of 25 million Indians, especially those who are below the poverty line and other social and economically backward communities. However, due to lack of proper administrative management and corruption, many Indians are not in a position to own a house of their choice. Though the 11th Plan and various other policy perspectives suggested the evolution of a number of schemes, India is far behind in providing a right to shelter in terms of a dwelling house that people need in terms of development as held by the Supreme Court in the Chameli Singh case. In order to help the populace, especially the needy sections and the employees sector, the government should take lands in huge bulk than to encourage the private sector and construct houses and distribute to people. In the case of employees, instead of asking the employees to get loans and paltry tax exemptions, the government or its agencies should construct the houses and deduct the income from their salaries directly. In such case instead of paying the House Rent Allowance (HRA), the government can take such amount with additional amounts that require a very less interest rate to recover the money. It would be a wise thing to do as it would avoid lots of hardships and scams wherein government companies like LIC are involved (*Indian Express*, 2010). In fact, such a policy perspective certainly brings down the scarcity of not only housing, but the escalating rental and land values in the Indian market. The government needs to consider this as a priority social security measures, otherwise a day may come like China which is currently on the brink of collapse in the housing sector.

Taxation is another important area where in the government has to have a serious consideration to bring changes in its policy perspective which may promote much needed social security to middle and upper middle-class families to save for their future needs without much governmental interference. Though the government has considerably reduced the rates of income tax to be paid by individuals over the years, the present rates are also high, especially, for employees who are in the higher bracket of pay scales. The present rate of 30 per cent charged to individuals at par with corporate sector is certainly high with fewer exemptions to individuals compared to that of corporate sector. Apart from the 30 per cent income tax to employees in the higher bracket, the introduction of a number of indirect taxes such as Service Tax, Value Added Tax (VAT), education cess and a host of other taxes without much needed social security provisions undoubtedly constitute as burden on the civil servants or government employees. The tax structure needs to be rationalised along with the inflation index. Though it may appear to be silly, this is an important perspective, which not only encourages social security policies but also reduces corruption in the society largely. Such a reform would certainly be within the realm of constitutional ethics of the welfare state.

Another important area is pension, which provides social security to civil servants. The pension scheme was introduced in the government sector for its employees. Considering their long service, responsibilities and loyal services rendered for a long time, the state has assumed the responsibility to protect their old age as a measure of socio-economic justice, which includes social security. This was even supported by the Supreme Court in Nakara v. Union of India. However, in the wake of economic reforms, considering pension has became burden to the exchequer to meet its other social security requirements of public at large, the state discontinued the guaranteed pensions scheme for employees joining the government services on/after 2004. The National Pension Scheme, introduced in 2013, is a deferred pension scheme depending on the market volatility, which has no guaranteed returns like the previous pension scheme. With the increasing life expectancy, the post-retirement pensions assume a critical role for employees in the absence of strong social security mechanism in various sectors, like that of developed countries. The deferred income scheme of pension with fewer perquisites to civil servants compared to that of the private sector employees will have an adverse impact in rendering their faithful services; this will certainly have an adverse impact on good governance. Further, the irony of it is that on one hand the government cites burden on the exchequer to pay pensions to employees after retirement. And on the other hand, the state increases the salaries, perks and other allowances, including pension time and again, of members of Parliament and members of legislative assembly (MLAs), citing a number of reasons, though their period of service to people is limited compared to that of government employees. Would it not amount to deviation from the welfare state model of governance as advocated by the Constitution?

Conclusion

For social security to develop as an important factor in the development of good governance, the government has to provide the platform for its development. Many times the governments either at the Union or at the state level are of the view that investing in sectors such as education, health, housing and other basic needs of the people is non-productive and there are no much returns. But the truth is that an investment today in these sectors will make these the highest yielding sectors of tomorrow for the sustainable developmental growth of the country. This is what the Western societies did long ago and became high stake nations of the contemporary world.

Models developed by the ILO, other institutes and the Western world may be studied to draw the thrust of social security schemes and social insurance schemes. Apart from that, for an affective commitment to discharge the constitutional and international obligations, the Government of India should become a party to the Social Security (Minimum Standards) Convention of 1952 of ILO. Also, it has to become a party to other relevant social security conventions of ILO. By joining in such conventions its workforce will certainly be in an advantageous position to enjoy benefits that are applicable to their counterparts in the developed world. In fact, some the conventions certainly impose obligations on the government to bring in necessary amendments to its existing social security legislations in the labour front. Though the government may think negatively by joining or ratifying such treaties and conventions, which may increase its burden in many ways and means, its thinking process requires a change which will adopt welfare policies that are suitable to its societal conditions. In the changing contemporary era of a globalised world, better conditions to workforce and other sectors of society mean better income to the people and less dependence on the state. Social security is a powerful tool to achieve the concept of good governance and contributes to a cohesive workforce and overall growth and development which bolster the living standards of the people; hence, the government needs to give a serious consideration to gauge its social security policy. Amartya Sen (2009), in all his works, especially in his book on *The Idea of Justice*, insists that the role of the state has to be a leading one in bringing welfare to the people which automatically makes the societies less unjust (Weiss, 2010). This is what has been advocated by the UN in its millennium goals (Sen, 2009) or near home, as rightly visualised by the former technocrat President of India Dr A.P.J. Abdul Kalam.[17]

Notes

1. For detailed discussion on the concept of governance, see en.wikipedia.org/wiki/Governance (accessed 25 October 2010).
2. Declaration on Right to Development, UN G.A. Res.41/120, 4 December 1986, Article 1 states the right to development is an inalienable human right by virtue of which every human person and all peoples are entitled to participate in, contribute and enjoy economic, social, cultural and political development, in which all human rights and fundamental freedoms can be fully realised.
3. Report of the Commission of the Global Governance: Our Neighborhood. Available online at http://www.itcilo.it/english/actrav/telearn/global/ilo/globe/gove.htm (accessed 1 November 2010).
4. For details, see UNDP, *Human Development Report 2010*. Available online at www.undp.org (accessed 5 November 2010).
5. Available online at www.undp.org (accessed 5 November 2010). The ILO constitution adopted in 1919 used the term only to cover the rights of the workers. Only in 1944 in Philadelphia it has been extended to cover a number of rights and recognising it as a universal right. For details, ILO, Social Security Guide, 2010, p. 25.

6. According to Article 22 of the UDHR everyone, as a member of society, has the right to social security and is entitled to realisation, through national effort and international cooperation and in accordance with the organisation. Article 25 states: (a) Everyone has the right to a standard of living adequate for the health and well-being of himself and of his family, including food, clothing, housing and medical care and necessary social services, and the right to security in the event of unemployment, sickness, disability, widowhood, old age or other lack of livelihood in circumstances beyond his control. (b) Motherhood and childhood are entitled to special care and assistance. All children, whether born in or out of wedlock, shall enjoy the same social protection and Article 9 of the International Covenant on Economic and Social Rights clearly imposes an obligation on the states to adopt steps in which every individual could realise the right to social security including social insurance.

7. For detailed discussion on Social Security Policy of the Government of India and the states see NCRWC, vol. II, Book 1, pp. 55–285.

8. Ibid., pp. 55–281.

9. 'Social Security Is Your Investment in the Future', Ministry of Labour, Government of India. Available online at www.labour.nic.in/ss.welcome.html (accessed 15 November 2010).

10. AIR 1994 SC1844.

11. Olga Tellis v. Bombay Municipal Corporation, AIR (1986) SC180.

12. Paschim Banga v. Union of India, AIR (1958) SC 731.

13. For details, see UNDP, Human Development Report 2010. Available online at www.undp.org (accessed 5 November 2010), pp. 26–27.

14. www.indiatalkies.com/2010/09/ahluwalia (accessed 20 November 2010).

15. For details, see UNDP, *Human Development Report 2010*. Available online at www.undp.org (accessed 5 November 2010), pp. 129–60.

16. Chameli Singh v. State of Uttar Pradesh, Air (1996) Sc 1051.

17. Detailed discussion on Millennium Goals; available online at www.UN.org.millenniumgoals. Also, 'A.P.J. Abdul Kalam: India Vision 2020', available online at www.Indiavision2020.0rg (accessed 20 November 2010).

References

Agarwal, S.K. 2008. *Towards Improving Governance*. New Delhi: Academic Foundation.

Chowdhury, N. and C.E. Skarstedt, 2005. 'The Principle of Good Governance', Open Draft for Review, United Kingdom: Oxford. Available online at www. worldfuturecouncil.org/.../user.../CISDL_P5_Governance.pdf (accessed 15 October 2010).

Frontline. 2010. 'Stunted India', *Frontline*, 10–23 April, Chennai, pp. 3–32.

Ganguli, Kisari Mohan. 1883–1896. *Mahabharata*. Available online at http//www. bharatadesam.com/spiritual/mahabharata/index.php vol. 18 (accessed 22 September 2010).

Hagemejer, Krzysztof. 2010. 'World Social Security Report', *Times of India*, 16 November.

ILO. 2010. *World Social Security Report*. Geneva: ILO.

Indian Express. 2010. 'The Recent Housing Scam of LIC', *Indian Express*, 25 November, Pune, pp. 1–2.

Kashyap, C. Subash. 2003. *Concept of Good Governance and Kautilya's Arthashastra*. New Delhi: ICSSR.

Margaret, Karns P. and Mingst A. Karen. 2005. *International Organisations: The Politics and Processes of Global Governance*. New Delhi: Viva Publications.

Planning Commission. 2008. *Eleventh Five Year Plan 2007–2012*. vol. II. New Delhi: Oxford University Press.

Rao, M.V.K. 1958. *Studies in Kautilya (2nd edn)*. New Delhi: Munshiram Manoharlal.

Sabharwal, Y.K. 2006. 'Role of Judiciary in Good Governance'. High Court of Haryana and Punjab, Chandigarh. Available online at www.highcourtchd.gov. in (accessed 1 October 2008).

Sastry, R. Shama. 1961. *Kautilya's Arthasastry Sastra*. Mysore: Printing and Publishing House.

Sastry, T.S.N. 2009. 'Good Governance and Right to Health', in K.K. Bagchi (ed.), *Good Governance and Development: An Indian Perspective*, pp. 370–86. New Delhi: Abhijeet Publications.

Sen, Amartya. 2009. *The Idea of Justice*. England: Penguin.

Sharma, S. Kumar. 2006. 'Good Governance in Ancient India: Remembering Santi Parvam in Mahabharat', *Meerut Journal of Political Science and Public Administration*, 6 (1): 109–23.

Theiler, Tobias. 2010. 'Societal Security', in Myriam Dunn Cavelty and Victor Maurer (eds), *Routledge Handbook of Security Studies*, pp. 105–23. London: Routledge.

Weiss, J. 2004. 'Poverty Targeting Programmes in Asia', Asian Development Bank. Available online at www.adb.org/documents/PRM/Working_papers (accessed 22 November 2010).

World Bank. 1992. *Governance and Development*. Washington, D.C.: World Bank.

Wyman, Miriyam. 2011. 'Thinking about Governance', a Draft Discussion Paper prepared for the Commonwealth Foundation Citizens and Governance Programme. London. Available online at http://www.education.gov.mt/youth/pdf_cyf/CYF_Themes_Concept_papers/cg_governance_papers.pdf. (accessed 15 September 2010).

II

Civil Service Reform in India

Civil service reforms in India are a continuous process. There are scholarly studies and elegant expressions of experiences by former bureaucrats who worked in different regimes and systems explaining the nuances of change. Reform of any existing institution or system is always aimed at bringing in a better transformation with amendments to the existing structures to facilitate development. The civil services in India were subjected to reform on the basis of Appleby Report in 1953 after Independence. A full-fledged commission known as the First Administrative Reforms Commission (FARC) was appointed in 1966 to make recommendations to adopt the administrative organisation to implement the development and welfare programmes of the government. The FARC has made far-reaching recommendations in 10 areas consisting of the kind of machinery, centre–state relations, economic and financial administration, and machinery for agricultural development required and so on. It has also touched upon the personnel, recruitment and training aspects of the executive. Along with the FARC, there are several other commissions and committees, such as Committee on Prevention of Corruption or Santhanam Commission, Pay Commission, Expenditure Commission, etc., that have also made references to the administration of the government that included civil service. The need for a CVC along with administrative vigilance wings in departments and the Lokayukta were some important proposals that were put in to operation by the government.

In the area of recruitment, the recommendations of Kothari Commission in 1976 have brought in a new phase in the staffing of civil service by opening up of the system to all categories of people, based on the merit obtained not only in general studies but also in select subject areas. The economic outlook of the government has undergone a change in the 1980s and international institutions, such as the World Bank, started giving advice on models not only in economic sphere but even made suggestions as to how the reforms are to be carried with the kind of administrative mechanisms. There are several developments in countries, such as the UK, where political changes have brought in ideas such as New Public Management in civil service on the lines of business organisations. It has affected the nature of civil services to be brought in relation to the needs of the kind of government in power and issues such as agencification of departments have been put in to practice in countries like Australia. Keeping in view the worldwide developments in the area of reforms, the government appointed the Second Administrative Reforms Commission (SARC) in 2005 and the Commission gave its report in 2008 on personnel administration.

The 10th report of the SARC in 2008 related to 'Refurbishing of Personnel Administration-scaling new Heights' is related to civil service reforms. The report after deliberations at different levels, including the interactions with retired civil servants, has recommended some changes and hinted at some new ideas in civil services. It has noted that the 58 group (a) central services and (b) services such as DANICS (Delhi, Andaman Nicobar Island Civil Services) are the largest cadre compared to the AIS, such as IAS, IPS and IFoS that are both central and state services. In addition to the above general services, there are technical services. The government has brought constitutional reforms to facilitate local and Panchayat Raj institutions through 73 and 74 amendments. The economic reforms brought in the year 1991 have liberalised the economy and either amended or abolished several government regulations to facilitate rapid industrialisation, trade and development. This required a new set of institutions and personnel to manage and administer the restructuring.

The *steel frame* of the civil service which was known during the British Raj for its depersonalisation and rule of law is found to be not conducive for quick and pro-liberalisation outlook. Therefore, it was felt that the system of administration needs to be changed and some regulatory frameworks were put in practice in all economic operations. But the civil service or public service is different from other private or corporate managements where the manager is responsible for his acts to the limited liability of corporate board while the civil servant is accountable to the minister under whom he works. The accountability of the civil servant is not limited to the minister, through him he is related to the people of the country and the legislative process that includes annual reports, questions and debates depending on the parliamentary process. Unfortunately, some experts and the reform-oriented civil servants do not realise that civil service in India is different from others as the authority and power of the civil servant in India flows from the provisions in the Constitution. It is not a hire and fire system of recruitment of a corporation where the manager can be sent home if he fails to bring in results as per his agreement. It is possible in the present system to measure the outcomes and output and evaluate his performance as per the parameters. Therefore, some reform enthusiasts wanted the same kind of outcomes in civil services and did away with the inputs and resources used in the system to measure performance earlier.

There is lot of debate and discussion on the kind of framework needed to assess the performance of the civil servants in India. Many suggested that the civil servant be given freedom to take decisions as per the outcomes agreed upon, such as Performance Appraisal Management System, and not base it on the Annual Confidential Report (ACR). It is also found that several serving officers are critical about the process of empanelment which is subjective and wanted an objective transparent mechanism for joint secretary to secretary-level positions in government. There is a shift now from the old archaic mechanism of ACRs to a system of quantified attributes on a 1:10 scale as followed in the armed forces in India. It is also noticed that there are some reforms affected by the government through service litigation in Central Administrative Tribunal (CAT) and the apex court, such as providing opportunities to the employee to give his reactions to the assessment given to him by the reporting officer. The suggestion that the performance appraisal format should be job specific, rather than a general format as is now practised in most departments, would go a long way if introduced in the reforms of civil services.

The concept of accountability, according to some, is vague in the absence of parameters and defined rules. The idea of accountability to the minister under whom the civil servant works and provides advice is now landing some civil servants in jail. They attribute the troubles to lack of clarity and civil service law. But there is a wild reaction from the public against the majority of the civil servants who are arrogant to the needs of the people and in relation to the powers they enjoy. There is a need for an in-depth study on the issue as the civil servants are given protection under the Constitution and the powers they enjoy are derived from the same Constitution. It is an irony that a number of civil servants think that they get this power because they got selected on merit by UPSC. This is not correct. The powers, wherever the civil servant works, are drawn from the rules framed as per the constitutional provisions. It is not a private property owned to get this privilege but due to the will of the people who elect a government through democratic process. The government thus elected is empowered to give this privilege to anyone, not necessarily the civil servant selected by a due process of recruitment. There is a thinking that if the government passes an Act to empower an agency allowing lateral entry of officers from any source to the executive, they do also enjoy the same power and privileges and they may be a better source of personnel in translating the agendas of the government than the permanent staff of civil servants. There are cases where officers from other services are brought for general administration and they perform better than the generalists such as IAS. This outlook of the government is not challenged by anyone on considerations of merits of the case but through indirect bureaucratic techniques of alleged sabotage and political maneuvering by the privileged few.

Discussing the ethics of equal opportunities in her paper, Susan Corby (2000) mentioned that

> the research evidence, however, is less sanguine. For instance, a report on civil service promotion procedures found that many line mangers were unaware of the potential for discrimination on grounds of gender, ethnicity and disability in staff appraisal reports and that there were departmental variations in the provision of training for line managers and in briefings for promotion board members and chairs.

She has explained the issue, by citing the Organisation for Economic Co-operation and Development (OECD) report, that ethical practices such as equal opportunity for gender, race, etc., are essential parts of administration as it leads to a fair participation. This ethical principle employed in the European context is more relevant in India due to the multiple and complex identities. But the record of our civil servants in this respect seem to be far from satisfactory as revealed in the number of litigations pending before courts. It is also found that many of the civil servants once they leave the LBSNAA forget about the constitutional provisions and the authority that it gives for their supremacy in the system. Therefore, it is necessary to motivate not only the young, but even the senior civil servants to get appraised of the various dimensions of the provisions that come to their rescue if adhered to rather than slavishly following the powers for personal gains.

There are four chapters in this section, discussing and analysing the need for reforms in civil service in India. Some of them seem to have been carried away by the Western thinking and, in the excitement, the reform agenda of the government in 1991. They seem to have a genuine desire that the civil service as it exists becomes dysfunctional and undergoes reorientation. That does not mean we should copy the West in all respects; the civil service is there to provide assurance of the government programmes to Indian citizens who live on our soil and not elsewhere. This may be taken into consideration while devising our own reforms based on our ethos to avoid the present confusion and judicial scrutiny of the executive. The reforms that are suggested by commissions and experts need to be scrutinised in order to bring order, discipline and development in the country.

Reference

Corby, Susan. 2000. 'The Ethics of Equal opportunities', in Richard A. Chapman (ed.), *Ethics in Public Service for the New Millennium.* Aldershot: Ashgate.

5

Accountability in Public Service

N. Vittal*

Accountability Is the Soul of Public Service

The expression *public service* can be interpreted broadly as any activity which contributes to providing services to a large number of people or a large number of citizens. The term *service* itself can be further looked at from two angles. The first is rendering services, which meet the (non-physical) needs of the citizens, such as health, education and security. The second relates to providing goods needed by citizens and, thus, which meet their physical needs, for example, food through public distribution system. In both types of public service, availability and accessibility are important. Ensuring that the citizens who are consumers of the public service get proper satisfaction is a sine qua non for rating the quality of service.

The term *public service* can also be interpreted to include the act of governance which leads us to the issue of public administration.

Accountability means responsibility. In fact, accountability is literally the soul of public service. If providing goods or services is the input of public services, meeting needs or aspirations of citizens is the output. The dynamics of public service in the ultimate analysis depends a lot on two

* Ex-Central Vigilance Commissioner, Government of India.

factors. The first element is the input and the second essential element is the sense of accountability or commitment. If the same idea has to be expressed in the form of equation: 'O' output, in terms of quality or level of satisfaction of the people or citizens, is equal to 'I' input multiplied by 'A' accountability.

$$I \times A = O$$

Output will depend upon what the parameters are that are measured when it comes to public service in the context of governance for public service in terms of providing goods and services to the citizens. The quality of output can cover a wide range of factors. So far as commercial activities are concerned, parameters have been evolved for measuring customer satisfaction. In fact, quality itself can be defined as fulfilling the promises underlying any services. When the concept about the quality evolved into the concept of total quality management, this concept of satisfaction was further enhanced to delight the customer and provide him/her a pleasant surprise. So far as business is concerned, Mahatma Gandhi emphasised the fundamental significance of the customers by pointing out that he/she is the very essence of business. Business thrives because of the customer. Peter Drucker (1954) distilled the quintessence of business as finding a customer and retaining him/her. While in the case of business, the concept of satisfying the customer and exceeding his/her expectations for delighting him/her with pleasant surprises may appear very pragmatic, when it comes to public governance, however, a similar concept has been only slow in evolving.

The relationship between the state and the people depends a lot on the nature and ideology of the state. It used to be said that in the UK people are subjects. In France, they are citizens. In the US they are tax payers. What is said of the US is true of practically all countries. In democratic states, the respect for the individual and his/her dignity is the essence of it. It relates to human rights and is more sensitive. On the other hand, in totalitarian regimes, the citizen is treated as a con in the wheel and an instrument for fulfilling the objective of the state. In the Indian context, therefore, in any discussion of public service and accountability in public service, it is necessary to bear in mind the basic spirit of democracy which is rooted in the dignity of the individual and the need for ensuring that respect for the individual is maintained and an environment is shaped where and by which his full potential can be realised. After all, every individual has some talent. Ideally in a democratic liberal set-up, the environment in terms of organisations, systems and procedures, rules and regulations must be such that the individual is able to rise to his full potential.

We may now examine the left hand side of the equation $I \times A = O$.

The inputs would be of two types. These are, to borrow the terminology of information technology, software and hardware. The software of the inputs for providing any public service depends primarily upon the people who provide the services and run the organisations providing them. The human element is the most significant input, so far as public service is concerned. Software aspect of the inputs would also include aspects of organisational culture, the attitudes and the training of people providing the public services. The hardware aspect of the inputs would cover the organisational structure, rules and regulations as well as the systems and procedures for selection of people to run the organisation and their training, the shaping of their attitude and nurturing the values for the organisation.

We then come to the second element on the left side of the equation $I \times A = O$.

Accountability, as mentioned earlier, constitutes the soul of effectiveness and quality of public service. In the ultimate analysis, accountability should and can be fixed and focused only on individual human beings. An organisation is after all an artificial person and an impersonal entity. Fixing accountability on organisations does not really make the practice of accountability meaningful. In any analysis of accountability in public service, we must never forget the fact that accountability is on the individuals. It is when we focus on the individual human element that we will be able to fix accountability and in case of failure rectify the system. In fact, if there is a single element that is responsible for the prevailing poor quality of governance in our country or the quality of services in any sector, we find invariably, it is the lack of sense of accountability. There are number of reasons why this situation has emerged over the years.

At this stage it is worthwhile to list the factors that generally contribute to erosion of accountability and difficulty in fixing responsibility when the public services fail. So far as the government or the state is concerned, one main cause of lack of accountability has long been known. It is the impact of what is called the Parkinson's Law. Years ago, soon after the Second World War, Professor Northolt Parkinson discovered that the size of the British Navy in fact became much larger after the Second World War than during at the height of the War. He identified that work expanded to fill time available. It is this counter intuitive fact which drives the continuous expansion of the number of people in government organisations. The psychological reason for increase in the number of public servants or the bureaucracy is manifold. A general assumption could be that this is due to the increase in the quantity of service to be provided; Parkinson's Law shows that even when there is no ostensible reason by way of increasing load of work, the bureaucracy has a tendency to expand because work expands to fill time available. Nature abhors vacuum and perhaps this is true of every other area also. That is why the British Navy expanded after the end of the War.

The very expansion in the number of public servants lays the foundation for lack of accountability. Accountability is easy and clear, if as mentioned earlier, it is focused on the individual and the task to be performed is clearly defined. However, when the task remains the same and what was being done by one person is to be done by three or even more people, then the immediate victim is the goal clarity. When there is lack of clarity about the objective or the goals or the functions to be performed, then accountability to that extent gets diluted. It may be possible to overcome this problem by clearly defining the functions. But by the very nature of the function, new demands and new situations may arise. It is not possible to anticipate all developments and cover them and have a rule for every situation. No wonder *work to rule* becomes an instrument of labour action to press demands on par with striking work or refusing to do work.

This highlights the fundamental paradox about fixing responsibility and brings us to another aspect. In the ultimate analysis the sense of responsibility has to be nurtured and it has to come from within the individuals. Perhaps the universally known excellent example for accountability is the mother. A young girl, once she becomes a mother, suddenly develops a spirit of accountability for the newborn. She becomes a caring, protecting and multitasking mother. This innate capacity to feel responsible for the output or results and protecting the object of care is at the soul of spirit of accountability. This is true for every activity, be it providing a service, meeting the customer's demand or meeting an emergency situation or whatever. Rules and procedures are needed for running organisations but, by the very nature, the rules and procedures can also come in the way of performing a function effectively.

The letter of the rules and procedures and their spirit have to be clearly understood. Unfortunately, in large organisations, especially government organisations, the focus ultimately turns out to be on the letter of the law rather than the spirit of the law. The Comptroller and Auditor General (CAG) focuses on an organisation based on the letter of the law and ultimately the emphasis seems to be on doing a thing rightly than doing right things. In fact, for getting better results when situations are changing, especially in areas of public service, doing the right thing, even by breaking the law, may be necessary. As has been rightly mentioned, one can never make an omelette without breaking eggs. Many a times, I have found that rules and procedures are eggs which have to be broken when there is a greater demand of meeting the needs of implementing the projects. And this is where a sincere public servant faces a dilemma about doing the right thing while at the same time not doing it rightly. In order to overcome the hesitation and the problems that may arise in the case of post audit, the best strategy to adopt is to record in real time the reasons why a particular course of action was adopted in the context of the rules, which may not entirely permit it. Recording such detail is the best solution for being accountable and at the same time, not becoming a unintended victim of audit procedures, which in our system is very common.

Poor System for Reward and Punishment

Another major reason for the lack of accountability is the system of rewards and punishment. Most governmental systems emphasise the written rules and procedures and as mentioned earlier, situations when an effectively performing public servant has to go beyond the letter of the law, faces the danger of becoming a victim. This may lead to situations where a person who doesn't take a decision or delays a decision and as a result causes greater harm to public service may make a better progress in his individual career than a public servant who takes an initiative and is compelled to break the law once in a while. In order to nurture a sense of accountability, therefore, systems have to be put in place. The rewards and punishments must be directly related to performance and taking initiative instead of blind conformity or ineffective mechanical approach to providing the services. The government is expected to be a model employer and keeping this in mind, the Indian Constitution provides a double guarantee to the permanent civil servants under Article 311 of the Constitution. Article 311 ensures that no one once employed can be removed from service unless the following conditions are satisfied:

> **Article 311 (2)**: Dismissal, removal or reduction in rank of persons employed in civil capacities under the Union or a State:
>
> (1) No person who is a member of a civil service of the Union or an all-India service or a civil service of a State or holds a civil post under the Union or a State shall be dismissed or removed by an authority subordinate to that by which he was appointed.
> (2) No such person as aforesaid shall be dismissed or removed or reduced in rank except after an inquiry in which he has been informed of the charges against him and given a reasonable opportunity of being heard in respect of those charges.

This sense of security may be justified to ensure that the public servant takes the initiative to meet situations as may arise in performing the role of public service, but what has happened is that once a person becomes a government servant, it becomes practically impossible to fire him. As a result, the greatest measure of punishing poor performance or lack of responsibility or lack of accountability gets blunted. In fact, it has been suggested that in order to improve performance, the Article 311 has to be modified and withdrawn and replaced by a rolling contract system so that at any given point of time, the relationship between the public servant and the state is a contractual one and in terms of the contract depending on the performance.

Weakness of Annual Confidential Reports System

One method of rating the performance of a public servant is through annual performance reports. We have a system of annual confidential reports. Under this system, while feedback on good performance is not given, adverse remarks are communicated. Thanks to the impact of Article 311, the protection given to the government servant, reality is that any reporting officer, who gives a honest adverse remark in the ACR is more often placed in the abode. Many reporting officers, therefore, choose the path of least resistance. There is inflation in the rating of performance. The situation has become ridiculous. For a government of India's servant, *good* means average or even poor!

Another complicating factor is that many government servants belonging to the reserved or backward classes, many a time advance the fact of their caste and accuse the reporting officer of prejudice in defending their case against adverse remarks. In Andhra Pradesh, when Mr Chandrababu Naidu was the chief minister (CM), an attempt was made to make this rating of performance as objective as possible, but the impact is not known. It may not be possible to quantify all public service precisely.

Lack of Transparency

Another major factor for lack of accountability is lack of transparency. In the corporate sector, the recent debates about the need for corporate governance has brought into sharp focus the fact that if a business enterprise has to be run under the principles of good corporate governance, three factors are important. First, there should be transparency. Transparency is the best guarantee to ensure that no malpractices take place. The greater the transparency, greater is the accountability so far as decision-making is concerned. One common complaint about governmental systems has been the lack of transparency. Rules and procedures are not transparent and the decision-making process is not clear. As a result, the citizen does not get the information that he/she needs nor can be sure that he has been treated in a just manner. In this context, the enactment of the RTI Act 2005 has been a great blessing and an important step forward in the Indian government system for ensuring accountability of public service. Recent review of the experience under the RTI Act 2005 highlights the teething problems of introducing a transparent system of governance and decision-making in an administration set up by the British colonial system where secrecy reigned supreme. There was an Official Secret Act but no Right to Information Act. As experience in corporate governance principles show transparency helps in fixing accountability and fixing accountability is the first step in ensuring a fair reward and punishment system so far as delivery of public service is concerned. If this is done in a very meaningful effective manner, it will ultimately lead to the greater satisfaction of the public.

Corruption

Perhaps the most significant factor that comes in the way of account-ability in public service is corruption. Corruption has been defined as use of public office for private gain, by the World Bank. The concern over corruption in public services gathered momentum universally towards the end of the 1990s in the 20th century and the adoption of UN Convention on Fighting Corruption, 2003, marks an important step forward. In the context of the public governance system, the focus on fighting corruption ranks very high because corruption has been a universal experience. Transparency International, the Berlin-based non-governmental organization (NGO), has been publishing from time to time annually the Corruption Perception Index. The direct correlation between reduction in corruption and greater accountability in public service is obvious. The measures to fight corruption, therefore, can be considered as measures that improve accountability in public service. For tackling corruption, one can adopt the same strategy as adopted for tackling any disease. If the cause of any disease is known, then corrective measures can be initiated to ensure that these causes are tackled and to that extent corruption will be reduced and greater accountability introduced.

In the Indian context, so far as bureaucracy is concerned, corruption is due to the following reasons:

1. Lack of transparency arising out of unclear rules and procedures and nurtured by a culture of secrecy under the ambit of Official Secret Act
2. Red tape arising out of complicated procedures leading to encouragement of corruption by way of speed money. It is true that the procedure which causes delay, called red tape, was seem to be done. But as happens in many human situations, the path to hell is paved with good intention.
3. A poor reward and punishment system
4. Fourth is the universal human tendency of groupism or brotherhood. Thick as thieves is a very common expression. Nobody talks about thick as *thick as honest people*. It is the tribalism of the corrupt and the brotherhood amongst them that gives them strength within the organisation.

Each of these four reasons can be effectively tackled and so far as developing alternatives are concerned, I would suggest that the standard basic principles of industrial engineering, consisting of the following options, are explored in every situation to improve procedures:

1. Elimination
2. Combination
3. Resequencing
4. Substitution
5. Modification

This exercise can be extensively used to bring better transparency and reduce to a great extent the scope of corruption. Equally important in fighting corruption is availability of information technology. We have seen in this country the tremendous impact of information technology, improving the Railway Passenger Reservation System, which benefits crores of people every day. Governance using information technology in various governmental organisation systems and procedures is another option that can be considered for reducing corruption and improving accountability in public service. Nevertheless, one cannot forget that no machine can be cleverer than the human mind. As Dr Radhakrishnan pointed out that the mind that invented the atom bomb is more powerful than the atom bomb itself. Experience in Andhra Pradesh, for example, in the computerisation of land record system show that even the registration system could be simplified and procedure could be speeded up and human intervention in putting data can be a source of corruption.

New Public Management

Above approaches for fighting corruption and bringing of transparency and accountability in public service all entail working within the given system. In recent times, especially after the experience of Margret Thatcher and John Major in Britain, the concept of new public governance has been becoming increasingly popular, thanks to the effort of the British government. The theory of public choice is also being discussed and an option for providing public service. Instead of depending only on the government as an agency to provide public service, we can visualise alternative agencies such as an NGO, even the private sector or better still public–private partnership, for evolving new models for providing public services.

Professor Pradip Khandwalla, former director of IIM Ahmedabad and a highly respected intellectual has come out with a thought provoking book *Transforming Governance through New Public Management* (Khandwalla, 2010). He begins with a highly perceptive comment:

> [W]hen there is poor governance, people tend to blame politicians and administrators. But the root cause of poor governance may lie in the design of the democratic-administrative form adopted by a country rather than in the character of the people governing the nation. If the design is inappropriate, the wrong kinds of people will keep on exercising authority, and the wrong kinds of conduct will be perpetuated. Unless the design is rectified, governance will tend to remain poor and even worsen. The alternative is not dictatorship but a democracy purged of its disease inducing genes.

He then proceeds systematically to prescribe how our democracy can be purged of disease inducing genes—through NPM.

NPM originated in the US and Britain. What started out as an effort to bring into governance private sector efficiency and accountability for performance, has now become a much more participatory, stakeholder-centric, humane, professional and innovationist paradigm of governance that has on the whole delivered good results across the globe.

It will free the prime minister (PM)/CM from the day-to-day pressures of political volatility and empower him to implement policies of public interest. The PM/CM so elected can induct talented people from different fields to become ministers and run the various ministries and departments. It is not necessary that, as at present, the ministers have to be legislators. This is the second radical suggestion that the great advantage of this change is that all talent available in the nation can be harnessed by the PM/CM. The legislators can devote their energies to the legislative function. Farcical instances such as our national budget being passed in a jiffy by the Lok Sabha will not happen. The third suggestion relates to the electoral system. We now have the British system of the first past the post becoming the winner, even though he may not have won the majority of the votes polled. Professor Khandelwalla suggests that this must be replaced by a system where the winner has to get the majority of the votes polled. This means that if in an election the winning candidate does not get 50 per cent +1 votes of the total votes polled, there should be a run-off between the top two candidates to be held soon after the election to decide the winner. So, as far as the administrative system is concerned, Professor Khandelwalla recommends the Margaret Thatcher Model of extensive agencification.

This means setting up executive agencies under professional managers who are domain experts, each with a stakeholders' board to transfer out to such semi-autonomous bodies some two-thirds of departmental functions and transform all undertakings and bodies into executive agencies. But who will implement these ideas?

Let us hope that the Indian intelligentsia will initiate a wide ranging debate and make NPM possible one day in India. NPM has a brief in element of accountability for public services.

Competition can be one method of improving public services. Whether competition to the government police services can be provided is worth examining. The dramatic improvement in telecom services when the monopoly of Department of Telecom was introduced from 1994 is an excellent example of the potential for improving public services.

Conclusion

At the age of 75, I am still optimistic. My optimism is not based on what Alan Greenspan would say as irrational exuberance. I am optimistic that the quality of integrity in public life will improve in our country. Incidentally, the accountability in public service will also improve. The following are the reasons:

To begin with, we have to recognise that we are a democracy and we are a society in which there is a very high degree of freedom of expression. We have an alert media, both electronic and print. This environment gives an opportunity for countervailing forces to develop and corrective action to be taken. Engineers talk of self-correcting or servo mechanisms which are based on the feedback, correcting themselves.

At least three examples readily come to mind. Perhaps, the greatest threat to democracy as we have seen from 1947 was in 1975 when Indira Gandhi imposed Emergency. But within two years the system corrected itself and it will be extremely difficult for the future PM of our country to impose emergency. One of the consequences of Emergency was that an amendment to the Constitution so far as imposition of President Rule in the states is concerned was made. Before Emergency in 1977, Congress was the dominant party and at the drop of a hat, President's Rule and Article 356 could be imposed on states where the Congress government at the Centre felt uncomfortable. This is no longer possible. Imposition of President's Rule, therefore, has become rare. The correction in the form of a constitutional amendment for gross abuse of the powers is an experience we have.

At a lesser level, when organisations have failed to check malpractices, the judicial intervention had forced corrections. Again, three examples can be thought of. The Hawala Scam led to the Vineet Narain case and the famous judgment of justice Verma in the Supreme Court of December 1997. This led to the CVC becoming a statutory body with powers over supervision of the Central Bureau of Investigation (CBI) and the

Enforcement Directorate, the two key agencies of the government dealing with corruption and the black money.

Structural changes in organisation and institutions, therefore, have been induced in our country to correct gross malpractices and there is no reason to believe that this process of self-correction will seize to exist, whenever blatant violation takes place. One recent example is the recent Spectrum scam so far as the auction of 2G Spectrum is concerned. This in turn led to open debate about the auction to be conducted for 3G and the net result is there for everybody to see. Not only was the 3G Spectrum transparent, it was done in such a way that against the budget of ₹35,000 crores, the Government of India is going to receive more than ₹60,000 crores as the result of the excellent response to the 3G auction. In this case, the growth of technology has created situations which have gone a long way to reduce corruption. The information technology applications by way of railways for the passenger reservation system have given relief to crores of Indian passengers from facing corruption daily while booking their tickets. An extension of this technology explosion is combined with the liberalisation policies of the government and has seen the incredible telecom revolution in the country; where from a teledensity of 1 in the year 1990 when the National Telecom Policy was announced we have reached to a more than 53 by 2010. The telecom sector's growth has introduced the basic principle that where there is competition, monopoly fails and not only the customer get better services; corruption also is reduced to the minimum. This has happened in the telecommunications and it will happen in every sector where government introduces competition, under the overall policy of economic liberalisation.

The success of activists and NGOs is another reason for rational optimism of the future of our country. Two professors from IIM, Ahmedabad used the well-known tool of the Public Interest Litigation (PIL) and thanks to the 2004 judgement of the Supreme Court based on their petition, today we know every candidate to election has to declare their criminal record, wealth and educational qualification.

The above analysis on accountability in public service leads us to fundamental points. Ultimately, the level of accountability in any service depends on three factors. First and the most important are the individuals in the organisation. As mentioned earlier, the concept of accountability cannot be diluted and it has to be always the individuals. It is by proper selection and training of people who come and occupy public services that will be able to nurture a culture of accountability.

Equally important in this context would be the development of the codes of conduct. For thousands of years, the Hippocratic Oath for doctors stood the test of time. 'Above all, do no harm.' Introducing an element of awareness about ethics in professional courses, as has been done for example in Tamil Nadu in engineering courses, is a step in the right direction.

After all, accountability is essentially an ethical issue and injecting an element of ethical thought in education and also in human resource (HR) programs after recruitment in an organisation will go a long way in nurturing a leitmotif of accountability which goes beyond mere rules and regulations and build a culture where the quality of public service will improve greatly.

Note

The suggestions given by the author on agencification has also been examined by the Moily Commission. Some bureaucrats who have used the NPM philosophy seriously are alleged to be landed in troubles. There is a rethinking about the concept and its application to large countries such as India.

References

Drucker, Peter. 1954. *The Practice of Management*. New York: Harper Business.
Khandelwalla, Pradip N. 2010. *Transforming Governmet through New Public Management*. Ahmedabad: Ahmedabad Management Association.

6

Corruption in All India Services

Bhure Lal

Corruption means improper or selfish exercise of power and influence attached to a public office. It is the antithesis of an orderly and just way of life both in its spiritual and material aspects. It includes acceptance of gratification or valuables for illegal considerations, misuse of power and authority in a dishonest and fraudulent manner, misappropriation of funds, abuse of position as a public servant for pecuniary advantage, possession of assets disproportionate to the known sources of income, etc. Society expects that each individual should perform his/her social/official responsibility honestly and the violation of this tenet would amount to an act of corruption. The PC Act defines corrupt practice as:

> Whoever, being a public servant, accepts or obtains or agrees to accept or attempts to obtain for himself, or for any other person, any valuable thing without consideration, or for a consideration which he knows to be inadequate, from any person whom he knows to have been, or to be, or to be likely to be concerned in any proceeding or business transacted or about to be transacted by such public servant, or having any connection with the official functions of himself or of any public servant to whom he is subordinate, or from any person whom he knows to be interested in or related to the person so concerned, shall be punishable. (Prevention of Corruption Act, 1988)

Corruption has been with us ever since man learnt to organise himself collectively. It existed even in ancient India but its extent was very small as compared to what it is today. In independent India, huge funds are disbursed through public agencies for developmental purposes. With this, the floodgates of corruption have been opened. Efforts made by governments to check the malady and bring the erring officials to book have not kept pace as they have touched only a small fraction of the incidence of corruption among government officials. As a consequence, corruption has destroyed the socio-economic structure of our society. Stringent measures are needed to stem the rot and contain the monster of corruption. The cancer-like growth of corruption in public administration is a matter of concern for all right-thinking men interested in preserving the sanctity of public institutions. It is disastrous to allow corruption to flourish in the mistaken belief that corruption in one form or the other has always existed and even the most developed countries in the world suffer from this malady. The canker of corruption must not be accepted as it is an obnoxious weed and springs because of lack of moral integrity.

We have failed to bring about an administrative system suiting Indian values and Indian ideals. A number of administrative reforms commissions were set up but their reports seldom saw the light of the day. Consequently, we have also failed to put officials with strong patriotic sense in the administrative chairs. Our administrative standards are going down day-by-day and corruption is having a heyday. The worst combination is a corrupt bureaucrat and a corrupt politician. Unfortunately, this combination is getting common and nobody knows when such a situation would come to an end. The late Jai Prakash Narayan used to say that the economic system which has been established in our country would only give rise to corrupt bureaucrats. It would not be out of place to mention here that Shri Jai Prakash believed that bureaucrats play the political game from behind the curtain. The bureaucrat and the politician both are interested in perpetuating corruption because both have ulterior motives. The politician has to collect funds and he/she needs the assistance of the bureaucrats to make rules and regulations in a manner which give the colour of legality to his/her money-making corrupt practices. In the bargain, the bureaucrats also take their share. Both have become so strong that it is difficult to separate them. Their unholy alliance can only be broken when we have a very strong central government having a firm political conviction that the administrative set-up must be rid of corruption and that the administrative machinery would not be used for political advantages. It is doubtful whether politicians will venture such a plan of action. There is a lack of political and administrative will to improve things. Corruption has many shapes such as corrupt conduct, intellectual dishonesty, mental dishonesty and dishonesty in framing policies.

There is a tendency towards collusion between bureaucrats, business-men and politicians. Financial purity and moral probity are the casualties in our present set-up. Badly drafted restrictive laws on political funding have encouraged parties in Italy, Spain, Germany and France to grant political favours in exchange for surreptitious transfers of cash. Tempting cash prizes coming from business and industrialists make the Indian governmental machinery to function tendentiously.

Every case of non-enforcement of law is an act of discrimination and arbitrariness. Every such case involves violation of Article 14 of the Constitution of India. Corruption is one of the copious causes of economic poverty. The poor and unfortunate people of India are being deprived of their assets by the avarice of those occupying the upper decks of political power in this country. Whereas the poor cannot earn even meagre livelihood, the corrupt are rolling in luxury and wealth. This becomes a breach of the constitutional right of the vast masses of people in this country who are deprived even of livelihood and a humane and dignified existence.

Sycophancy is also a form of corruption because songs in praise of a corrupt superior falsely build up his/her destructive morale. A man given to sycophancy will not arrive at correct decisions which may affect the society adversely. The sycophants understand the weakness of the boss and exploit it for their personal corrupt ends. They are rewarded both by their 'bosses' in the government and also by succeeding in capturing top slots in private sector.

Lucrative jobs in the private sector are the happy hunting grounds of retired civil servants. The most prized persons in the job market are the bureaucrats and technocrats just preparing for retirement. The private sector tycoons build up dossiers and files on superannuated old 'red tape artistes' who benefited them during the course of their tenure as civil servants. A large number of them have been hired by private companies to exploit their political and administrative links. They don't feel any-thing odd sitting on the other side of the fence and seldom hesitate in condemning the very bureaucratic machine they came from.

The Santhanam Committee (1964) observes:

> It is generally believed that such employment is procured on a quid-pro-quo basis for favours shown by Government servants while in service. It is also feared that highly placed Government servants who accept such employment after retirement may be in a position, by virtue of their past standing, to exercise some influence on those in service who might have been their colleagues or subordinates.

Corruption in public life of India is a fact. It has become a recognised way of life. It is a malady permeating every sphere, every layer of society and all levels of bureaucracy, including the AIS and the central services. It has infected every part of governmental machinery, including politicians and ministers. Gunnar Myrdal in his *The Asian Drama* talks about the experiences of western businessmen in India. Narrating their experience, he points out that it is 'necessary to bribe high officials and politicians in order to get a deal through,' though such a contention was dismissed by Mrs Indira Gandhi who regarded corruption to be 'a global phenomenon'. Interestingly, Myrdal finds businessmen are willing to bribe—'French, American and specially, West German companies are usually said to have the least inhibition about bribing their way through. Japanese firms are said to be even more willing to pay up' (Mydral, 1968).

Corruption is rampant in the lower echelon of the public services. The middle levels are also in the grip of corruption and it has made its impact felt in the apex buds of our administrative services. The AIS have ceased to be Caesar's wife and quite a significant number of them live a luxurious life. The motto of service to people and their welfare is becoming irrelevant. The Santhanam Committee (1964) on the PC Act observed in 1964 that corruption in certain areas had spread even to that level of administration from which it was conspicuously absent in the past. Our administrative structure portrays a much worse picture today with the ranks of corrupt IAS officers swelling every year.

Integrity—'the differentia specifica' of AIS—is no more their ornament. The reputation for sound integrity enjoyed by them is in doldrums. The young IAS and IPS officers were in great demand for postings in the states. They had also won the faith and confidence of public at large. The directly recruited young officers in other services also enjoyed similar reputation. It is unfortunate that this image and reputation have been badly shattered and the number of IAS officers with unsavoury reputation is on the increase. IAS officers with impeccable integrity have become very scarce. The service is on the path of degeneration from being an honest service into a dishonest one. Tushar Talukdar, a senior IPS officer of West Bengal, in his book *Ghus Niley Bir* (The Bribe Taker Is a Hero), laments the shattering of his hopes and points out that IPS officers who have indulged in corruption all their life and auctioned *thana*s (police stations), reached up to the level of DGP. Narrating the case of a senior officer, he asks him, 'How much more wealth do you intend to amass before you stop taking bribes?' The officer replied, '[I]t will never happen, I will die if I stop taking bribes' (Lal, 2002). Talukdar further points out that corrupt IAS and IPS officers instead of feeling ashamed have become aggressive and 'proclaim that those who are corrupt are brave and those who do not accept bribes are cowards'. At the time of expiry of the assembly term, the Bihar speaker presented each MLA with a gold plated watch. Four MLAs out of 325 refused to accept the watch. They were termed as 'hypocrites' by the remaining 321 MLAs. Thus, corruption is being institutionalised with no accountability around. Policies initiated by such institutions and persons will only demolish the remaining vestiges of upright conduct. The structural policies and adjustments will be so devised as to destroy righteousness. Honesty is being forced to fly like a white scared dove chased by hunters. The 'Scam' was initiated by policy changes. The sugar scam and the rumors of payoffs in a large number of deals relate to the new policy initiatives.

The illegal practices that led to the scam could not have been tolerated, had the officials and executives in the nationalised banks not been paid off. This situation is fraught with grave dangers and would ultimately result in the abrogation of the rule of Law. In Jammu and Kashmir (J&K), majority of government employees maintain links with militants. Connivance between the two is proving a big hurdle to normalcy. Crippled bureaucracy is completely in the grip of malaise and suffers from agony of backlash from militants. A dishonest official cannot be punished for transgression of law since he/she has resources and the best possible counsels on his/her side while on the other hand an honest official has no support despite acting in a lawful manner. A dishonest official, if caught in the act of accepting bribe, will ensure his/her acquittal by bribing, whereas an honest official, if implicated maliciously, might have to go to jail. Thus the corrupt administrative services will help in creating a situation in which people will be denied rights granted to them under the law and the dishonest persons will go scot-free without any stigma.

The laws affecting the notorious sections of society will remain a dead letter. This has completely eroded the credibility of administrative services and institutions. People have lost confidence in the ability of administration and even the wildest accusations of corruption against officials at the highest levels are readily accepted without any reservations. Harshad Mehta had corrupted and subverted the entire banking system for personal gains, made accusations of bribery against the highest public officers and this wild accusation found a ready acceptance in a large section of our population. This portends an ominous threat, a breakdown of our administrative machinery and its credibility. The man in the street is willing to believe the worst of the men in positions of power and influence. Economic crimes, bribery, embezzlement, abuse of power, influence peddling and arbitrary enforcement of laws have aroused resentment among people and the general feeling is that corruption has reached alarming, epidemic proportions.

The perpetrators and the beneficiaries of corruption are politicians and bureaucrats. Both are fattening themselves at the cost of people and the nation's wealth. Unfortunately, people have learnt to live with corruption in general. They do not feel shocked when corrupt deeds of politicians and bureaucrats are divulged. The magnitude of black money is beyond imagination. It is no longer measured in lakhs, it is calculated in lakhs of crores. In the Hawala Case, Jain has not only paid off very senior politicians but he had also bribed bureaucrats and kept a record of payments. The entries have been denied by all concerned persons as false and malicious. It is a sordid story reflecting the way the public regards politicians and bureaucrats today. People are sick of corruption but do not want to put a full stop to it. People have a right to make kings and the king made by them along with the servants (politicians and bureaucrats) are looting them.

The administrative system is a hostage to corrupt politicians and bureaucrats. Bureaucrats and politicians with integrity are unable to carry the masses with them because of an all pervasive environment in which the corrupt have flourished. People are complacent about corruption. There is an erosion of public standard and integrity even amongst members of the most elite civil services in the country. The situation becomes particularly painful when press openly reports about the lack of integrity and probity even amongst the officers of the Indian Administrative Service and the collusion between top administrative officers and politicians.

So far as officers belonging to AIS are concerned, according to figures available with the CBI, the Bureau registered 100 criminal cases between 1969 and 1994, against such officers for their involvement in corrupt practices. The year-wise details are given in Table 6.1.

Table 6.1

Pendency of Cases with CBI

1970	1975	1980	1986	1990	1992	1993	1994
1	3	4	16	9	8	3	4

Source: Corruption in the AIS—a background paper for the CVC's meeting.

The aforesaid criminal cases were registered by CBI against IAS officers involving

1. two DGP of two states
2. a chief secretary in one of the north-eastern states, who was found in possession of properties worth crores of rupees
3. a special Inspector General of Police (IGP) in one of the western states who was found in possession of substantial assets besides cash of more than ₹25 lakhs
4. a regional development commissioner, Ministry of Steel and Mines, who was found to possess assets running into crores of rupees
5. a young IAS officer posted in Delhi for having properties valued at more than a crore of rupees
6. a senior police officer posted as executive director in one of the public sector undertakings for collusion with his subordinate officer for extorting money from private contractor
7. a joint secretary in one of the ministries of Government of India for possession of hard cash amounting to ₹28 lakhs besides other assets

8. an AIS officer on deputation with Central Investigating Agency (CIA) for collusion with seeking pecuniary benefits from accused persons
9. a secretary level officer in one of the eastern states for showing undue favours to a private firm in certain purchases, etc.

A number of cases pertaining to possession of disproportionate property issues have been registered against officials holding very high positions. The aforesaid statistics are not exhaustive and certainly do not indicate the magnitude of corruption prevalent in the AIS officers. These cases relate to the 100 officers.

The officers were either posted with the central government or were on deputation to the central public sector undertakings. The CBI can take cognizance of the activities of only those AIS officers who are serving the Government of India. The strength of these officers is only about one-third of the entire cadre strength. The remaining two-thirds serve in the states under the control of the respective state governments. The CBI cannot undertake any inquiry against the officers posted under the control of the states unless a request is made by the state government concerned to the central government for taking up an inquiry. The problem of corruption in the state governments is also very grave and it is difficult to have a true and comprehensive picture of the problem. Usually, the inquiries are hushed up because of the involvement of high-ups and patronage and power wielded by the AIS officers. The IAS and the IPS are powerful pressure groups and the investigating agencies find it difficult to proceed against them. The state governments usually withdraw the consent under Section 6 of the Delhi Special Police Establishment (DSPE) Act. The sanction for prosecution as required under Section 197 of the Code of Criminal Procedure (CrPC) is not granted, delayed or withdrawn, nullifying the efforts of investigating agencies.

Recently officers of the rank of DGP in Haryana and Uttar Pradesh were placed under suspension for corrupt, malpractices in the matter of recruitment of police constables. There is a price tag for recruitment of constables, assistant sub-inspectors (ASIs), etc. Whatever we have discussed so far is offending and bitter but we must not lose heart and feel diffident.

We must have faith in the system that the rule of law will prevail even against the mightiest. We must realise that despite our shortcomings we have the capability to reform ourselves. We must make a beginning in the correct direction to stem the rot. There may be quite a few amongst us whose conscience would revolt if they are forced to deviate from the course of Civil Service Neutrality and Civil Service Reforms law. Persons holding high offices and interfering in the course of justice would face highly embarrassing situation. Our conviction must be to uphold the highest moral values and impeccable integrity. We should not permit anyone to have the courage of advocating or practising corruption in any form. Our emphasis should not only be on economic and social uplift-ment but also must include moral regeneration of our society.

It is thus expected of us to be honest in our dealings. For an administra-tor honesty is not the entire virtue. It is only one aspect of his conduct. An honest officer without being effective is like a soldier without a gun. The most cherished combination is an honest and an effective officer. Unfortunately, this is a rare phenomenon.

Liberalisation and Corruption

Liberalisation or no liberalisation, corrupt practices will remain an inte-gral part of our social behaviour if the people at the helm do not combat the problem of corruption with a firm conviction to eradicate it. People in dire need will always approach men of influence and power to derive concessions and benefits not permitted by law.

Corruption is rampant in every sector of our society, private as well as public, and it is doubtful whether liberalisation or privatisation will help in controlling this monster.

Complete liberalisation is a myth. Reasonable restrictions and regula-tions can always be imposed in the interest of public health, morality, peace and tranquillity. The person who will decide this aspect can make a fortune and thus, corruption will get confined to the decision-making levels.

After independence, there has been a complete bureaucratisation of economic processes resulting in arbitrary use of discretionary controls. This has given rise to a class of power brokers and made our entrepreneurs dependent on politicians and bureaucrats who always cornered a dispro-portionate share of the national cake. Deregulation and liberalisation are intended to put an end to all such distortions. Liberalisation may help in shrinking the base of corruption. It may also help in curtailing harassment to people as the government has initiated various measures to amend the Income Tax Act, Foreign Exchange Regulation Act (FERA), Export and Import Act and so on. Various controls provided under these Acts have been simplified or removed. FERA was regarded a draconian Act and since been abolished.

These measures have reduced the nuisance value of various law enforcing agencies. This coupled with the lower taxation rates of customs, excise and income tax will create an environment in which the tax payer will also cooperate with the tax authorities as the amount of tax and the amount of bribe may be equal to his tax liability. On the other hand, the tax authorities will collect the tax according to the provision of the law as the client does not want any illegal favours. This will result in reduction of the regulatory functions of the state. Moreover, liberalisation implies deregulation and decontrol which will ultimately result in termination of the Licence Permit Raj. According to the provisions of the new industrial policy, licences are required only for 15 industries as compared to over 200 earlier. The government has also announced a scheme of rewards to the extent of about 20 per cent of the value of confiscated gold and contrabands such as narcotics. In addition to the informer, the employees are also eligible to get the reward. This coupled with the reduction of controls will help in reducing the quantum of black money generation. Liberalisation will demolish the source of patronage. The hitherto so-called lucrative posts will lose their glamour. Liberalisation, thus, may help in reducing the base of corruption but it will not affect corruption at the key policy formulation levels. It is also clear that in some way or the other, the regulatory mechanism will continue and this will act as an ally to corrupt practices. The opposite may also happen. As the possibilities of money making dry up on the regulatory front, the officers/officials may tend to make much more money out of the funds allocated for other poverty alleviation programmes, such as the Jawahar Rozgar Yojana (JRY).

Corruption cannot be cured by liberalisation alone. The need of the hour is men and women of probity in public life. So long as there is corporate funding of political parties, corruption will manifest in all our decisions. Even T.N. Seshan admits the role played by slush money in elections. The cost of fighting an election is enormous. The candidate requires a huge amount of money on travel, posters, handbills, stickers, jeeps, loudspeakers, flags, canvassers and the like. The canvassers need extravagant treatment like free and rich food, drinks and vehicles at command. The candidate has to spend a lot on election agents at each polling booth, their allowance and accommodation. It is a fact that in our type of democracy many candidates deploy private armies to terrorise the opponents from voting against them. The criminals are hired to capture polling booths. Therefore, to meet all the expenses, the political parties collect funds. These funds are made available by the industrialists and tycoons on a quid pro quo basis.

Political funding is prevalent all over the world. Parties are financed by businessmen. It is the same system anywhere you go. No company is willing to pay through a cheque. This implies that Indian elections are fought entirely on black money. The businessmen oblige politicians; the politicians and the ministers reciprocate by doling out favours to them. This sets in motion a chain which extends all the way to the bottom. Ministers have to depend on bureaucrats. Once the secretary starts accepting money then the lower and clerical bureaucracies cannot remain honest and we end up with a situation where they demand kickbacks merely to perform the jobs that they are supposed to do.

Administrative Challenges

Industrialists make sure that the decisions result in furthering their own interests or hurt their rivals. At the Mumbai conclave of industrialists, it was pointed out that if the liberalised policies do not suit industrialists, they would not contribute funds to the ruling party for election purposes. Industrialists today are talking about a level playing field, meaning there is no discrimination between Indian industrialists and foreign investors. Government policies can be formulated in a manner to benefit a particular class of industrialists or a particular industrialist—Indian or foreign. It is thus discriminatory aspect which gives rise to corruption. It is easy to misuse the rules to favour a few and discriminate against others. Government policy on investment in power, telecom, petroleum and roads come under fire. The charges of actual or intended corruption in the award of contracts have been rampant. It may be building of a road or buying a railway track, there is a take in the globalised cake.

We must not also forget that we are still a long way away from achieving the ideal state of transparency in decision-making. The first weapon against corruption is transparency of information and publicity. In a democracy, it is not enough to make the right decisions. The reasons for the decision must also be understood by people. It will be a determining factor with Indian decision-makers, who command much financial clout with the people who rule or hope to rule the country. The decision-makers will make decisions handing out favours to that group or class of people who furnish substantial amounts to the coffers of political parties to contest elections. Thus, it is clear that liberalisation alone will not help in curbing corruption. It is the moral and not the tangible effects of the government's economic reforms that seem to be fuelling disenchantment among people. Liberalisation is being perceived as an enhancement of opportunities for corruption.

This was evident in the recent election results and the central government policy-makers had to think about the human face of reforms. The bank scam and the sugar scam rocked the country in the post-liberalisation era. Corruption comes in handy to industrialists and tycoons to curry favours at the hands of the powers that be. It manifests through arbitrary award of contracts, sanctioning of deals and investment projects without competitive bidding and transparency. The Licence Permit Raj has been replaced by the Tender Raj. It is, probably, in this context that Arjun Singh mentioned in his resignation letter: 'A perception has emerged that liberalisation of economic policy perhaps has become liberalisation of corruption' (Lal, 2002, p. 174). It is an international phenomenon. Liberalised economies such as Japan, Italy, Belgium and France have all fallen prey to corruption and corrupt practices, so much so that the gamut of corruption extends to the top executives, including presidents and prime ministers. Incidents of corruption involving even the presidents and prime ministers were eye-openers. Therefore, corruption has nothing to do with the type of economic system that we have in the country. It is directly related with the type of persons who man the affairs of the country and flows from top to bottom. Another inevitable deduction is that elections and its funding by industrial houses perpetuate this malaise. In the words of late Madhu Limaye: 'Corruption on the grand scale is provided by the ruling parties drive for election funds.' The fund collecting activity not only destroys our moral values but also the vitals of our economy and polity and creates a set of moral values which percolate down to the lowest strata of society (Limaye, 1995).

The Santhanam Committee on the PC Act pointed out in 1964 that 'corruption can exist only if there is someone willing to be corrupt and capable of corrupting. We regret to say that both willingness and capacity to corrupt is found in a large measure in the industrial and commercial classes'. The industrial and commercial classes possess huge amounts of unaccounted money and resort to corruption to promote their business activity.

Our politicians have forgotten Gandhiji's teachings; while writing in the *Harijan* (23 April 1938), Gandhiji had advised, 'the ministers and the legislators have to be watchful of their personal and public contacts. They have to be like Caesars' wife, above suspicion. They should not make private gains either for themselves or for their relatives or for their friends' (Gandhi, 1938).

This axiom is not adhered to by any politician in this country. Even the bulk of prominent businessmen admit that some kind of corruption may be inevitable, but the dilemma is elsewhere—in Bribonomics—on which a full session was devoted at the Davos congregation in 1995. The deliberations indicate that corruption and crime, such as money laundering and drug peddling, are increasing around the globe. The costs of global crimes for business in developing and developed economies are enormous. According to one estimate, corruption is costing American companies alone about US$500 billion a year. At the Trade Meet (January 1995) at Davos, the chief of Interpol pointed out that Bribonomics was prevalent from India to USA and Japan to Venezuela. This illustrates the lack of business ethics and honesty. It is unfortunate to mention that some countries have given their concurrence to write-off bribes for tax purpose. Then where is the incentive for businessmen to change? Globalisation of business can also result in globalisation of corruption. *The Report of the South Commission* (1990) points out that

[c]orruption has been on the increase in many countries—in all parts of the world. In the West, it tends to be associated with big businesses and such activities as manipulation of stock markets, in socialist countries and the south, overregulation and the absence of effective systems of public accountability

make it tempting to resort to corrupt practices. Over Centralisation, limited administrative capabilities, laxity of tax administration, and authoritarian tendencies has combined to provide fertile conditions for corruption in many developing countries.

Raysmond Kendall, secretary general of Interpol (the police intelligence network), while addressing the Davos Summit in 1995, cautioned that he had 'indications of a very dangerous slide down the slope of tolerance of dishonesty. It is not just in the developing world, we can't say we are any better in our world'. The United Nations Development Programme's (UNDP) Human Development Report 1992 cautioned that 'much of the corrupt money flies out of developing countries to be parked comfortably in the banks of the industrial countries.... There should be international system to monitor the arrival of dubious money' (Lal, 2002). Thus there is a need to ensure that liberalisation does not imply corruption by other means and that globalisation does not result in increasing the size of the cake.

Liberalisation has not resulted in any fundamental transformation of our natural psyche. The evil of insular mindset still dominates our actions. Liberalisation has not shaken off the manacles that shackle the mind. The process of economic reforms has not introduced any fundamental transformation in our consciousness. Western consumerism is corrupting Indian spirituality. Market economy cannot discriminate between right and wrong. It understands only demand and supply and purchasing power. It cannot categorise level of thinking. Plain living and high thinking have no place in market economy. Free play of market boosts consumerism and this has no connection with our moral well-being.

It was envisaged that corruption would be curtailed by liberalisation, democratisation of the economic system and transparency brought about by an aggressive media. Unfortunately, it has not happened. It is because of the international monetary movement which takes place very fast. A sizeable portion of this finds its way back to the donor countries by way of kickbacks and commissions, thus aggravating the economic problems of the third world economies. Even the World Bank realised that about 30 per cent of economic aid made available to Indonesia during the regime of Sukarno found its way back to donor counties by way of kickbacks and commissions.

Corrupt Practices

There are many ingenious ways of making illegal money—from counting of the proverbial current to the sophisticated Swiss bank account—by misusing authority. Persons occupying high offices indulge in corrupt practices with a view to favour some at the cost of others. They do not do it as an individual but in connivance with others. The prerequisite is that a convenient atmosphere must be created politically and administratively. Once such an infrastructure has been created, then they start acting in an arbitrary manner. These arbitrary acts are based on considerations of bribes and are in violation of rules, laws and conventions. These acts cannot stand the scrutiny of good honest conduct and are immediately rewarding in nature—both politically and financially. Persons in power refrain from taking decisions in the lawful discharge of their duties and thus compel the needy to approach them for expediting the decisions. This is normally against consideration. India spends thousands of crores of rupees on government and public-sector purchases. The requirements and specifications for purchases are tailor-made to favour only a few suppliers. This gives the supplier a monopoly status. The experts' team often does it against a consideration. Thus, a substantial part of the deal goes to the persons empowered to take decision with regard to such purchases. Moreover, there are middle men in large government contracts. These contracts are awarded and kickbacks are received. In some cases, the agents are done away with and the commissions are received directly by the persons striking the deal. Such kickbacks are often received in hard currency abroad. The government corridors are also frequented by power brokers and wheeler dealers. It is difficult to establish corruption in such cases because no hard evidence is available. The evidence may also not be available within the country as kickbacks have been received outside the country in Tax Havens where Indian laws are not in operation and the depositors are protected by the rigid secrecy veil.

The Santhanam Committee on PC Act has pointed out that in all contracts of construction, purchases, sales and other dealings on behalf of the government, a fixed percentage is paid by the suppliers which is shared in agreed proportion amongst the various officials concerned. Often inferior quality goods are purchased. After independence, poverty alleviation programmes were undertaken on a large scale. These programmes might not have made the targeted groups rich but they have come as a boon to the persons implementing them. In most departments there is a kickback starting from the point of supply of funds.

Junior officials have a fixed rate of kickbacks—the share of junior engineer will be 5 per cent of the total amount of the transaction and the assistant engineer's share will be 3 per cent and that of the executive engineer 2 per cent. In government offices, a similar system operates. The clerk will refuse to type a letter or to post it unless he/she has been paid bribes amounting to 5 per cent of the transaction. At the lower level, peons will refuse to inform a official that a visitor wishes to see him/her unless they have been tipped. It is unfortunate that the well-intended schemes like JRY and National Rural Employment Programme (NREP) have come under attack because of percentage share cut at the levels of DM and beyond.

Tender Raj is replacing the Licence Permit Raj. Every tender has a cushion and the amount is distributed between politicians and bureaucrats. If the amount has been received abroad it finds its way back to the country to non-resident Indians and becomes transparent. The recent flow of money into the country may be on this behalf also. Misappropriation of government land by bureaucrats and politicians has been a great source of money making.

According to the then land commissioner, Delhi Development Authority, K.L. Alphons: 'Bureaucrats and politicians have encroached upon land worth ₹10,000 crores in Delhi' (Lal, 2002). In the states, the revenue departments headed by the DMs have failed to check the scandals in allotment of government land. Bhumidhari rights are being conferred upon fictitious persons. This amount is shared between different concerned authorities starting from the Tehsil.

Normally the transactions take place in the shape of land, that is, in kind. The nominees of the officials get the *pattas* (title) and become owners of the land. Best illustration of such scandals was illustrated by one Moti Goel in Ghaziabad and Bulandsheher districts of Uttar Pradesh who grabbed land worth hundreds of crores by forging the records in connivance with revenue officials.

A particular prescribed authority of the Urban Land Ceiling Act had devised a novel method to receive bribes. He took no action on the representations of people who requested for exemptions and according to the proviso of the Act if no cognisance was taken by the prescribed authority within a stipulated period, the exemption would be deemed to have been granted. The prescribed authority deliberately took no action and struck a deal with the parties that a certain number of plots would be registered by the colonisers in the name of the persons nominated by the authority and the authority would receive the proceeds thereof from such nominees. Thus the authority did not come into the picture anywhere and made huge fortunes. Similarly, the conversion of land from agriculture to industrial and commercial use is a big money spinner and people have made huge fortunes over night as the value of land multiples by several hundred folds. The IAS officers often give the colour of legitimacy to their misdeeds in connivance with the other departmental officers. Excise contracts, mining contracts and allotment of scarce commodities are done against illegal gratifications. The money is often paid in cash to the nominated agents of concerned authorities. There will be as many ways as there are individuals to receive slush money. Interested parties also take care of the education of the wards of officials. Postings and transfers of officials have become an industry. Posts carry a bid and the highest bidder gets the post.

Many instances have been reported in the press about the lack of integrity and probity even amongst the officers of IAS, indicating moral decay. Officers have been prosecuted by the government for connivance and collusion with their political bosses to defraud the government of several crores of rupees in deciding the procurement of costly equipments. A young officer was prosecuted for misappropriating crores of rupees in executing a project meant for the welfare of weaker sections of the society. In Maharashtra, an IAS officer was charged with drawing more than ₹13,000,000 from the government treasury for disbursement to land owners in a land acquisition case. He did not disburse the amount in time. An officer of Assam and Meghalaya cadre was convicted by the court and sentenced to one year imprisonment for misappropriating government funds amounting to ₹52,000. In Bihar, an IAS officer did not invite quotations for procuring certain materials of the value of ₹1,300,000. Again in Maharashtra, two officers were charged with irregularities in purchase of stores valued at ₹9,500,000 and ₹400,000, respectively. Instances have also come to notice where officers made purchases without budgetary provisions. In Bihar, an IAS officer was the kingpin of the scam of flood-relief distribution, misappropriating the relief in league with the politicians.

It is thus clear that the conduct of civil servant is not above board. He/she is influenced by the prevailing socio-politico-economic ethos of the prevailing climate; the civil servant has compromised with the sense of responsibility not expected of him/her.

Problems Faced by an Honest Officer

It is difficult to fathom the agony and frustration of an honest officer. He/she has to walk through an unfriendly and hostile environment. In the discharge of his/her impersonal duties, he/she ends up creating personal problems and legal battles. His/her superiors and government drop him/her like a hot potato. To break his/her morale, he/she is confronted with a plethora of anonymous complaints, stage managed fictitious documents and officers with unsavoury reputation are put in charge to investigate matters pertaining to him/her. Material is collected against him/her in an unfriendly, hostile and zealous manner. Intelligence Bureau (IB), Research and Analysis Wing (RAW), Directorate of Revenue Intelligence (DRI), Central Board of Direct Taxes (CBDT) and CBI are put against him/her. Officers, who paid him/her obeisance till yesterday, frown and humiliate the person and question him/her in a bid to find out something against so that the word 'honest' is obliterated from the memory of people. Midnight transfers, surveillance of movement and eavesdropping of telephone are ruthlessly employed. Fellow officers feel scared to associate themselves with such an officer. Even the family members think that the officer has done something wrong. An environment is created where the person starts hating himself/herself. Thus, an honest officer suffers, along with his/her family members, physically, mentally and financially. This is the price he/she must pay to live up to his honest convictions. His/her firm faith in God and perseverance will stand him/her in good stead. Ultimately, no harm comes to him/her and he/she triumphs. The agony suffered by him/her and his/her family is the price he/she must pay.

An honest officer's well-wishers are the poorest of the lowest rung, for whom politicians and corrupt officials have little sympathy. An honest and an effective officer is not liked by his/her superiors and subordinates as he/she is a roadblock in their evil designs. He/she is forced to subdue his/her personality. Willingness to do wrong things is regarded as a sincere demonstration of loyalty. Conversely, failure to do so involves the wrath of superiors and politicians. The future of honest civil servants becomes a tragedy once political power is usurped by corrupt politicians who have the authority not only to control the civil servants but also to transfer them, suspend them and put them under investigation. Favours flow only to pliable civil servants. After retirement as well they are heavily rewarded by way of appointments to high posts like governors, ambassadors, advisors and chairmen of commissions.

Unfortunately, under the present circumstances, honesty, merit, diligence, efficiency, forthrightness are at a discount and extraneous considerations such as community, caste and commitment to individuals have become very rewarding. How can such an administration take judicious view of things based on truth, honesty and national considerations? Politicisation of administrative services has derailed the bureaucrats from the correct path. It has made them corrupt, narrow-minded, selfish and characterless. The administrative set-up is functioning today as a keep of corrupt politicians. Every bureaucrat has a godfather who not only protects his interests but also comes to his rescue when the bureaucrat acts in violation of law. Thus, there is a complete understanding between corrupt bureaucrats and the administrative challenges of corrupt politicians. The two would go together in taking government decisions which promote narrow political interests rather than national interest and justice. For probity to get the respect that it deserves, some odd inquiries in a high handed manner are no solution. Values must be promoted and the political leadership has a big role in this. If it does not accept this responsibility then the insensitivity to corruption and misuse of authority will grow exponentially.

Investigating agencies develop cold feet while dealing with the corrupt acts of top bureaucrats and politicians. Commenting on the sluggishness on the part of the CBI in the famous Hawala Case, the Supreme Court observed, 'The credibility of our system is at stake'. The corrupt officers can get even the evidence tampered and witnesses intimidated. On the other hand, an honest officer, fraudulently implicated, may find it difficult to arrange sureties to get a bail. In the prevailing atmosphere in the country of all pervasive corruption it is impossible for a public servant or any public officer under government to carry an impartial and independent interrogation and investigation because of the threat to his career and future prospects. The record of investigating agencies has been dismal.

The frustration of an honest officer is difficult to understand when he/she sees a corrupt officer reaching the apex of an organisation. His/her stooges make him/her a man of great virtues, ability and expertise, dedicated to the cause of national good. Official machinery is used to legitimatise corrupt practices and officials with integrity are hounded with impunity. Public good is farthest from the minds of corrupt officials. The fight between honest and dishonest officers is a fight between two unequals. An honest officer feels greatly disillusioned when he/she sees his/her superiors, politicians and colleagues in their true colour. In Italy, Judge Antonio Di Pietro spearheaded the anti-corruption drive with the zeal of a crusader. But he was a sad person while resigning from his post as political manoeuvring had made his work impossible. The symbol of justice, while submitting his resignation, he expressed, 'I feel used, exploited, pulled in all directions, thrust into the headlines every day, either by those who wish to use me against their enemies or by those who wish to see a non-existent political agenda in my normal work' (Lal, 2002).

Reward and Punishment

A conscientious civil servant should be indifferent to rewards. A dedicated service well performed is highly satisfying. The officer should have conviction to safeguard the welfare of the people. It will earn him/her good will and esteem which no money can buy. Self-satisfaction should be the most cherished reward. It will give him/her contentment which is probably the best prize in life. The wages of every noble work are blissful and the reward of one duty is the power to fulfil another. Selfless deeds are always virtuous and blessed are those who perform them. An officer motivated by the greed of reward will lose his effectiveness because his eyes will always be fixed on the reward and not on the nature of his act.

In Uttar Pradesh, the government introduced the system of rewarding the DMs for achieving the targets in family planning. The entire energies of the district administrative machinery were diverted to this activity only at the cost of other developmental activities. There was unhealthy competition, force was used, figures were fudged and persons who were not in the eligible category were also sterilised. As a consequence, the programme earned a bad name and the system of reward had to be abandoned.

The reward of a thing well done is to have done it and the fruit of our duty is our duty. A generous action is its own reward. Motivated action with a view to win award can seldom keep company with virtue. A soldier who sacrifices his life to uphold the integrity, honour and prestige of the country creates for himself a place of reverence in the hearts of people for all times to come. The virtue is in the struggle, not in the prize. People manage to get decoration/awards even in fraudulent manner by arranging false encounters or ambushes. Even the army is no exception to this malady.

The object of punishment is prevention from evil. The activities of a dishonest officer if not checked and punished will spell disaster for administration. If a dishonest officer goes scot-free, it will imply weakness of administration and absence of government. Crime and punishment grow out of the same stem and punishment must follow the guilt. Disgrace is as much in the punishment as in the crime. A dishonest officer must understand that a day will come when he/she will have to pay for dishonesty.

The above two paragraphs describe the ideal situation which seldom exists. Under the present circumstances an honest and effective officer is the most troubled, scared and attacked person having no support either from the clan or the politicians. The obsession with persons who matter and powers that be is—how do they benefit from the impartiality of an honest officer? He/she is of no use to them. He/she is a dejected and rejected lot. Putting him/her into uncalled for difficulties does not prick the conscience of senior officers who are willing to be used as tools at the instance of politicians. Destruction of such officers will let loose the reign of terror and anarchy. It is, therefore, essential to maintain and uphold the morale of such officers. Fellow officers, instead of acting out of jealousy, should exhibit a sense of espirit-de-corps and appreciate the actions of their comrade in arms. High morale and high spirits of an honest officer will further strengthen his/her convictions and thus he/she will fight the malaise of dishonesty with greater vigour. The officer will not yield to the dirty environment all around him/her.

A dishonest officer has all the things at his command. A civil service band of like-minded loyalists will make a great hero of the person. First rate qualities will be attributed to him/her, civic receptions arranged and decorations and praises showered. He/she can even manipulate rewards. It will be a great achievement if the modern administrative system succeeds in protecting the honest officers, even if it fails to reward them.

There is a general feeling among people that an IAS officer does not acquire fortune; the fortune acquires him/her. This feeling of fortune acquisition deprives the officer of all the pleasure of doing well to people for whose service he/she has been appointed. He/she does not command the joys of benevolent friendship and people do not regard him/her with esteem. Such an officer does nothing constructive during his/her tenure in government service. People detest him/her but he/she derives sadistic pleasure in gazing at the money in his/her chest and the more he/she has, the more he/she desires to have.

It is difficult to say at what point of time an IAS officer turns corrupt. Some officers resort to corrupt practices from day one, some turn corrupt after learning from the environment in which they are placed, some are led to corruption because of covetous desires and insatiable love for riches, some want to lead a luxurious life, some want to be conspicuous and some are led to corruption because of unequal comparisons. Once an officer yields to the temptation, then his greed will know no bounds breaking all the sinews of faith of the administrative system. Corruption will, thus, spread like a general flood and drown all virtues.

When does an officer turn corrupt? He/she may be unaware of it. The situation is like a fish in water. When does the fish drink water? It may not be aware. Similarly, corruption is honey-coated poison pill at the tip of tongue of an officer. When will it enter his/her body? He/she may not be aware and thus the best person turns the worst. The idealism of young officers evaporates soon and the venom grips him/her completely. Poverty alleviation programmes, such as JRY, have enriched some young IAS officers along with others. At the junior and middle levels, financial dishonesty dominates. At higher echelons, intellectual and financial dishonesty rules the roost. Policies are framed to benefit certain industrial tycoons against considerations and the officers are used to give them legal clothing. They may or may not have share in the booty.

The situation is gloomy but not without hope. There is no dearth of good, honest officers, though they are in a minuscule minority. Such officers must keep their spirits high and muster courage to organise service in the true sense. It is entirely an individual officer's choice whether to remain honest or turn corrupt. An honest officer earns goodwill of people which no money can buy. He/she keeps his/her back straight and chin up. It is, therefore, high time that we choose the path of goodness, righteousness and lead the service towards virtue.

Corrective Measures

Our freedom fighters had dreamt free India to be a nation with the highest of values. The new government would promote the highest moral values and people holding the reins of administration would have an impeccable integrity. Nobody would have the courage to advocate or practise corruption in any form. But dreams have shattered. In independent India corruption has captured all walks of our life and values have been thrown into the dustbin.

Despite the existence of a large number of agencies like CVC, CBI, State Vigilance Commissions and vigilance set-up in each department, corruption has flourished. It is a sad commentary on our administrative system. We must realise that empty threats in a culture of corruption are not likely to pay. We have to remedy a fundamental cause—the Indian way of life which makes all laws and institutions function defectively. We shall have to make our home environment, education system and institutions healthy and effective. Our children must not acquire any corrupt tendency ab initio. We shall have to create a climate against corruption and corrupt people till the time corruption becomes a universally detested word.

Recruitment to the service should not take place after 25 years of age and probationers should be placed under officers who are known for sound integrity so that they imbibe the right attitude. A person who joins the service after having worked in lower capacity may learn the tricks of the trade and may compromise with integrity because he/she has remained part of the environment which thrived on corruption. The emphasis should be twofold—the institution and the individual. If our intention is to have a good tree, then we should ensure purity of the seed and the purity of the environment, otherwise the results are likely to go astray.

Certainty of punishment will create the right atmosphere. Any IAS officer who abuses his power should be proceeded against. Any officer against whom prima facie case is made out even during investigation should be suspended and further action pursued. It must also be ensured that action is taken swiftly as delayed action is not likely to prove effective. His Lordship, Justice V.R. Krishna Iyer said:

> [T]o punish such super offenders in top positions, sealing of legalistic escape routes and dilatory strategies and bringing them to justice with high speed and early finality is a desideratum voiced in vain by Commissions and Committees in the past and is a dimension of the dynamics of the Rule of Law. (UNDP, 1992)

Governmental action alone is not enough to curb corruption. Anticorruption activities should become a movement with the people. If each individual makes up his mind not to get corrupt or indulge in corruption the problem of corruption will vanish. They should organise peaceful dharnas and conduct agitations, the issue must be kept in public focus.

An independent investigating agency is a prerequisite. A weak investigating agency will be ineffective to bring the white collared offenders to book that will remain unruffled by the law. The agency must not come under pressure of any kind—administrative or political. It must not lose its aura of credibility. Officers should try not to yield to temptation and lead a life of morality and probity. We must understand that the IAS is a service not a profession. In a profession, majority of the people keep self-interest above everything. The average officer has distanced himself/herself from good conduct and is thus advancing on the path of evil and corruption. Honesty, and not corruption, should be the guiding principle of our political and administrative system.

Transparency in functioning and accountability for the action will improve the image of the officers and the service will not come under the heavy weight of corruption. Officers at all levels must also ensure that the public gets its due in the normal course without resorting to 'speed money' to get their work done by various government agencies and public undertakings.

An agency like Lok Ayukta or Lokpal is not likely to deliver the desired result if the incumbent is a political appointee. He/she cannot act in an impartial manner. Therefore, an investigating agency comprising people who are not government or political appointees is imperative. A committee consisting of eminent persons from various fields like judiciary, academics, administration and social scientists not under the control of government should decide about the course of investigation. The committee must deliberate and scrutinise the evidence available before taking further action. Such an independent body cannot be subdued or bulldozed by the political and administrative apparatus. Such an arrangement will take care of lethargy and self-interest which have weakened the governmental machinery and its independent action against the corrupt officials and politicians. This is likely to create conditions of purity in public life. The governmental machinery will act more promptly and efficiently, be it running of telephone services or power supply or postal delivery.

The autonomous independent committee will not only proceed against the corrupt politicians and bureaucrats, but also take care of the fact that no agency or person is allowed to abuse or misuse the monopolistic powers of an investigating agency.

The State Anti Corruption Bureau, including the CBI, experiences difficulties in conducting investigations against AIS officers because such officers are appointed by the president of India and their service conditions and cadre management are regulated by the central government. The central government may consider extending the jurisdiction of the CBI to AIS officers, irrespective of their posting whether with the state governments or central government. Likewise, the State Anti Corruption Bureau can also be empowered to have jurisdiction in respect of officers of the AIS in the states if they are not already under the purview of the Bureau.

As far as possible, discretionary powers should be defined, and limits of these powers should be laid down. Officers at times play havoc with the rules and procedures while acting under discretionary powers.

The scope of discretionary powers must be curtailed in the management of the economy. This will help in reducing the temptation for arbitrariness. It may be difficult to dispense with the discretionary powers altogether; built-in safeguards must be provided to check their misuse by the authorities.

An atmosphere should be created in which an honest officer should be recognised. Integrity must be given due weightage while considering an officer for appointment to a Administrative Challenges sensitive and prestigious post. Conduct rules relating to submission of information concerning employment of near relatives in companies or firms, acceptance of gifts, transaction in movable or immovable properties must be rigidly followed. The government must arrange to scrutinise this information and seek clarifications wherever necessary.

Anti-corruption Establishment

Tackling corruption is a high priority item on the agenda of the Government of India. Various agencies engaged in curbing corruption are:

1. the CBI
2. the CVC
3. the organisations within government departments and public sector enterprises
4. Anti Corruption Bureau and the Lok Ayuktas in states/union territories

The obvious negative impact of corrupt and unethical practices is on productivity; the responsiveness, legitimacy and transparency of governments, the effective implementation of policies and efforts to bring about recovery and development in general dictate that concerted action by all concerned must be taken upon to deal with this debilitating problem.

Dealing successfully with this phenomenon requires a deeper understanding of its underlying causes. The various authors who have attempted to give a plausible explanation for the problem have often singled out one dimension or another as being the most crucial factor. One maintains, however, that the matter is not that simple and that political; cultural and economic factors all lie at the root of this multidimensional problem.

Can the Situation Be Remedied?

Repeated attempts have been made over the years to combat corrupt practices and ethical violations. A common feature of those is the enactment of codes and establishment of institutional mechanisms to enforce ethical behaviour. The real crux of the problem is the implementation which has been far from satisfactory.

The salient questions remain: why have these measures been generally unsuccessful, and, given the extent of the malaise of unethical conduct and the hitherto limited success in dealing with it, is it realistic to expect that this situation can be remedied? The answer is a firm 'yes' provided there is political and administrative will and an awakened civil society.

In the first instance, these measures have failed because they were introduced in an overall political and policy environment that was not sufficiently conducive to enable the success of the measures. When grand corruption is rampant at the top level of government and politics, the nature of governance has basically remained undemocratic, unaccountable and patrimonial, and where patronage systems have remained intact, one can hardly expect to enforce measures against unethical behaviour with any degree of seriousness or that the enforcement systems and institutions will be left to function without interference. Thus, the nature of the state and governance and commitment at the highest political level are crucial prerequisites for any successful drive to curb and punish ethical violations. If the objective of political parties is to capture the seat of power, by hook or crook, and civil service is utilised as a tool and an instrument to achieve this objective, the situation can never improve. The civil service will be preoccupied with designs to give the colour of legitimacy and legality to the evil designs of politicians. Second, the measures that have been introduced have been partial in nature, focusing mainly on sanctions and concentration of power and authority. The regulatory measures were designed not to improve the enforcement and fixing accountability. They were designed in such a way as to leave scope for mischief and discrimination.

Third, many of the institutions that were established to promote ethics and accountability often lacked the resources, public visibility, impartiality and public support that are critical for their success. Perpetrators of evil got the seal of approval of such institutions and carried on with their activities detrimental to public welfare.

The enormity of the task to deal with corrupt practices and to promote ethics and accountability in the civil service is not to be underestimated. In spite of setbacks experienced in this regard, it is still possible to score gains in a meaningful manner. Central to this is the need for the dedicated and sustained implementation of comprehensive, broad-based and self-reinforcing measures and not merely partial solutions—by the government and the public to deal with the multi-dimensional nature of the problem, within the framework of democratic, responsive, transparent and accountable governance otherwise political instability, possibility of a military cum civil strife, social unrest and anarchy will be inevitable.

A comprehensive agenda to promote ethics and accountability in contemporary civil services ought to comprise

1. fostering and promoting enabling conditions of service to enhance professional and ethical standards;
2. advancing and affirming sound policies on recruitment, training and public personnel management;
3. encouraging public service associations to play catalytic role in institutionalising professional values and defending occupational interest;
4. promoting a psychology of service in political and public life;
5. creating, strengthening and upholding the integrity and effectiveness of public institutions of accountability;
6. cutting down on excessive centralisation and bureaucratisation;
7. enacting, improving and effectively enforcing legal instruments, codes of conduct and regulations promoting ethics and accountability;
8. establishing coalitions of business associations and civil society to expose and fight corruption;
9. mass education campaigns on the extent and cost of corruption and unethical behaviour;
10. the systematic and impartial prosecution of violators; and
11. fostering popular participation to ensure the responsiveness, accountability and transparency of governance. This last element

of the comprehensive agenda deserves further mention. Even the best of safeguards and practices under democratic systems of governance can give way to abuses, as the experience of developed countries has repeatedly demonstrated.

For this reason, a crucial safeguard of high standards of public ethics and accountability has to fall on the ability of the citizens and people's organisations and associations to hold public officials and politicians accountable for their acts and also to ensure that public institutions fulfil their functions properly and responsibly.

Finally, the international dimension to the ethical crisis ought not to be neglected. Bribery of public officials in developing countries has often been used by businessmen in developed countries as fair and legitimate method for business promotion. Many governments in industrialised countries ignore bribery; some openly promote it and a few even make it tax-deductible. There is an urgent need to enforce ethical behaviour at the international level if grand corruption in developing countries, as a result of international business transactions, is to be curtailed. In recent years, Transparency International has been playing an appreciable role in raising the alarm about this problem and demanding that action be taken to remedy it. Any meaningful progress in this direction would require an agreement on and the strict enforcement of international conventions, punishing corruptors, strengthening international integrity systems, establishing disclosure of external accounts laws, and repatriation of wealth and payments amassed through international corruption. The international community is, however, far from any consensus that is likely to institute such measures.

The discussion above shows the need

1. To develop civil services as a neutral, professional, merit-based, accountable and essential instrument for good governance
2. To delineate public service values
3. To define code of ethics for civil servants
4. To empower public services for good governance. It is relevant to point out that for any civil services reform in the country there are three most important components:

- fairness in recruitment
- putting in place a regime of stability of tenures
- Good governance and better public service delivery, which is free of corruption

5. As regards recruitment to public services, it should be fair and through open competition—subject to conditions such as probation, citizenship, qualifications, character and health, etc. The competition should be merit based and open. There should be equal access to public services to all eligible citizens. However, a dangerous trend is creeping in the services—casteisation and communalisation of services. The first and Administrative Challenges foremost criterion for recruitment should be choosing a person suitable for good governance. At the same time the need to promote lower strata of society cannot be denied. But such promotion should not be based on vote-bank criterion. Instead of caste-oriented recruitment to civil services, we should adopt some other objective criterion like poverty and extend it to all Indians including Muslims, Christians and all others who are in Antayodya/Below Poverty Line (BPL) category. Such a step will help civil services to be neutral.

The problem starts when the officers are not given a reasonable tenure and the selection for a particular post is done on considerations other than merit and suitability. The stability of tenure is required as it

1. is the key to good governance,
2. enhances effectiveness of administration,
3. keeps the morale of the services high,
4. enables the member of service to gain experience in respective fields for his/her career prospects,
5. provides protection to officers and
6. prevents use of postings as a punitive measure.

In the past the need for stability of tenure has been always felt and there have been several recommendations on the issue:

1. Establishing security of tenure in the central government—well laid out tenure policy approved by the Appointments Committee of the Cabinet (ACC), CSS and Central Silk Board (CSB)/ACC.
2. States are advised from time to time to ensure stability of tenure.
3. Some states, for example, Maharashtra, have evolved comprehensive law to regulate tenure; Karnataka on policy on transfer and Uttar Pradesh on Civil Services Board. But they are ineffective.
4. Other states have some mechanism for ensuring stability of tenure.
5. Overall result is that there is no security of tenure and ad hoc transfers are made.
6. Amendment to AIS Rule 7 to provide for a minimum tenure of two/three years for certain posts has been suggested.
7. The tenure of a district officer—DM/superintendent of police (SP)—should be a minimum of three years in a district. This should be made mandatory and they must not be prematurely removed except on the grounds of graft and incompetence determined in an objective, laid down procedure.
8. The Civil Services Board should be set up in each state whose advice must be binding in matters of transfer. Autonomy and independence of this Board must be ensured.
9. Empanelment of civil servants at the Centre at the level of joint secretaries and above is another important area which needs attention and improvement. The process of empanelment has become a political game. Names are added and deleted at will and reviews are conducted without any basis. The process of empanelment at the level of additional secretaries and secretaries has become opaque. This has resulted in inefficiency, indiscipline, misuse of power and corruption. The system has to change. The process of empanelment must be independent and autonomous, capable of maintaining integrity of the system, and the recommendations need not be altered except on the ground of integrity. It will be appropriate to entrust this job to UPSC or an autonomous body outside government.
10. Post-retirement appointments must cease to be a political-spoil, to be distributed amongst political favourites, as it is fraught with dangers of politicising the civil service. An autonomous/independent committee comprising eminent retired civil servants

having representatives from judiciary and academics should be entrusted the job of shortlisting probable retired/retiring officers with sound administrative track record and efficiency imparted by them to the system. Appointments like election commissioners, CAG, members of UPSC, members of tribunals, information commissioners, including principal information commissioner, and other high-ranking post-retirement appointments in various bodies, commissions, etc., should be made out of this list only. The list prepared by the committee will be forwarded to the PM/CM, as the case may be, who can then choose the best man/men out of this list. This will result in utilising the best of bureaucratic talent leading to greater efficiency and accountability.

11. Some posts have been notified to carry a fixed tenure such as the cabinet secretary, the home secretary, the defence secretary, the IB and CBI chief. It is a healthy practice to provide certainty of tenure. It will certainly lead to eliminate unhealthy cut-throat competition among officers to capture these posts, particularly when an officer is picked up in the 60th year of his age—the age of superannuation. Providing a two-year fixed tenure in such circumstances will imply giving an extension through the back door. It must, therefore, be ensured that an officer picked up for the above fixed tenure has two years to superannuate and no back door extension is granted to him/her in contravention of rules.

The above proposed measures will also need amendment to the AIS rules, 1954, flowing from the All India Services Act, 1951, to provide the necessary legal back up for implementing the above reforms.

Reforms will be incomplete until recruitments to state civil services are insulated against political interference. The writ of the State Public Service Commissions does not run and they get cowed down under extraneous and undesirable pressures. The recent happenings in some of the State Public Service Commissions, such as Punjab, Bihar, Haryana, Maharashtra, do not inspire confidence at all.

Elevation to IAS/IPS/IFS from state service cadres is a naughty problem giving rise to unwarranted, prolonged litigation, destroying the service ethics and environment. It will be appropriate to conduct a limited examination, restricted to the job profile of eligible officers followed by an interview before preparing a panel for up gradation. This will help in picking up not only the best but also ensure insulating the service from extraneous considerations in matters of such as recruitments/selections. A study conducted by the CVC on 290 officers revealed a wide gamut of lapses among civil servants. They have also indicated a possible linkage between the officers accused of conniving with their political masters.

The government's future reforms could thus be directed towards putting a proposal to impose any penalty in a case with a vigilance angle. This would ensure objectivity and fairness in complex issues with more open and transparent procedures. The CVCs on one hand follow uniformity of approach from case directive basis and ban a post-gender negotiations (except to case) on the other; this would not lead to the objective of achieving the organisation's L1 (L1 is the lowest value). Such efforts need to be accompanied with purview. The commission would provide the much desired other reforms that reduce areas of discretionary decision. One of the findings of a study on supervisory failures and lack of accountability said that

> apart from making annual confidential reports more effective, another system needs to be revived. Up to about the middle of the last century, the Central as well as State Governments had an excellent system of inspections in place. Every supervisory officer mandatorily had to inspect the functioning of each of his subordinates at least once a year. Over the decades, this system has fallen into disuse. (Lal, 2002)

There is an old adage that man does only what his boss inspects: nothing could be truer. If a factory manager is ready to accept cloth of the width of a ribbon, the workers would not think of producing cloth of the width of a curtain. It is, therefore, imperative for all supervisory levels in the government to measure performance of their immediate subordinates and comment on the shortcomings noticed by them. This is how subordinates will improve. Further, such inspections would constitute a much more solid basis for writing annual confidential reports than mere impressions. The inspections could also unearth vigilance lapses on a systematic basis. Governments would, therefore, do well to revive this institution.

Last but not least, there has been thinking in certain quarters that there has been too much vigilance in government and that this phenomenon impairs decision-making. This study does not support this conclusion; on the contrary, it clearly indicates that there has not been too much but too little vigilance, especially preventive vigilance. At no cost officers/officials with poor integrity be allowed to continue in service. The government should have extraordinary powers to terminate the services of civil servants with poor integrity.

References

Gandhi, M.K. 1938. *Harijan*, 23 April.

Government of India. 1988. Prevention of Corruption Act, Section 11.

Lal, Bhure. 2002. *Corruption: Functional Anarchy in Governance*. New Delhi: Siddharth Publications.

Limaye, Madhu. 1995. 'Political Safety Is Hostage to Rocketeers', *Mainstream*, 7 January.

Myrdal, Gunnar. 1968. *Asian Drama: An Enquiry in to Poverty of Nations*, Vol. II. New York: The Twentieth Century Fund.

Santhanam Committee. 1964. *Report of Santhanam Committee*. New Delhi: Government of India Press.

South Commission. 1990. *The Report of the South Commission on the Challenge to the South*. New Delhi: Oxford University Press.

UNDP. 1992. *Global Dimensions of Human Development*. New Delhi: Oxford University Press.

7

Institutional Reforms in Indian Civil Service

P.K. Saxena*

With a few exceptions, most institutions in India have emerged from the colonial legacies of the past. These are circumscribed by colonial laws, rules and regulations, practices, modes and also by thinking. The institutional designs were, both in the public and private sectors, evolved by the colonial motives and operations. Till 1990, the institutional network was fully geared up to govern the masses for the convenience of the institutions. The legal network was not able to support the masses for their constitutional rights and the duties in most of the matters. The institutions, both in the public and private, were ruling the masses. The 1991 economic crisis of fiscal deficit, problem of balance of payment (BoP) and political instability, which were also the results of failure of colonial institutions, brought the changes in the economy by the introduction of the New Economic Policy. Further, the General Agreement on Tariffs and Trade (GATT) and the operations and practices of the World Trade Organization (WTO) have forced the government to redesign the institutional network in the country. In the reorientation processes, it was also difficult to bring changes without making any change within the institution, such as reduction of staff, change in the bureaucracy procedures and also sentiments. Further, the masses were

---

* Professor of Public Administration, Rajasthan University, Jaipur.

not prepared to accept the institutional reforms for globalisation and market economy. Moreover, the steel framed bureaucratic apparatus, designed during the colonial times, is still a bottleneck for any reform proposal. The Indian bureaucracy is not able to become market friendly and is not prepared to open its decision-making system to the public for transparency in the implementation of public policy, supply of information, reduction in the staff, cost-benefit system and accountability in its performance. In India, institutional reforms are not so easy at the political level due to democratic political system. The existence of the coalition governments, lack of political consensus on institutional reforms and politics of vote banks in the design of the economic policies hamper the speed of the institutional reforms. In a democratic system, as the elections are held, coalition partners of the government disfavour government policies, decisions and programmes and, hence, the process of institutional reforms is stopped. The federal system of governance also creates hurdles in the process of reforms. The federal units (states) are to undertake the programme of institutional reforms on the basis of party interests, ideology, local conditions, local vote bank and local people. The state governments are, to some extent, autonomous in the implementation of the directions of the Union government. Similarly, local self-governments in the states are, to some extent, equally free to bring or not to bring institutional reforms. It would be an uphill task to bring national consensus on globalisation, privatisation, disinvestments or downsizing the government both vertically and horizontally in the present democratic system. Last but not least, politicians are also not in a position to avoid the above-mentioned factors due to overriding factors. Therefore, the process of institutional reforms in India is not similar to China, Japan or Malaysia. It is much different to these countries in terms of motives, strategies, choices and designs.

Motives

In South Asian region, India is a major power block with an economic model of reforms. In Asia, India has also some regional responsibilities as well as liabilities of power balance and competition with China and

Pakistan. The presence of military power in the neighbouring countries, such as Afghanistan and Pakistan after the event of 9/11 in the USA, has also forced the country to redesign its motives for economic reforms. The increasing military interference of Western powers in Asia will certainly affect the economic situation not only in the region but also in the country. The shift in politics of India from the Congress Party to the coalition-led BJP has affected the liberalisation and globalisation policies significantly. First, the emphasis on the protection of Indian products and the industry in the era of globalisation as the emerging corporate sector in different fields would crush the Indian industry; and, secondly, disinvestment in core or profit-making sectors like petroleum is to be done cautiously. Further, liberalisation and opening of some sectors for the foreign direct investment (FDI) be avoided like in media, domestic consumer market, etc. And last, but not least, Indian culture and heritage be protected in the era of liberalisation. It must be noted that globalisation and liberalisation are being considered by the masses as the reason for erosion of Indian values and culture. Therefore, any move to bring any change in the reforms package, culture and values are given weightage in any policy of government. Beside this, the move to create an atmosphere and supportive system of institutional reforms was half-hearted; the 73th and 74th constitutional amendments for restructuring the federal polity and decentralising the local governments for the emerging economic system were not able to empower the local governments for the coming economic burden. Resource crunch, lack of skilled and trained manpower, and overcontrol of the state governments could not prepare them for the institutional reforms within themselves. Moreover, the very critical aspect of the Indian institutional reform is the Indian colonial bureaucratic system which is a big hurdle in any institutional reforms move. The incapacity of the Indian decision-makers at the political level to abolish the colonial bureaucratic structures has crippled the fruits of the market economy and the corporate sector. These structures are hurdles in the path of emerging markets as institutions of the decision-making system of the country. The unfriendly procedures and attitudes of the bureaucracy towards the markets have put negative effects upon the new entrants in the market economy. The strategy of market reforms was full of doubts, confusions and lack of supportive system due to over-bureaucratic structures. Further, the Indian bureaucracy is not supportive to non-state organisations and players. Therefore, the distribution process is highly centralised, over corrupt and dominated by the anti-distribution elements. The legal system is not reformed to support the non-state organisations. The colonial rules and regulations are also in force to suppress the functioning of the non-government/state organisations. The privatisation move to reform the institutions was also full of corruption, over cost and poor services to the masses. The losers of the privatisation move were also deprived of their rights and compensation. Competition between public and private is still absent in terms of quality, services, cost and technology. A public–private mix system could not emerge in any sector of the economy. Last not least, the social institutional reforms were over occupied by Indian culture and values. The laws relating to family, marriage, property, woman–man relationships and individual identity were completely biased and anti-development system. Overprotection of women in the Indian laws and regulations, religion-based family and marriage system (like Hindu/Muslim/Christian Marriage Act), rigid property laws and their poor delivery in the property reforms, rigid social system based on caste, kinship and heritage, etc., have also contributed in the negation of globalisation and liberalisation. In spite of the prevalent situation, India has shown its commitment towards the GATT and different agreements to pave the way for globalisation and liberalisation. However, the motives for the institutional change have been designed to suit the above-mentioned situations and conditions. No government can go against the old traditional and colonial institutions, if it wants to remain in power. The motives of any change are decided by the political masters in government for the interests and welfare of the country and the public.

In deciding the motives of the institutional reforms, the prime consideration has been that the basic structures of the institutions, staff and budget will not be altered and the staff will be protected fully in liberalisation and privatisation process. Further, the burden and cost of liberalisation and privatisation will be met out within the limits and adjusted within the process and no institution or person will bear it extraordinarily. Moreover, the coming problems emerging from the institutional change and reforms will be sorted out by the government at its own budget and resources. Lastly, the relationship between the institution and the public should be made more transparent, flexible and simplified for quality services. The emphasis of the motives is upon the institutional efficiency and service.

The motives of institutional reforms were mainly centred on the following: First, every institution should be able to adapt to the global trends, practices, behaviour and modes of exchange in order to deal with the emerging situations. Liberalisation and privatisation form the base of institutional reforms and no institution can ignore it. The institutions should be prepared for liberal economy and private sector cooperation; for this, FDI and private capital be acquired in all sectors of economy in order to avoid capital shortage, resource crunch and technological assistance; market economy is the growth engine of the development strategy. Hence, the function of resource allocation will be transferred to the market shortly from the government-owned institutions; the government will limit itself to the regulation which would also be autonomous and independent and facilitate the market players to play within the limits of law and rules and regulations. Secondly, institutions be developed 'out of the planning and budgetary constraints' through privatisation of institutional services and processes. Further, non-state organisations and NGOs will be allowed in the Indian economic sectors in order to provide alternatives of the institutions and move participation of masses in the economy. The budgetary provisions will be mainly used to provide the services for the deprived and poor masses or the core priorities of the institution. Moreover, more investments will be made in those institutions which support the market economy or the market institutions in different ways and means. Such institution would facilitate in building social safety net, price competition, fiscal balance, etc. The ownership of such institutions may be in the form of non-government, non-private and private sectors but governmental ownership is to be avoided. Thirdly, the internal management of the institutions should be designed on the more scientific and management principles in order to develop professionalism, commitment, honesty, transparency, etc., so that a non-bureaucratic and efficient system of management be developed. In the scientific management of the institutions, autonomy and independence of the institutions will be preserved. Fourthly, performance of the institutions in terms of assets, capital, staff, investments and trust of public in the institutions would be enhanced and government would provide extra capital for such tasks if institutions face crisis situations. The government support to save the institutions is to provide institutional and political cost. To avoid crisis situations in the economy, the demand for new design institutions will be fostered so that the existing institutions, wherever, they have failed, could be supported by the new institutional structures. Such new institutions are mainly in the sector of supplying perfect information to the markets, regulatory institutions, government and the masses. The market variations, price variations, quality, technology, manpower planning, etc., could be managed for the projections and demands. Last but not least, corporate restructuring is also in the agenda of the government for the institutional reforms. During the 1991 economic crisis and the problem of BOP, it was realised that corporate sectors be restructured to reform the financial sector. Such restructuring includes: elimination of tax and tax relating institutions, reduce legal and regulatory impediments, strengthening prudential regulation, establishing procedures for out of court settlements, resolving inter creditor differences, improving financial disclosures, scientific governance of corporate sector, emphasising on public asset management company than bank-led institutional arrangements, disciplining the budgetary support to the weak and ill corporate sector, deciding the principles of amalgamation of different corporate sectors, deciding the entry of foreign takeovers and evolving alternative strategies of restructuring of corporate sector. However, it would be the effort of the government that losses during restructuring would be either adjusted in the tax exemptions or the budgetary support in order to provide time to the weak corporate sectors to emerge in the market. Attention would also be paid on cash flow, recapitalisation of the markets, protection of the workers, suppliers, contractors, interest rates and the fair operations of the markets. In spite of this, corporate sector restructuring requires very cautious approach as the market risks, losses and the cost of restructuring is increasing and the alternative paths are adopted by the anti-corporate restructuring elements due to liberal market and legal network. The Government of India is very keen on this aspect and is making efforts to take the help of the international financial institutions, such as the International Monetary Fund (IMF), World Bank, etc., to avoid the failures in the restructuring and also to seek new alternative strategies.

On the whole, the motives of the government in the institutional reforms are mainly centred around the preparation of ground for globalisation, liberalisation and privatisation of the economy and to hand over the decisions of the economy to the markets rather than to the government. The government would like to remain a fair regulator of the economy; further, all institutional reforms are aimed to bring change without hurting any side of employees, cost and institutional structures; separation of government functions from the market in order to liberalise economy and budgetary allocations would be mainly aimed mainly to the poorest masses, security measures and to those sectors which are left or avoided by the private sectors; legal network reform is in the least priority of the government which would hamper the growth of institutions in long run, lastly, to prepare the federal polity tiers for example the state and the local governments to reorient their systems and institutions for the international dealings and biddings. However, all such reform efforts are circumscribed by the capabilities of the country and the adoption of the masses. If the institutions fail to deliver goods, the masses may revolt against all such reforms.

Institutional Choices

The Indian Constitution has provided some institutions for fiscal administration like Comptroller and Auditor General, Finance Commission, etc., to indicate the tendency of centralised network in a federal polity. The above institutions are responsible for planning and devolution of resources that facilitate markets and governments to function through a central administrative structure. Further, state governments are much free to initiate fiscal reforms, market reforms, plans and administrative services at their own under the constitutional provisions. The local governments are although reformed under the 73rd and 74th constitutional amendments in 1994 but much has to be done to strengthen them for global and liberal economy. In other sectors also, the rules and regulations have existed since the colonial time and much has also to be done to reform the legal network of the country for the liberal economy. For example, the banking and social insurance sectors need an overhauling of laws and institutions. The social safety net is also weak to protect the poor and the weaker sections of the society in the present and future emerging socio-economic system in the liberalised economy. The cultural aspect too has to be focused under the reforms packages. Culture is a very sensitive issue in the Indian socio-politico system and may put several hazards to the Indian polity and government. The religious and social organisations are opposing vehemently the liberal and global economy on the pretext of cultural erosion of the country. Moreover, the population pressure, over poverty ridden masses, non-cooperation of monsoon and climate, natural calamities and incapacities of using the natural resources properly, like water, solar energy and natural products, have put a burden on the existing institutional network on the one hand and also created obstacles in the path of reforms on the other.

In spite of all this, the government is committed for the reform in the tune of international demands, standards and perfect system of market economy. The institutional reforms done in the past 10 years are known as the first-generation reforms in the Indian economy which was aimed to clear the deck for the second-generation reforms. The main characteristic of the first-generation reforms was to create a support system for the coming economic reforms. Although the support system was improper and weak due to several inherent limitations, it has no doubt enabled the reforms psychology preparing for the market economy. The first phase of reforms has created regulatory framework that monitored the disinvestment effects on the performance of administrative organizations. Such efforts have indicated some of the trends in the economic reforms; for example, budgetary support would be to the poor masses, defence, deficit control and contingency demands; privatisation of most of the infrastructural facilities like electricity, water roads, railways, etc.; down-sizing the government structures and number of employees; protection of consumers in the global economy, reducing quantitative restrictions both in import and export, allowing foreign direct investments in the core areas except media, insurance and public protection system, increasing more expenditure on education, technology, health, etc., enlarging the tax net in many service sectors; fiscal autonomy to states in many areas. Such trends show that the government is committed to the basic spirit of globalisation and liberalisation. Although the government's efforts were aimed to develop a climate of market economy, bold steps for economic reforms were absent. However, the reasons of such absence may be attributed to the political scene in which a coalition government was working. Over population, poverty and cultural side of reforms were also factors which make the government over cautious in the market economy.

The second-generation economic reforms (2000–04) were introduced with the following vision: first, market economy would be the base of further development strategies in which market perfections would be brought through new institutional mechanism that is regulation, corporatisation and technical cooperation. In some sectors institutions were created to facilitate the market. But the trend shows that the government was more interested in creating the regulatory devices instead of corporatisation or technical cooperation. Further, the regulatory institutions were manned by the permanent civil servants belonging to the IAS. Consequently, most of the newly created institutions were the changed versions of the government departments/ministries and lacked the professional outlook for the market economy. The bureaucratic dominance in the regulatory institutions has generated a tug of war between the ministries and the institutions and the very purpose of the regulatory institutions was demolished. Moreover, the scams in the capital market, decreasing size of Indian investments, over expenditures on the public services and poor management of the capital have generated debate on globalisation rather than on the reforms in the institutional operations.; corporatisation of economic sectors was also done half-heartedly as it might hurt the Indian capitalists interests as well as the political purposes of the privatisation. The corporate sector was also not very cooperative in the liberalisation and globalisation of the economy due to its own self interests. Foreign investors were not much able to influence the Indian corporate lobbies due to their own reluctance and failures in the Indian markets. One of the hurdles was also the over control of the banking sector, interest rates and financial transactions as well as of the financial institutions. Consequently, corporatisation in the economic sectors could not emerge and the scattered efforts to boost the economy have not been very successful. Similarly, technical cooperation was liberalised by removing quantitative restrictions and quality control measures but paucity of funds as well as bureaucratic procedures have crippled the purposes of the liberalisation. Technical cooperation was mainly promoted by the Indian resident investments but FDI in technical cooperation was not energised. For example, the fund starving educational institutions, agricultural development projects, scientific furtherance of research in basic fields where FDI could only be a solution, was not encouraged. The terrorism has diminished the prospects of technical cooperation. Moreover, the atomic experiments in India during 1998 have put a very bad effect upon the technical cooperation measure.

Secondly, disinvestments in public sector enterprises were emphasised with a view to generate more capital in two ways, one by saving money on public enterprises and the other by selling the enterprises in the market on the basis of international bidding. The capital generated by disinvestments policy was also not considered the part of budgetary resources (although the World Bank is emphasising upon such capital as the budgetary resource). The investments in the Public Sector Enterprises (PSEs) in the last 50 years were made out of budgetary allocations and by sales in most of the cases. The government wants to use the money for emergency situations in the country, including the war, drought, flood, failures of crops and economy. In any case, the disinvestments were not adopted timely and quickly. The disinvestments policy ignored the market sentiments, changes and demands. Therefore, the disinvestments policy has not been very successful. Moreover, the policy generated more unrest in the PSEs and the share of PSEs in the total production and sales in the market have gone down. The economic recession both at the national and the international level has further severely affected the PSEs. In some of the vital sector of the economy, like petroleum, gas, media, disinvestments were kept pending and decisions were not taken till recently. The profit earning nine diamonds of the PSEs were still not covered in the disinvestments policy. In the overall liberalisation framework, disinvestment, FDI, etc., in the media sector are considered risky in view of the culture and traditions of society. Petroleum was also similarly considered a vital sector and a source of revenue generation for the government through custom excise duty. The FDI in the petroleum sector was allowed but disinvestments were opposed by the coalition partners of the Union government. Further, disinvestments in the service sector were also not much pursued due to heavy risks in the service sector. The banking sector was untouched although FDI was allowed. Foreign sector banks were allowed in the country but the Indian banking industry was not much reformed which needs special reforms more particularly in the second generation reforms strategy. The inefficiency in the service sectors, such as banking and insurance, was not reduced under the reforms packages. The electricity, water and roads service sectors were being privatised but FDI in these sectors have been very low and this diminished the prospects of disinvestments.

Looking at the FDI policy, the government is also very cautious in allowing FDI in the vital economic sectors. Although the committee on the FDI has recommended up to 75 per cent FDI in most of the sectors but the opposition from the coalition partners in the government has restricted the implementation of the FDI policy in full swing. Further, the policy of protecting the Indian industry from foreign capital has also affected the FDI. Comparing the FDI in Indian and China, the figures are surprising and eye-opening. India is lagging behind in FDI in comparison to China. The reasons may be attributed to the decision-making system, bureaucratic system, politico-administrative process and the efficiency level in the industrial sector followed by the legal system. The cultural side is also very important in the Indian context. Further, the FDI is also dependent on other factors, such as peace in the South Asian region, supportive international economic system, expenditures on defence, currency exchange rate, bank interest rate, foreign exchange management system in the country, capital market operations, etc. In India, much has to be done on the front of FDI and its use; also, sectoral reforms, institutional capacities and market perfections are the need of the hour. Moreover, the incentives to the FDI, legal simplifications and full convertibility of currency are the critical issues where India has to decide.

Structural adjustments programme is also a point of choices. The government has chosen those fields/sectors where Structural Adjustment Program (SAP) does not put much burden on the government vis-à-vis finance and cost effectiveness. The reasons may be attributed to the cost, number of employees, trade unions and the lack of technical expertise to initiate programme in the economic sectors. Further, the involvement of private sector in the SAP is also a point of debate in the Indian economy. The limitations and inherent problems of private sector, labour laws and the judicial decisions also prohibit the government to initiate SAP in most of the economic sectors. However, where the SAP was initiated, was not very conducive. In some of the Union ministries, SAP was not very successful due to protest and opposition from the staff side; the results of the SAP were not very encouraging too. The mode of SAP was to reduce the number of organisations, employees, laws, plans and programmes in order to decrease the burden of the government. The strategy of implementing the SAP was evolved in those areas where industrial production or service sector existed but some of the important sectors such as banking, insurance, civil services, education and health were left untouched. The SAP was introduced in electricity, water, environment, information technology, roads, construction and in similar sectors. The results of SAP in electricity sector were very discouraging and were misused by politicians and administrators for their own purposes. The benefits are yet to reach the masses. In the SAP, the government has not taken a very thoughtful strategy and concentrated on the political benefits rather than benefits for all. In some of states, such as Rajasthan, SAP was limited to the replacement of organisations by another organisation but institutional reforms were ignored. The staff was not changed; procedures were not changed; administrative behaviour was not much changed and the SAP was known as old wine in a new bottle. The political reasons in the SAP dominated. The masses were not very much served.

Reforms in Civil Service

Looking at the civil services side, the situation is not also encouraging. The continuation of the colonial structures, services and the rules and regulations have left very limited choices and motives for institutional reforms. The colonial civil services with steel framed structures are carrying the burden of economic reforms and it may be a question of efficiency and effectiveness. The government is spending a big amount of budget on civil services. Besides this, all colonial evils of bureaucracy are to persist. Hence, it is difficult to believe that the bureaucracy inherited by the colonial practices and behaviour would be successful in bringing market economy and institutions compatible to the global trends. It is also expressed that the institutions, whatever being created in the country, would not be as competitive as existing at the international level. Further, the civil services are not ready to surrender their power, prestige and facilities in the market economy. In such situations all efforts of civil service reforms would be futile. An assessment of the civil service reforms in the last 10 years shows that the bureaucratic organisations have been replaced by other bureaucratic organisations. In the Union ministries, agency system, involvement of NGOs and voluntary organisations were not properly considered. A heavy reliance upon the bureaucracy is marketed in all government plans and programmes. Besides this, the government has also neglected these aspects in its reforms. In spite of all this, it is seen the Indian bureaucracy is preparing itself for the reforms if a strong government will prevails.

Last but not least, the judicial reforms are required urgently in order to provide support to the market economy. The colonial laws and outdated Acts are to be abolished. A drastic change in the market related legal procedures, liabilities and information is required. Some of the efforts by the law ministry may be welcome initiatives but a very heavy exercise is required.

Social organisations are to be supportive to the market economy. However, if the market economy fails to deliver the goods and fruits of the globalisation, the social system would oppose the institutional reforms.

On the whole, institutional reforms in India have taken a long time and have a long way to go. The question of capacity building through institutional reforms would be a question of debate. Further, the fruits of market economy reaching the masses would be doubtful. It is also being expressed that the colonial bureaucracy would not allow much institutional reforms in the country due to its fear of loss of power in the administrative change. In the institutional reforms, multistage holders would threaten the bureaucracy which would be disliked by the bureaucracy. Moreover, the social system based on religion, caste and other social factors would not be supportive in the market economy. To add fuel to fire, the politics of votes would also avoid much institutional reforms. Several examples are cited when institutional reforms were avoided; for example, entry of foreigners in the media and FDI in several economic sectors were denied on the pretext of social deterioration. Besides this, NGOs and similar organisations will not be allowed to be autonomous to support the socio-economic change through institutional reforms. Last but not least, there will remain unanswered questions as to what extent the judicial system would support the market economy aimed reforms. The history of the country clearly demonstrates that drastic reforms initiated by any regime were rejected by the Indian society and the culture. Now, the fate will be of market economy reforms is left to the future.

Bibliography

Elster, Jon, Claus Offe and Ulrich K. Preuss. 1998. *Institutional Design in Post Communist Societies: Rebuilding the Ship at Sea*. Cambridge: Cambridge University Press.

Islam, Roumeen. 2002. 'Institutions to Market Support', *Finance & Development*, 39 (1): 48–51.

Kettl, Donald F. 2000. *The Global Public Management Revolution*. Washington, D.C.: Brookings Institution Press.

Knack, Stephen and Philip Keefer. 1995. 'Institutions and Economic Performance: Cross-Country Tests Using Alternative Institutional Measures', *Economics and Politics*, 7 (3): 207–27.

Lee, Doowon. 1997. 'Flying Geese in Asia: Comparative Study of Asian Development Models', proceedings of 12th ADIPA Bienniel Meeting, Bali, Indonesia. Asian Development Bank, Emerging Asia.

Porter, Tony. 2002. 'Politics, Institutions, Constructivism, and the Emerging International Regime for Financial Regulation', *The Review of Policy Research*, 19: 53–79. Policy Studies Organisation, Opinion, USA.

Saxena, Pradeep K. 1995. 'Gatt: Prospects of Productivity Improvements in Public Sector in India', in Arie Halachmi (ed.), *Public Productivity through Quality and Strategic Management*. Brussels: International Institute of Administrative Sciences.

———. 1997. 'Strategies of Development in Developing Economics', in *Strategic Planning and Development*. Sheffield: Sheffield Hallam University Press.

Qian, Yingyi. 2000. 'The Institutional Foundations of China's Market Transitions', paper presented at the Annual World Bank Conference on Development Economics, 1999. World Bank.

8

Reinventing the Civil Servant*

Madhav Godbole[#]

It has been a decade since the economic reforms were launched in the country in mid 1991. During this period, we have taken a fresh look at how we transacted the business of the government and reviewed a number of rules, regulations, licensing procedures and grant of approvals in the government. But, one crucial area which has remained untouched by reforms is the civil service and the big bad bureaucratic machine which has retained its tight grip over the economy of the country. This paper attempts to look at the role of civil servants in a deregulated economy.

The first forty years since Independence were marked by the State occupying the "commanding heights" of the economy. The socialist policies pursued by the government arrogated to the government superior wisdom in all fields and led to totally unguided use of all discretionary powers. The license and permit raj of this period gave enormous powers to the civil servants. Postings in all economic ministries were keenly sought after as even lowly civil servants in these ministries enjoyed enormous discretionary and other powers. The system of licenses and permits was misused not just by the politicians and the bureaucrats but also by the industrial houses to pre-empt grant of licenses to their competitors. Large licensed capacity often remained unused and unimplemented, thereby denying

---

* This chapter was originally published in *Diamond Jubilee Souvenir* in 2001.
# Former Home Secretary, Government of India.

the benefits of the same to the competitors as also the general public. The powers enjoyed by the Directorate of Technical Development (DGTD), for example, were to be seen to be believed. The licensing committee, the capital goods committee, the foreign investment board and a host of similar other committees in the government could dispense favours to all and sundry. Since these were decisions of the committees, hardly any one officer could be held responsible or accountable. Inevitably, this gave rise to the generation of a large amount of black money. Political and administrative corruption was rampant. In fact, there were those in the political hierarchy who argued that there was nothing wrong in taking a percentage cut in foreign exchange for the favours granted to foreign companies. This led to proliferation of numbered accounts in Swiss banks and in similar other tax havens. The single most improvement reform brought about by economic liberalisation was to do away with this system of license and permit raj.

But, this by itself was not enough. There had to be transparency in all decisions made by the government. The rules of the game must be clear to all those participating in the game, if there is to be a departure from the previously announced rules. The reason, therefore, must be made clear to everyone by issuing a "speaking order." It is not surprising that a large number of visiting foreign trade and industry delegations have highlighted this point in their observations to the government from time to time during the last ten years since the onset of economic liberalisation. The role of a civil servant in the new milieu has to undergo a qualitative change from being regulatory to promotional, developmental and facilitating. As the capital investment by the government gets reduced perceptibly, its place will have to be taken by the private sector. One interesting feature of the new development is that backward states such as Orissa and Madhya Pradesh are now in as good a position as some of the developed states to attract new private sector investment. These forces will gather further strength if the civil service in these erstwhile backward states is able to imbibe the new changes much faster than the states which have been the traditional destinations for attracting such investment.

By way of illustration, it will be useful in this context to refer to the power sector reforms in Orissa. This small and backward state took a lead to launch power sector reforms in the state and was the first state in the country to privatise the generation and distribution of power. As a result, it was able to attract much larger investment in the state. Many other states are now following the lead given by the Government of Orissa.

Much remains to be done in the deregulation of the economy. As is widely accepted, that government governs the best which governs the least. This would effectively mean reducing the role of the government by downsizing the same. This may require taking a fresh look at the primary responsibilities of the government. Looking to the serious constraint of financial resources faced by the government, it is time to give a serious thought whether the government ought to be doing all that it has been doing so far. It would appear that the government should concentrate its limited resources on some of its primary responsibilities such as maintenance of law and order, administration of justice, provision of rural services such as primary education, primary health, drinking water supply and so on, and protection of and provision of a safety net for the economically and socially weaker sections of society. All other duties and responsibilities are, in a sense, optional. In all other areas, the government should encourage the private sector and co-operatives to play their role in meeting the needs of society. An important challenge facing the civil services is how to downsize the government and at the same time to encourage the other non-government sectors to fill in the gap. Looked at in one sense, this is a pioneering role for a new civil servant. His success or failure will mark how soon we are able to make a transition to a rapidly growing economy and to qualify for being in the ranks of middle-income countries in the world.

As a part of these efforts, the government will have to divest itself of the activities which can be contracted out to the private or the co-operative sector. This will require a bold vision and a firm commitment to usher in the requisite changes at a fast enough pace. Since higher civil servants are in charge of a number of institutions and organisations as also government departments and ministries, they are better suited to bring about these changes through enunciation of appropriate policies and programmes. On the contrary, as has been seen time and again, a disinterested bureaucracy can be a positive hindrance to the process of change.

In the new environment of change, the government will have to be made more open, transparent and accountable. This objective will be met by placing on the statute book an effective right to information law. Ideally, such a law should pertain not just to the government sector but also to the private sector, co-operatives, trusts, organisations registered under the society's registration law and other diverse organisations and institutions. Under such a law, it must be the responsibility of the government to share as much information as possible with the public periodically on its own, without anyone having to approach the government for it. It would also, *inter alia,* mean the government identifying all areas of discretion so as to formulate the guidelines for the use thereof. The areas of exception from the purview of the Act must be kept to the barest minimum. Old record must be made public as soon after the decision is taken as possible, without waiting for a statutory period of thirty years to expire. Unfortunately, the Bill on this subject introduced by the Government of India in Parliament leaves a great deal to be desired. It is hoped that the report of the Parliamentary Standing Committee on the subject will suggest some major modifications in the Bill.

A civil servant, working in a deregulated economy, will have to be sensitive to the impact that the actions of the government will have on the economy. Since the main engine of growth will be outside the government, any such adverse impact may result in the economy being adversely affected leading to the slowing down of the economy. In this sense, there is a mutually reinforcing action and reaction to all decisions of the government.

This is also evident from the fact that the government and its organisations will have to stand the scrutiny of the market from time to time. Such scrutiny is in the form of credit rating of the institutions. Government's actions will be assessed and reassessed by credit rating institutions. As a result, certain actions such as budget management and fiscal responsibility will also come in for scrutiny by these institutions. Thus even items of work which were once upon a time considered as within the sovereign realm of the government are no longer outside the pale of scrutiny. The role of the civil servant in this sense will be much more accountable to society at large.

Deregulation of the economy will imply taking a fresh look at the laws, rules and regulations in the country. A recent review of the laws by the Government of India showed that literally hundreds of laws have outlived their utility. Even basic laws such as the India Penal code, Criminal Procedure Code and the India Evidence Act are out of step with the changing times. Several laws contain restrictive provisions which are no longer in keeping with the liberal and deregulated environment which we seek to promote. The punishments, particularly the monetary punishments, prescribed in several laws have lost all significance with influx of time. It is pertinent to ensure that this aspect of the liberal environment and deregulated economy is not lost sight of and speedy steps are taken to repeal, amend and/or modify the laws suitably and to keep them continuously under review.

It is necessary to understand that free market forces do not mean free for all operations of the markets. In fact, a free and deregulated economy often means an economy which is well regulated through appropriate laws and institutional mechanisms. The present controversy surrounding the Securities and Exchange Board of India (SEBI) and its weaknesses in controlling the share markets brings this out sharply. Protection of small investors and strict vigilance against insider trading will have thus to be the hallmarks of the regulatory efforts of SEBI, as is the case in respect of similar institutions in the USA. Yet another step that is long overdue is to set up regulatory bodies for various fields of activities such as public transport, public health, education, water supply and so on. We, as a country, have just made a beginning in this direction by setting up electricity regulatory commissions at the centre and in some states. But, even here the experience is a mixed one. A number of states have sidelined the commissions and have unilaterally taken decisions in respect of electricity tariffs. In certain other states, all powers as visualised under the relevant central legislation have not been given to the regulatory commissions. In all these matters, the civil servants will have a special responsibility to take an enlightened and forward-looking view in the matter and to advise the political leadership appropriately.

A deregulated economy has to be, by definition, a decentralised economy. This would imply bringing in democratic decentralisation at several levels. Unfortunately, in spite of the 73rd and 74th Amendments of the Constitution, the pace of ushering in these changes is far too slow and faltering. Delegation of powers, both administrative and financial, is pertinent in this behalf. Even though large funds are now flowing to these bodies, their own efforts to mobilise the resources are, by and large minimal. The audit of these expenditures also leaves a great deal to be desired. The financial health of decentralised sector will have to be assessed on the basis of the capacity of these institutions to garner resources and to spend them diligently.

In the new liberalised environment, the civil servant will have to be sensitive to the impact of his actions on the society, much more than in the days of the *Mai-Baap Sarkar*. But it must be ensured that he retains his independence, objectivity and political neutrality. This would imply that he must not only stand for all these qualities but must be seen to personify these qualities. Thus, suggestions which are made from time to time to bring about closer relationship between civil servants and the private sector by way of sending civil servants on deputation to the private sector for a duration of 3–5 years must be scrupulously resisted. A civil servant must not be seen to be aligned with or under the influence of one industrial house or the other.

Managing this change is by no means an easy task. It will call for a cultural change in the mindset of a civil servant, in his capacity to look at issues in a detached manner and more than anything else, to understand his secondary and subsidiary role in the new and larger scheme of things. This will require training, new orientation and a capacity to adjust to the rapidly changing times. A suitably redesigned basic training for the probationary period as also the orientation courses during the service should help in these endeavours. For if the civil servant is not reinvented to suit the new liberal and deregulated environment, such a new environment itself may be found wanting essentials.

III

Functioning of Service Commissions in SAARC Region

The SAARC region consisting of eight counties, Afghanistan, Bangladesh, Bhutan, India, Maldives, Nepal, Pakistan and Sri Lanka has a population of 1,368 million as estimated around 2010. It is just about one-fifth (20 per cent) of the total population of the world. Realising the need to have cooperation to promote the welfare of the people of the region and to accelerate economic growth, the SAARC was formed by the heads of state of all the countries, except Afghanistan, in 1989. Afghanistan joined the group later (2010). The region has a long shared history and culture that dates back to several millenniums. Though India had a lengthy history of civil service, it was the British who had introduced the Western form of bureaucracy through its Government of India Act 1858. The civil servants were recruited through the Civil Service Examination held in England till 1922. The leaders of the Home Rule movement protested against this and wanted the examinations be conducted in India. Therefore, the ICS examination was organised in India on behalf of British Civil Service Commission. After Independence, the Federal Service Commission was named as UPSC in India. Pakistan still calls it Federal Public Service Commission (FPSC*)*. The service commissions and the recruitment policies of other countries in the region have broadly barrowed from these two commissions with necessary inputs from each country's requirement.

Public or civil service commissions play an important role for the quality, integrity and continuity of civil service in South Asian countries. Civil service commissions in the region are not only responsible for recruitment but also for the promotion, transfer, discipline and appeals of civil servants, vested with the commissions. Thus, the study of service commissions in the region does provide us an understanding of the state of civil service in each country. An attempt is made here to provide information and analysis on each country in relation to the civil service commission. It is found that India, Pakistan, Bhutan and Maldives have stable establishments as far as governance is concerned and are pursuing a democratic form of government. In the case of Afghanistan, Nepal in the north and Bangladesh and Sri Lanka on the south of the subcontinent, we have varied and different forms of government and some of them are in transition. Therefore, we have commissioned a comparative study on the five countries to bring out salient features and contrasts in the operation of service commissions in the countries which are dissimilar. The functioning of the service commissions in India, Pakistan and Bhutan are given in detail in the section on case studies.

Civil service commissions throughout the world have been subjected to reforms to suit the changing needs of governance. Though most of the countries pursue democracy, each country has set its own socio-economic targets within the broad parameters of its constitution. Some countries have constitutional provisions and status for the public service commissions while some have statutory status through legislative action. There is lot of difference between a statutory commission and a constitutional authority like the ones we have in India and Pakistan and others in the region. Several developments in the area of technology, rights regime (such as RTI), human rights, privatisation, outsourcing and alternative sources of acquiring supplementary capabilities have appeared in the process of governance over a period of time. It is also noticed that international organisations like the World Bank, WTO, OECD, United Nations Conference on Trade and Development (UNCTAD), etc., are taking interest in providing technical assistance to improve the administrative capacities of the emerging nations including skill upgradation, training and alternative models of recruitment policy.

The strength and authority of a civil servant depend upon not only on the credibility and legal status of the recruitment agency—the civil service commission—but also on the methods adopted to recruit people on the basis of merit, capability and integrity. A civil servant in a developing country needs broad understanding of the society, economy, political process, natural resources and international setting to advise the government on policies that bring tangible changes in the lives of the people. Some of the chairmen and the members of the civil service commissions have shown extraordinary enthusiasm and commitment to build an independent and transparent system of bureaucracy immediately after Independence. It was an enormous task to organise and reformulate the structures and policies relating to the recruitment of competent personnel for the governance of an independent country without any vestiges of colonialism. It was a challenging job for the first generation of chairmen. R.N. Banerjee and other officers who were drawn from the civil services have done commendable job in establishing structures, policies and traditions that still remain outstanding in the service of the nation. Yet, there are limitations in the formulation of policies for the recruitment of personnel to operate an independent and permanent system of civil service as several developments have taken place between 1950 and 2010 in the world that has bearing on the recruitment agencies and its policies. It is also found that the governments that came to power had differences in opinion with the systems that were permanent as agencies to maintain enduring structures. This has created tensions and unnecessary reforms to unseat people. There are also cases where the incumbent had to compromise with the government to implement changes suggested by the government and are alleged to have been responsible in diluting the stature and prestige of the organisation.

The contents of the chapter that is presented here explain the system and structure of public or civil service commissions in the region. Each country has given a different orientation to its examination system, interview method, syllabus, category of positions taken in to the fold of the commission. We can see that the status of the commission itself has varied from country to country. Maldives Parliament selects the chairman and the President of the country selects the Members of the Service Commission. In India, Bhutan and Pakistan, the President of the country appoints the chairman and members. It is also noticed that several changes have taken place in the structure of administration of the commission except in countries where there is a constitutional provision. The recruitment in to higher civil services in most of the countries was based on the elite background of the recruitees in the beginning. But slowly with the reform agenda of the governments and the democratic decentralisation of administration, together with the availability of alternative openings in multinational companies (MNCs), private sector, etc., the clientele coming in to the system have changed. Countries such as India, Pakistan, Bangladesh and Nepal have made stipulations to bring in diversity to different ethnic minority and gender considerations. The Indian government has appointed so far two ARCs to recommend changes in recruitment system, civil service code, evaluation methods of performance, ethics and administrative structures which will contain corruption and also to bring in accountability. The debate over the need for new structures to regulate the civil servant's public behaviour and the scheme of incentives to encourage the performers is publicly debated by intellectuals and common man alike in countries like India. This indicates that the civil service is no more limited to a select few and protected by the system. It is now the concern of every one in a democratic polity.

The chapter that is produced here would show the unity and diversity in the administration systems of the region as reflected in the functioning of the civil service commissions.

9

Comparative Study of Service Commissions in SAARC Nations: Bangladesh, Nepal, Sri Lanka, Afghanistan and Maldives

D. Francis*

The SAARC region has different styles of government that represent a democracy, a dictatorial system, a military junta rule and anarchy at different stages in some of the countries. However, there are countries that have stable governments as per the constitutional mandate with administrative structures that are exemplary in the world. We have selected here five countries in the region that are typical in their governance and growth of civil service systems. The previous chapters have provided the system of civil services in relatively stable and democratic governments. The present five countries have distinct characters that make them different from others and at the same time resemble amongst themselves.

---

*Teaching Asstistant, Department of Economics, Dr. B.R. Ambedkar University, Etcherla, Srikakulam, Andhra Pradesh.

Introduction

Governments in most of the countries of the world are making their best efforts to strengthen their political, economic, bureaucratic and other systems to achieve their goals in more effective and well-organised manner. Some of the countries in the region have been involved in various programmes to make their political and economic systems transform towards a more dynamic and democratic development. They seem to have realised the importance of the doctrine of good governance. It is expected that it would bring solutions for a wide range of international, national and local issues, including transnational global markets, national economies and their management, provision of human rights with special attention to marginalised and minority groups and other issues of governance. In this context, the civil service has been assigned a pioneering role to play in achieving these aims and aspirations of the entire civil society. During the past 25 years, as a common response to economic, institutional and ideological changes that were taking place in the world, public sector reforms became an important aspect for governments both in developed and in developing countries. As a part of reforms in public sector, public management has been emphasised and emerged as a recipe in developed countries. These management-oriented reforms have been labeled as 'Managerialism' (Pollitt, 1993), 'Market Based Public Administration' (MBPA) (Lan and Rosenblom, 1992), 'Entrepreneurial Government' (EG) (Osborne and Gaebler, 1992) and NPM (Hood, 1991; Kearney and Hays, 1998). This new paradigm or trend seems to have been popularised through the NPM. The NPM that emphasises on reforms of the central civil service apparatus has been introduced as a new administrative orthodoxy (Olsen, 1997) in several countries.

This chapter is about service commissions of Bangladesh, Sri Lanka, Nepal, Afghanistan and Maldives. An attempt is made here to study the functioning of service commissions of these five countries. Data relating to the constitutional status of civil service, its history, establishment, traditions and amendments are provided here for each country separately. The chief functions of a service commission are discussed and finally an evaluation is made basing on the data for each country.

Bangladesh

Introduction

Abdul Wahhab (2009) tells us that

> civil service of a country generally includes all permanent functionaries of government which distinctly excludes defense service, although some civil servants work in defense ministry and its various departments. A member of civil service is not also a holder of political or judicial office. The civil servants of a state are collectively called civil service. Civil service is a professional body of officials, permanent, paid and skilled. Policy formulation is the function of cabinet/ministry, but policy implementation, the main aspect of development is the function of the civil servants. Although policy formulation is the jurisdiction of cabinet/ministry, it depends largely on civil servants for the data of policy formulation. According to a British writer, in ninety nine cases out of one hundred, the ministers simply accept the views of civil servants, and sign their names on dotted line. So a state may run without ministers, but it cannot run a day without civil servants (Ahmad, 2003: 455). Here lies the importance of recruiting the best talents for civil service in order to make public sector a relevant, dynamic and powerful force of change.

Background of Bangladesh

Bangladesh was a province of united Pakistan from 1947 to 1971 and became independent in December 1971. Literally, the word 'Bangladesh' means the land of Bangla. In fact, Bangladesh is a country of Bengali-speaking people consisting of more than 98 per cent of total population. Bangladesh is one of the largest deltas of the world with an area of 157.579 sq. km. By size it stands 89th in the world, but in population it is 8th in the world and 5th in Asia. Male female ratio is 105:100 and literacy is 63 per cent of which male literacy is high.

Bangladesh is a unitary country with parliamentary form of government. Administratively Bangladesh is divided into six divisions and each division is divided into districts, called *zilla*s. There are 64 districts and each district is divided into sub-districts called *upazillas* (481). Every *upazilla* consists of several unions (4,466). There are local governments at *upazilla* and union levels. The urban communities are led by city corporations and municipalities. The people of Bangladesh prefer to join civil service because it is the biggest employer in the country.

Status of Civil Service

The Constitution of Bangladesh has granted equal employment opportunities for citizens. The Constitution declares: 'There shall be equality of opportunity for all citizens in respect of employment or office in the service of the Republic' (Article 29 [1]). 'No citizen shall, on the grounds only of religion, race, caste, sex or place of birth be ineligible for, or discriminated against in respect of any employment or office in the service of the Republic' (Article 29 [2]). However, under clause (3) of the same Article, the Constitution has provided certain exceptions that read:

> Nothing in this article shall prevent the state from (a) making special provision, in favour of any backward section of citizens for the purpose of securing their adequate representation in the service of the Republic; (b) giving effect to any law which makes provision for reserving appointments relating to any religious or denominational institution to person of that religion or denomination; (c) reserving for members of one sex any class of employment or office on the ground that it is considered by its nature to be unsuited to members of the opposite sex. (Article 29 [3])

The above constitutional provisions indicate that civil service recruitment policy in Bangladesh is the admixture of merit and quota. The clause seems to have been lifted verbatim from Article 16 (4) of Indian Constitution. Recruitment policy was first introduced in Bangladesh by an executive order in September 1972 called Interim Recruitment Rules 1972 before the Constitution came into operation in December 5 of that year. The recruitment to civil service in Bangladesh may be of various natures. They are: direct appointment through competitive examination, appointments by promotion, appointments by transfer and appointments on ad hoc basis and then regularisation. Here we shall deal with direct recruitment to the officers giving emphasis to cadre services.

Government employees in Bangladesh vertically belong to four categories, namely class I officers, class II officers, class III employees and Class IV employees. The officers are also classified as gazetted officers and non-gazetted officers. The officers whose appointment, posting, transfer, promotion, etc., are notified in government gazette, they are known as gazetted officers. All class I officers and some of the class II officers are treated as gazetted officers. Of the class I officers, some belong to the cadre services.

Cadre service means the organisation of civil servants in well-defined groups, services or cadres. Cadre service generally exists in countries with British colonial heritage. Cadre services are constituted under law with a number of position or structure and recruitment and promotion rules. Non-cadre services, however, are mostly based on position, with no definite structure of mobility, either horizontally or vertically. A cadre system entails organisation of civil servants into semi-functional occupational groups or cadres. Cadre service in Bangladesh was first officially recognised in 1981, and Bangladesh Civil Service Recruitment Rules were introduced in the same year.

Bangladesh Civil Service, more popularly known by its acronym BCS, is the elite service in the country. BCS inherited the Civil Service of Pakistan (CSP), which was the legacy of ICS, the most distinguished civil service in the world. Currently there are 28 cadres in the BCS. Some cadres are general, such as BCS (Administration), BCS (Foreign Affairs), BCS (Police), BCS (Food), BCS (Customs and Accounts), BCS (Information), etc., and others are professional/technical, such as BCS (Health), BCS (General Education), BCS (Technical Education), BCS (Economics), BCS (Fisheries) and so on. Among the general cadres, BCS (Administration) is the steering wheel around which the entire administration of Bangladesh revolves. It is like the IAS in India and CSP in Pakistan. The first appointment of a BCS (Administration) officer starts as assistant commissioner in the rank of assistant secretary. The BCS (Administration) officers in hierarchical order are assistant secretary, senior assistant secretary, deputy secretary, joint secretary, additional secretary and secretary, the highest civil post in Bangladesh government, excepting two—cabinet secretary and principal secretary. Originally, there were 30 cadres in the BCS. In 1990, BCS (Secretariat) was merged to BCS (Administration). In November 2007, lower judiciary in Bangladesh was separated from the executive. As a result BCS (Judiciary) has become a separate service known as Judicial Service and it is no more a cadre of BCS.

Bangladesh Public Service Commission

Recruitment is the process of searching for prospective employees and stimulating them to apply for jobs in the organisation (Flippo, 1984, p. 141). No element of the career service system is more important than the recruitment policy (Stahl, 1962, p. 51). Recruitment is the cornerstone of the whole personnel structure. Unless recruitment policy is soundly conceived, there can be of little hope of building a first rate staff (Stahl, 1962, p. 51).

Broadly, there are two major methods for recruitment to civil service: (a) merit system through competitive examination and (b) spoils system. Under the typical civil service law, the central personnel agency commonly called Public Service Commission is responsible to conduct competitive examination. Spoils system (also known as a patronage system) is an informal practice where a political party, after winning an election, gives government jobs to its voters as a reward for working towards victory, and as an incentive to keep working for the party—as opposed to a system of awarding offices on the basis of merit, independent of political activity.

Bangladesh Public Service Commission, shortly known as BPSC, is a constitutional body (Articles 137–41), like its predecessors in British India and united Pakistan. The Constitution has assigned PSC to conduct tests and examinations for the selection of suitable persons for appointment to the services of the Republic. The PSC is also empowered to advise President in framing recruitment rules, promotion and other matters related to civil service. The chairman and members of PSC are appointed by the president with the advice of PM and their tenure is five years or attain the age of 65 years whichever is earlier. Currently, the PSC consists of a chairman and 14 members.

Constitutional Provisions for Establishing One or More PSCs

Accordingly after independence of Bangladesh, two types of PSC were constituted. The PSC (First) meant for the recruitment of class I officers and PSC (Second) for class II officers. But the two commissions were merged into a single one in 1977 through the PSC Ordinance of that year and the number of members was fixed between 6 (minimum) to 15 (maximum), including the chairman. Before 1982 no competitive examinations, in present sense, were held in Bangladesh. Civil servants were then recruited either only with interview or with short written examinations and interview by the PSC. But majority of the officers were appointed on ad hoc basis and latter they were regularised by PSC. Regular competitive examinations began since 1982 when BCS Recruitment Rules 1981 was introduced.

Functions of BCS

BCS recruitment process consists of the following steps that are stated below:

1. Multiple choice questions (MCQ) preliminary examination: It is a screening test of 100 marks on Bangla, English, General Knowledge, Bangladesh and International Affairs, General Science and Technology, Mathematical Reasoning and Mental Ability and Everyday Science.
2. Written examination: According to the Second Schedule of BCS Recruitment Rule 1981, BCS examination consisted of 1,600 marks. But it was reduced to 900 marks in 1984; and again it was increased to 1,000 (Ali, 2007: 61–62), which is still going on.
3. Viva-voce
4. Result publication for selected candidates
5. Medical test

6. Police verification
7. Appointment

Generally the respective ministries, directorates, divisions, departments and statutory bodies inform the PSC about the number of vacant posts through the Ministry of Establishment (MOE). The PSC through national newspapers invites applications for the vacant posts. The eligible candidates are asked to appear at a preliminary examination of 100 marks to drop out the less qualified candidates. The applicants who qualify preliminary examination are invited to appear at a written examination consisting of 1,000 marks, including 200 marks for viva and psychological test. Recently marks of viva have been reduced to 100 and another 100 marks of a written subject was increased. The candidates obtaining 50 per cent marks in written test are qualified for viva. The minimum qualifying marks for viva is 40 per cent. If a candidate fails in viva, he/she will not be considered for final selection. The merit list is prepared on the basis of written and viva marks. After completing merit list, the candidates are selected for different types of quota. The PSC sends the final list of selected candidates to MOE with recommendation for appointment to the vacancies. Police verification and medical check-up of the selected candidates is arranged by MOE respectively with the support of Home Affairs Ministry and Health Ministry. Final appointment is given by MOE through notification.

Evaluation

The above information on civil service recruitment policy in Bangladesh as narrated by Wahhab (2009) found some shortages and suggested some measures for better service to the people well as for good governance. It is noted that there shall be two PSCs, one is central PSC responsible for recruiting officers of two categories, namely All Bangladesh Services for the Centre and provinces, and central service meant for only the Centre. The other is provincial PSC meant for recruiting officers for provincial administration. If the above suggestions are not possible to implement, the present single PSC should be divided into PSC (First) and PSC (Second) like the earlier. The PSC (First) will recruit all cadres of BCS, including other class 1 officers and PSC (Second) class 11 officers. As a result, regular and timely recruitment will not be possible for smooth administration in the country.

Since the inception of PSC, with a few exceptions, the chairmen and members were appointed on political considerations. As a result there are allegations of recruiting candidates aligned to the ruling party. To avoid this criticism the appointment of chairman and members of an institution such as PSC must be from among the persons of high integrity, strong moral courage, personality and commitment with sufficient knowledge and experience on administration. Renuka Priyantha has conducted studies on the personnel management reforms in Sri Lanka and we have made use of the data for the present paper.

Sri Lanka

Introduction

Public sector reforms for the existing civil service in the third world countries are not a new effort or a new programme. In fact, the successive governments elected to power in most of the third world countries have undertaken different types of reforms since their independence. But in the 1980s, factors such as budget deficits, international influences and the emergence of market-based neo-liberal economic policies had affected governments to move towards the reforms in reducing cost and size of political–administrative mechanism (Hague and Harrop, 2001).

Sri Lanka is one of the developing countries that embarked on civil service reforms since the 1980s. Under the influence of the British colonial regime, the administrative structure of the country was highly centralised. With the bureaucratic approach to management, rigid ruling system became the norm and seniority rather than merit had been the main ground for promotion.

Most of the reforms undertaken during the 1970s were based on the decentralisation of government responsibilities and duties to local governmental authorities, but in the 1990s there was a remarkable departure and started to apply NPM strategies for Sri Lanka.

Background

Officially the Democratic Socialist Republic of Sri Lanka is an island country in the northern Indian Ocean off the southern coast of the Indian subcontinent in South Asia. Known until 1972 as Ceylon, Sri Lanka has maritime borders with India to the northwest across the Gulf of Mannar and Palk Strait, and the Maldives to the southwest.

As a result of its location in the path of major sea routes, Sri Lanka is a strategic naval link between West Asia and South East Asia. It was an important stop on the ancient Silk Road. Sri Lanka has also been a centre of Buddhism and culture from ancient times, being the nation where the Buddhist teachings were first written down as well as the oldest continually Buddhist country. Sri Lanka boasts a diverse range of cultures, languages and religions. The Sinhalese people form the majority of the population; Tamils, who are concentrated in the north and east of the island, form the largest ethnic minority. Other communities include Moors, Burghers, Kaffirs, Malays and the aboriginal Vedda people.

Sri Lanka is a republic and a unitary state which is governed by a semi-presidential system with its official seat of government in Sri Jayawardenapura-Kotte, the capital. The country is famous for the production and export of tea, coffee, gemstones, coconuts, rubber and cinnamon, the last of which is native to the country. Sri Lanka has been called the Pearl of the Indian Ocean. The island contains tropical forests and diverse landscapes with high biodiversity. The country lays claim to a long and varying history of over 3,000 years, having one of the longest documented histories in the world. Sri Lanka's rich culture can be attributed to the many different communities on the island. The country is a founding member state of SAARC and a member of United Nations, Commonwealth of Nations, G77 and Non-Aligned Movement. As of 2011, Sri Lanka was one of the fastest growing economies of the world.

Status of Civil Service

The Sri Lanka Administrative Service (SLAS) is the key administrative service of the Government of Sri Lanka with civil servants working for both in the central government as well as in the provincial councils. It was formed as the Ceylon Administrative Service (CAS) in 1963 as the successor to the Ceylon Civil Service which was abolished on 1May 1963. It is the senior of the public services.

The Provincial Council System was established in Sri Lanka in the year 1988 under the 13th Amendment to the Constitution of the Democratic Socialist Republic of Sri Lanka. Accordingly, the functions of the Central Provincial Public Service Commission commenced from 14 July 1988. The Central Provincial Public Service Commission's authority area consists of three administrative districts, namely Kandy, Matale and Nuwara Eliya.

Civil service is created to promote and support an efficient, disciplined and contented public service which will serve the public with fairness, transparency and consistency in an equitable manner, free of all negative influences, such as corruption, politicisation, waste, negligence, and lethargy, which support positively democratic governance.

Based on the British Civil Service the SLAS is the permanent bureaucracy that helps the elected officials on day-to-day functions of government. They are selected and promoted by the PSC. But top positions in the government, for example, permanent secretaries, are appointed by the president, in theory, on the recommendations of the PSC.

A permanent secretary is the top bureaucrat of the government ministry and is responsible for the day-to-day functions of the ministry whereas in theory the minister is responsible only for drafting policy. The head of the SLAS is the secretary to the president.

After 1 January 2005, the SLAS had introduced four grades, such as: special grade officers, class I officers, class II officers and class III officers. Below the 'senior officers' (special grade officers, class I officers), each individual department can put in place its own grading. The post of deputy secretary is only used in the Ministry of Finance and is ranked just below the post of permanent secretary.

Administrative Rules and Regulations

In Sri Lanka there are detailed and strict constitutional provisions and administrative rules and regulations of the civil service. The civil servants have emerged as powerful interest groups due to the fact that they were protected by the Constitution and by tenure provisions.

Within the civil service, there are different organisations having separate mandate, role and responsibilities and each of them has their own patterns of culture (Somasundram, 1997). The core of Sri Lankan Civil Service Structures, laws comprise the institutions of Civil Service. The Sri Lankan Civil Service Structure was created in Sri Lanka in the 1830s at a time when the colonial rulers introduced the constitutional reforms for the country for the first time. The situation of the civil service did not change even after the independence of the country. Rules, regulations, traditions and working methods are more or less based on the colonial system. Several attempts had been made by successive governments since the 1960s to make some changes. But still it can be observed that those reform proposals with little intent of bringing about any fundamental changes were limited to small galvanisations such as trivial financial incentives.

New Public Personnel Management Reforms

One of the prominent concerns of NPM is improving practices and techniques of personnel management system which are practiced in the civil service at present. According to the definition (Bratton and Jeffrey, 1994, p. 5), the prime objective of Human Resource Management (HRM) is to achieve the efficient and customer oriented organisation. NPM theorists expect to reform the current practices and aspects for better human resource management that can be utilised to accomplish overall objectives of NPM doctrine. Further, training is needed for enhancing the following qualities of the civil service, so that it will help improve the efficiency and the quality of service delivery.

1. Provide the necessary skills to the managers to deal with new responsibilities

2. Improve skills for customer-oriented civil service
3. Improve the procedures and standards of service provisions
4. Absorb modern techniques, methods and processes

The Sri Lanka government under the guidance of international organisations has been trying to implement the NPM principles in its civil service system.

Civil Service Commission

The origin of the PSC in Sri Lanka relates to the White Paper 197 issued by the colonial government in 1946, which set out measures to improve the quality and efficiency of the colonial service of the British administration. The setting up of PSC was proposed in its paragraph 21(xi) which mentioned that PSC should be established in the colonies. Subject to the general overriding powers of the secretary of state, the selection and appointment of candidates in the colonies to posts in the local service will lie with the governor of the colony. It is desirable that the governor should be advised in these matters by a PSC appointed by him and so composed as to command the confidence of the service and the public. The service commission is established under the Constitution which continued the legacy of the British for a long time and followed the same methods as were in vogue in the region.

The mission of the Commission is to establish and maintain a competent, efficient, impartial and highly motivated body of public officers, dedicated to serving the people.

Sri Lanka has achieved the dubious distinction of having the highest per capita staffing rate in South Asia, and one of the highest in the developing world. From 1990 to 2001, public sector employment grew at an annual rate of over 3.5 per cent.

The first dimension of strategies in implementing reforms is clarified by the overall goals of the reform programme itself. According to the Management Reform Policy Framework, the overall goal of the new strategies is to reduce the size of the state sector in order to facilitate the establishing macro-economic stability and fostering the private sector's contribution to the development process. The reduction of the size of the state contains two different but interrelated stands, viz., rightsizing the human resources and the role that has to be played by the state. Under the human resource management reform it was expected to reduce the number of the cadres in the civil service by introducing a voluntarily early retirement procedure with financial assistance. But no significant cadre reduction in the public sector has occurred in the period between 1994 and 2004. Just after a year of this reform programme implementation started, Shelton Wanasinghe explained the situation in the following words.

Thus Sri Lanka's administrative system remains in the same condition of low effectiveness of some years ago. It not only continues to be irrelevant to the task demands emanating from the economy and the society but also, even more threateningly, constitutes the most serious barrier to achieve her development aspirations. 'The restoration of the administrative improvement effort must thus become a priority task during the rest of the decade' (Wanasinghe, 1994, p. 12).

Evaluation

It can be inferred from the above data that reform implementation was a failure as there is no support from bureaucrats. The extent of the support of bureaucrats is very significant for reform implementation; they should be ready to work with innovations. First, there should be a capable institutional structure for such an implementation. Therefore, one aspect of such policy reform application from western countries to non-western countries is the taking into account of institutional conditions, and their capacity for implementing public sector management reforms. Rather than just considering the matter of what is to be applied from NPM universal package, it is more important to think of the matter of how it can be implemented. At present, it seems that in Sri Lanka, much attention has been paid on the contents of reform programme without sufficient analysis on operational arrangement of them.

Nepal

Introduction

Nepal has undergone two popular uprisings within a short span of 16 years. The first popular movement of 1990 overthrew the king-led undemocratic panchayat system and reinstated parliamentary democracy, which had been abrogated by the king. The second movement of 2006 caused the end of the kingship, the unitary system of government and the parliamentary constitution of 1990. The period in between the two popular movements is marked by political instability and turbulences erupting apparently due to inter-party conflict, intra-party feuds and the insurgency (people's war) launched by the Nepal Communist Party–Maoist (NCP-M). This has resulted in a painful and prolonged political transition—actual and perceived. Usually, transition is an opportunity to reform. So, after regaining democracy in 1990, successive governments had taken various governance reform measures. The civil service reforms and governance agenda in Nepal drawn from the studies of Madhu Nidhi Tiwari are discussed here.

Background

The Federal Democratic Republic of Nepal is a landlocked sovereign state located in South Asia with an area of 147,181 sq. km. Nepal is the world's 93rd largest country by land mass and the 41st most populous country. It is located in the Himalayas and bordered to the north by the People's Republic of China, and to the south, east and west by the Republic of India. Specifically, the Indian states of Uttarakhand, Uttar Pradesh, Bihar, West Bengal and Sikkim share border with Nepal, while across the Himalayas lies the Tibetan Autonomous Region. Kathmandu is the nation's capital and largest metropolis.

Nepal has a rich geography. The mountainous north has 8 of the world's 10 tallest mountains, including the highest point on earth, Mount Everest, called Sagarmatha in Nepali. It contains more than 240 peaks over 20,000 ft (6,096 m) above sea level. The fertile and humid south is heavily urbanised.

Hinduism is practised by about 81 per cent of Nepalese, making it the country with the highest percentage of Hindu followers. Buddhism, though a minority faith in the country, is linked historically with Nepal.

A monarchy throughout most of its history, Nepal was ruled by the Shah dynasty of kings from 1768, when Prithvi Narayan Shah unified its many small kingdoms. However, a decade-long civil war by the Communist Party of Nepal (Maoist) and several weeks of mass protests by all major political parties led to the 12 point agreement of 22 November 2005. The ensuing elections for the constituent assembly on 28 May 2008 overwhelmingly favoured the abdication of the Nepali monarch Gyanendra Shah and the establishment of a federal multiparty representative government.

Structure of Civil Service

With the regaining of democracy after 30 years of monarchy in 1990, the civil service had been drawn to serve the new political system that had many values contrary to the bureaucratic culture they were accustomed to. The civil service was developed in a system that believed in active role of the king, making the palace the nerve centre of political and administrative system. Now, the civil service was required to serve a system that emphasised the rule of law, the people's sovereignty, human rights, multi-party parliamentary system (for example, competitive politics and constitutional monarchy) as cardinal virtues of the system. This called for a drastic change in the governance ideas relating to civil service management.

Nepal's civil service was founded in traditional closed career model. Accordingly, in the higher civil service (gazetted categories) selection through open competition was permitted only in class III, which was the entry point. The ARC had suggested making provisions for filling 20 per cent of the vacancies in the higher civil service through open competitive examinations. The Commission had clearly stated that this will pave the way for the entry of highly qualified experienced and efficient people working at the non-governmental sector to enter the civil service so that the infusion of competent and efficient people who can carry on new ideas as per the change in governance ideas will be possible. The new Civil Service Act of 1993 has made provision to only 10 percentages of vacancies at the higher level—class II and I fill through open competition. Thus, the concept of open career is now accepted in a limited scale. From the prospective of the working civil servant it is a fast stream or fast track to climb the career ladder.

The syllabus of written examination has heavily incorporated the inter-related concepts of NPM, good governance and other contemporary issues. Thus, the successful candidates are found to have a sound and up-to-date theoretical knowledge about the development in the field of public affairs.

Personnel Management System

The training policy was revised with the objective of making it need based, dynamic and better utilised. Civil servants are unable to fully utilise whatever knowledge and skills acquired through training because of resistance to change and lack of a well-founded democratic culture (Pant and Shahi, 2009).

The above mentioned functions intended to improve employees efficiency and capability are, however, almost totally ignored. Under such circumstances motivating factors to go for training are:

1. To score marks for promotion
2. Economic gain through saving
3. Getting rid of monotony of work
4. Visit to foreign countries to see new places

The goal to enhance efficiency through acquiring new knowledge skill thus exists only in paper, not in deed. The Civil Service Record

Department had started the office automation by preparing a database of gazetted civil servants belonging to various services in early 1990s. This was made public by publishing the information so obtained in various volumes. It has facilitated increasing efficiency by making possible to use these records for making decisions relating to personnel management of the civil service.

As a measure to improve performance of the civil servants, the ARC 1992 had pointed out the urgency of introducing systematic job description of each and every post. It had also suggested making legal provision so that every civil servant will be required to prepare a performance plan (work plan) and summit it to his boss. The commission further suggested using performance evaluation as a measure to provide feedback to the employees about their strengths and weaknesses relating to job performance. These suggestions, besides infusing transparency in the civil service management, intended to start the performance-based management system in the civil service, which were completely lacking in the past.

With a view to bring gender equity in the civil service, the Ministry of General Administration (MoGA) and the Ministry of Women, Children and Social Welfare (MOWCSW) were called upon to devise new methods to strengthen recruitment, selection and promotion criteria, with particular attention to alleviating constraints and creating new opportunity for women. By amending the Civil Service Act in 2007, 33 per cent of positions to be filled through open competitions are now reserved for women candidates. Accordingly, for the first time, separate examinations were conducted in 2007.

Public Service Commission

The PSC was established in Nepal on 15 June 1951. The Commission is involved in selecting meritorious candidates required by the Government of Nepal for various vacant posts of the civil service. The continuity of PSC has never been hindered since its establishment. The present Constitution of Nepal 2007 (2063 BS) has designated the PSC as an independent constitutional body. As per Article 125 of the Constitution, there shall be a PSC in Nepal. The Commission consists of a chairman and members as may be required. The chairman and members of PSC are appointed for six years. The chairman and members may be removed from their offices on the same grounds and in the same manner as has been set forth for removal of a judge of the Supreme Court.

To suggest changes in the administrative system in congruence with the new governance ideas, an ARC headed by the PM was constituted in 1992. The Official Development Assistance (ODA), United Kingdom (UK); UNDP and ILO had provided services of advisors to the Commission. In its recommendations, the ARC pointed out the need to make the civil service accountable, transparent, result-oriented, efficient, downsized, highly motivated and free from the disease of corruption. It had proposed more than 100 recommendations to overcome the problems facing the civil service. The key recommendations, immensely interrelated, are as follows:

1. Redefine government's own role so that it can gradually confine itself chiefly to promotional and motivational activities
2. Downsize the civil service and inject the culture of competition by transferring many of the service delivery functions hitherto carried out by government through the civil service or public enterprises to NGOs, community organisations, private sector and cooperatives
3. Take measures such as: contracting out, lease out, gradual deregulation and disinvestments (privatisation)
4. Improve efficiency of the civil service so that it can facilitate, monitor, regulate and enable the non-governmental sectors to deliver services efficiently
5. Make civil service more capable /efficient and effective to carry on activities which are required to be performed by the government itself
6. Ensure job security
7. Infuse new blood in the higher civil service through open competitive examinations (through lateral entry)

The ARC 1992 had also prepared an implementation plan, which had stipulated the time frame and the organisation's responsible for undertaking various reform activities and also suggested constituting a high-level Administrative Reform Monitoring Commission (ARMC), directly under the PM for a term of three years.

The reform interventions proposed under Gross Rating Point (GRP) has many features similar to ARC's recommendations. However, it was also in favour of gender sensitive civil service. In fact, gender sensitive civil service was a major agenda of Mainstreaming Gender Equity Programme (MGEP) of the government, which was launched under the UNDP's financial support. Thus, GRP interventions along with MGEP intended to infuse elements supporting the concepts of New Public Administration (NPA), Responsive Governance and Representative Bureaucracy. The new public administration movement emphasises equity and social justice. It seeks to change those policies and structure that systematically inhibit social equity and, hence, it is supportive to gender equity. From the above description it can be safely said that the conceptual framework of the civil service reform was an amalgam of certain features of the NPM, the NPA, representative bureaucracy and the responsive governance.

Functions of Service Commission

The functions, duties and powers of PSC of Nepal are as follows:

1. It conducts examinations for the selection of suitable candidates to be appointed to various civil service posts.
2. Permanent appointment to any position in the civil service which carries the benefit of pension shall not be made except in consultation with the PSC.
3. The Government of Nepal is required to consult the PSC on the following subjects:

   - matters concerning the laws relating to the conditions of service of the civil service;
   - the general principles to be followed in the course of appointment to, promotion to and departmental action concerning the civil service or positions;

- matters concerning the suitability of any candidate for appointment to a civil service position for a period more than six months;
- matters concerning the suitability of any candidate for transfer or promotion from one service to another within the civil service or any other government service to the civil service;
- matters concerning the permanent transfer or promotion of any employee, working in any position of an organisation which is not required to consult with the Commission on matters of appointment, to any position for which consultation with the Commission is required; and
- Matters relating to departmental actions proposed against any civil servant.

4. Subject to the constitution of other functions, duties and working procedures, the PSC shall be regulated by law.
5. Every year, the Public Service Commission shall submit annual report on the works it has performed to prime Minister. Prime Minister shall cause such report to be laid before Parliament.

Process of Selection

The PSC conducts examinations for selection of candidates as per the Public Service Commission (Procedure) Act, 2048 BS by using one or more methods of selection as follows:

1. Open competitive written examination
2. Open competitive practical examination
3. Selection
4. Interview
5. Any other methods adopted by the Commission

In order to carry out selection process, the Commission publishes vacancy announcement for the concerned candidates in its weekly bulletins published every Wednesday as well as in the *Gorkhapatra*, a national daily. The Commission has also adopted an annual calendar of operation of its activities which incorporates all the details of phases of the selection process.

In order to maintain fairness and impartiality in the selection, the Commission has adopted a system of 'multi-blindness' in which setting and moderation of questions, checking of answer sheets, conduction of interviews as well as result of written examinations and interviews are carried out in a manner that officials involved are kept in anonymity to each other.

The PSC maintains a pool of experts and specialists for the purpose of selection. They are assigned to the specific selection tasks in a confidential manner. The PSC has also initiated the process of screening for certain posts where numbers of candidates are high. The candidates have to get through the preliminary examination in order to appear in the main examination

In 1995–96, the PSC had started the process of reviewing its curriculum of the entry examination (gazetted class III) of higher civil service. The method adopted for evaluation was a striking departure from the past in three ways. Firstly, it was gender sensitive. Secondly, it was interactive. Finally, the job analysis of various posts was done. Workshops were organised for job analysis. This was followed by individuals and group discussions. Special interactive sessions with the women groups such as civil servants, intellectuals and college girls were also organised. The purpose was to make a gender audit of the then existing selection method and other aspects of examination system. The above programs were conducted throughout the country. After three years effort made by the PSC, the curriculum of gazette III was revised on a scientific and gender sensitive basis. Thereafter, the success rate of female candidates increased.

Combating Corruption

In the late 1990s, with a view to obtain measures to control corruption the government constituted a task force to suggest ways to fight corruption. The GRP also endorsed its recommendations to strengthen the legal framework for combating corruption, enforcing its implementation and ensuring the involvement of civil society in the government's anti-corruption efforts. The major focus was on the strengthening the Commission for Investigation of Abuse of Authority (CIAA) in terms of enhancing the investigative capacity of its personnel and strengthening legal provisions. To ensure prompt and the decisive action against non-compliance, the government promulgated/amended various laws dealing with causes of corruption and abuse of authority by public officials. Accordingly, amendments in the CIAA Acts, PC Act, besides enactment of Special Court Act to expedite the hearing of the cases of corruption and Political Parties Act were undertaken. A new national vigilance council was created and is attached to the PM's office. Anti-Money Laundering Act is also enacted.

The Political Parties Act 2002 has made political parties responsible to keep records of their annual income and expenditure and also get their accounts audited. The amended PC Act has given special focus on preventive aspects. Consequently, besides the traditional punitive actions the CIAA is undertaking following activities:

Achievements

In 1974, the size of Nepalese civil service was 5,372 that reached to 100,632 within 70 years, that is 1990. However, due to various efforts made for downsizing, it has reduced to 76,609. This shows a tremendous success in bringing efficiency in terms of savings in salary, benefits and other expenses for the civil servants.

The following acts of forced retirement, reduction of retirement age and lateral entry have infused new blood with sound knowledge in high-level administration. Criteria for transfer have been codified for the first time. The civil servants have felt themselves more secure in their job. Abrupt dismissal without giving opportunity for self-defence is not possible, since the Supreme Court has emerged as the guardian of job security in case of unjust dismissal.

Civil servants considered the right to organise into a union as a positive development since it provided opportunity to express professional interests in an organised manner.

There is a favourable legal institutional framework for enhancing accountability. Practices of making closed-door decisions do not exist anymore. The interaction between civil servants, politicians and professionals through seminar and other interactive programmes before introducing a bill having an impact on their employment conditions has slowly been established. Practice of public hearing of civil servants performance is also increasing.

Right to information has become a constitutional right. Emergence of pressure group called for a more transparency leading to the more visible bureaucratic functions.

The government has given a high priority in bringing the non-governmental sector to take over many of the functions, which were traditionally carried out by it. NGOs are contributing in education, awareness raising, advocacy, community development services and economic services.

Evaluation

Despite long suffering and sacrifice for democracy, the democratic leaders are not showing the strong will to develop a 'system' which will enable the civil service assuming its responsibilities as per the norms of the democratic governance as per M.M. Tiwari. The leaders rather prefer to make the bureaucracy a parasite. The civil servants, particularly at the top level, are also equally responsible for this phenomenon. This is understandable from the fact that instead of discouraging politicians for such actions they rather encourage politicians to repeat such deeds so as to provide opportunity for them (bureaucrats) to favour their own relatives and friends, and at the same time make it possible to be in the good books of the political boss. The task of transforming the civil service from a non-responsive to a responsive one is therefore prolonged. The efforts for governance reform during the prolonged transition did not give fruitful results as yet.

Afghanistan

Background

The country is under transition from a war ravaged and politically devastated society—due to civil strife and fundamentalist forces for decades—to a more settled system of governance. There seem to be some stability after Karzai took control over the reign of power through some kind of a democratic process in 2004. Afghanistan is one of the ancient civilisations that share its legacy both with central Asia and south Asia. The modern Afghanistan was created by King Abdurrahman Khan during 1850–901. He had established the administration that existed till very recently.

Afghanistan has a population of 30.4 millions divided by different ethnic groups. Pashtuns constitute 42 per cent, Tajiks 27 per cent, Uzbeks 9 per cent and rest is from other smaller groups. The demographic composition of Afghanistan is very typical as only 2.4 per cent of the population belong to the age group of 65 plus.

Status of Civil Service

The civil administration in Afghanistan established by Abdurrahman Khan was put in shambles when the country was allegedly under the control of Soviet Union and later under North Atlantic Treaty Organization (NATO) forces. The old system of administration and civil service was totally ruined in the process of civil strife and the associated problems in the country. After the break with the past in the effort to rebuild the economy, society and the systems, the government has undertaken a massive reconstruction programme with the aid and support of UN agencies. One of the important programmes undertaken by the government with the support of UNDP is in the area of public service. An Independent Administrative Reform and Civil service Commission (IARCSC) is formed on the lines of civil service commissions in the region.

The UNDP project is undertaking the following measures of capacity building in Afghanistan.

The UNDP's Capacity for Afghan Public Service (CAP) project, being implemented in partnership with the Capacity Development Secretariat (CDS) of the IARCSC focuses on long-term capacity development (CD) and primarily skills development through coaching and mentoring and advising in the five common functions of Policy and Strategy Formulation, Project Management, Financial Management, Procurement and Human Resources Management. The key objectives of CAP are to provide: (a) coaching services for Afghan civil servants to strengthen core functions of government (CAP project is a pioneer in introducing coaching as a CD tool in Afghanistan in a systematic and comprehensive manner) and (b) advisory services to senior management in government to strengthen leadership and policy-making skills.

CD under the project is focused on the Government of Afghanistan's strategic priorities as defined in the Afghanistan National Development Strategy (ANDS) and the Public Administration Reform (PAR) effort and so on. The CAP project is designed, in particular, to support public administration reforms; 'government machinery', including the number of ministries, will be restructured and rationalised to ensure a fiscally sustainable public administration. The IARCSC will be strengthened and civil service functions will be reformed to reflect core functions and responsibilities.' The capacity development initiatives of CAP project contribute to the implementation of ANDS and achievement of its benchmarks, particularly with regard to 'Governance, Rule of Law, and Human Rights' and 'Economic and Social Development' with primary focus on governance.

The project supports the overall objectives for IARCSC capacity development initiatives in the area of PAR which are aimed at the analysis, restructuring and associated human resource management reforms to make senior civil servants/civil service more results and service delivery oriented and more driven by a clear code of ethics. The project seeks to improve public administration, strengthen democratic practices and implement priority reforms. The approach and institutional arrangement is in line with current thinking on CD reflected in the OECD Development Assistance Committee (DAC) guidelines on good practices for capacity development and the Paris Declaration on Aid Effectiveness (in 2005).

Constitution and Functions of Civil Service Commission

The civil service commission in Afghanistan is different from other countries, but follows the same structures. The IARCSC as the agency is comprised under Article 54 of the Afghanistan Constitution is a constitutional body. It has nine commissioners and one of them is selected as the chairman of the commission. Out of the remaining eight members, five members constitute the civil service appointment board and three are devoted for taking of the appellate functions.

Civil service in Afghanistan does not include military, judiciary and academic cadres. As of now 17 ministries are using the services of IARCSC. The selection process is based on open competition through an advertisement for the posts indicating the qualifications, job description, etc., after receiving the applications from the candidates, they are shortlisted and called for personal talk, group discussion, workshop, etc., depending upon the kind of job for which selection takes place. It appears that the process of selection resembles some of the western countries, for example, Australia.

Innovations of the System

The strategy to strengthen the system of civil service in the country has followed a unique strategy of providing opportunities to the expatriates. The Afghan Expatriate Programme (AEP) and the Afghan Lateral Entry Programme (LEP) have opened up the civil service system for capacity-building activity with the help of their countrymen with around 60 personnel who are evaluated as per norms.

The major achievement of both LEP and AEP, which underlines the importance and success of the initiative, was the kick-starting of the process of bringing Afghan professionals and associated expertise into the Afghan Civil Service to increase capacity, be it in advisory or line management positions. Several individuals remained in service with the Afghan Civil Service and are currently working in very senior positions, including ministerial appointments such as minister of finance, chief justice of Afghanistan, minister of mines, current chief of security counsel and ex minister of foreign affairs, deputy minister of foreign affairs, deputy minister Independent Directorate of Local Governance (IDLG), attorney general, minister of Hajj and religious affairs, director general (DG), High Office of Oversight on Anti-corruption.

The continued employment of these high quality individuals is a prime indicator of the significant contribution to sustainability that has been at the core of the AEP and LEP programmes. Equally important is the impact the programmes made in terms of laying down the groundwork in preparation for the Management Capacity Programme (MCP) which represented the next evolutionary step in the AEP/Reprocess and which encompassed a more clearly defined administrative approach and enhanced managerial rigour; for example, in terms of performance metrics which were more relevant and more closely monitored. Unsurprisingly, the elements of the LEP that could have been improved are identical to the structural and administrative issues outlined above with reference to the AEP. In neither case should these concerns detract from the overall success of the project. Along with major achievements, there were areas where the projects lacked rigour in terms of design and implementation.

The recruitment and selection policy, while praiseworthy in its commitment to transparency, objectivity and fairness, became overly complicated and bureaucratic. The prior review process by the World Bank added into delays which inevitably led to delays in recruitment and it possibly resulted in the loss of high quality potential recruits. There was limited synergy with other existing capacity-building intervention.

Though AEP and LEP produced significant achievements at the critical context of Afghanistan at that period of time, considerable lesson learned from AEP and LEP laid the foundation to the birth of a more solid and well-defined project of MCP. Among other key features of MCP, the positions are categorised to fit into specific criteria, the functions of the appointee will support particular organisational common functions, the posts are not advisors, but in line position functions which reflect more weight in hierarchical authority for implementation, as supposed to only giving advice.

Evaluation

The above information and the material available on the website of Afghanistan, IARCSC and other sources do not provide any clue that the system has achieved normalcy except that the presence of international agencies is felt in the projects undertaken for capacity building. Yet, the question arises whether Afghans are really given the opportunity to develop their own system based on their circumstances and culture or the Western models are enforced on them. The official delegation of the Afghanistan Commission seems to have met the UPSC, New Delhi, to have a memorandum of understanding (MoU) to strengthen their capacity in the areas mutually agreed to. This shows how the commission is conducting itself to strengthening institutional structure for a better system of recruitment of civil services. The outcome would come to light only after the country performs its usual functions on its own, may be after a decade later?

Maldives

Maldives is the smallest country in Asia with a population of about 3.5 lakh people. It is a republic with unitary type of government. It is an archipelago in the Indian Ocean close to the west coast of India. It is in deep trouble due to environmental problems, particularly after the 2004 tsunami that hit the country severely and is now under a great threat to its physical existence. The land mass of the country is just four feet above sea level. The major part of the Gross Domestic Product (GDP) comes from tourism and stands at around US$2.84 billion and the per capita income is US$5,973. However, the Human Development Index (HDI) of Maldives comes in the middle-income range and stands at 109, above India.

As the country was a colony under the Portuguese, Dutch and British, it has inherited some of their administrative mechanisms. During 1980s and through 1990s, the President's Office implemented several projects to reform the government service. Some were externally funded projects with foreign consultants and advisors contributing to them. A number of committees were instituted at working and consultative levels. During the two decades (1980s and 1990s), comprehensive government service rules were formulated and implemented; procedures were established for recruitments, promotion, transfers and termination, pension and staff development. Staff appraisal was introduced and tried out. Classification of positions and salary structures were introduced. Compliance audit committees were formed and several visits were conducted. However, values such as impartiality, honesty and integrity never picked up. With the unprecedented expansion the country was experiencing and the consequent pressures the organisations were subjected to, these values even deteriorated further. Aistath Rasheed has provided some information on 'Government and the Civil Service Commission in Maldives' to explain the situation in Maldives that is supplemented by other sources.

The Government Service

During the 800 years of sultanate rule, the government was run by the sovereign assisted and executed by ministers and chief justice. The ministers were responsible for the discharge of government, while the chief justice for judiciary and tenets of Islam. Affairs of government were conducted by two levels of Regal Councils, comprising the nobles called the Kilege and the ministers called the Fansafurdhaaha. The affairs of the atolls were conducted by appointees of the sovereign call Kangathi. A constitution-based government was instituted in 1932 with cabinet of ministers with portfolios of a modern government. The customs, practices and procedures remained traditional.

The Public Service Division (PSD) and the Deterioration of Standards

The PSD was created in the President's Office in 1999. The aim of the creation was to increase efficiency and effectiveness of the government machinery to meet the demands of the social and economic development of the country. These were to be met by training, innovation, values and improved discipline. A myriad of objectives were formulated by the division. They were implemented. The creation of this division brought hopes to those who were aspiring for a technical and professional civil service in the country. From 2003 until the enforcement of the Civil Services Act in 2008, the division conducted recruitment, promotions, termination and all its businesses with little regard for the standards, the rules, procedures and practices established prior to its creation. The advocated values were sidelined in decisions. Political motivation became a crosscutting factor in decisions. Hence, prejudice, partiality, favouritism and nepotism crept into official business as never before. This feature was intensely prominent between 2006 and 2007 till end of February 2008. Positions were created irrespective of mandate and the organisation structure. Promotions were distributed in double, triple and quadruple jumps with no relation to performance. Consequently, motivation of the hard-working qualified and deserving staff plummeted. Morale and work discipline were adversely affected in many organisations.

The Civil Service Act

Although the idea of creation of a professional and technical civil service in Maldives was floated by consultants and the technical teams of 1980s and 1990s, it was never picked up by the government. The Civil Service Act was the result of an initiative by a private member of Parliament who submitted the bill to the Parliament in 2007. The aim of Civil Service Act is to make the civil service independent functioning under an independent commission, the Civil Service Commission (CSC).

The Act gives the CSC responsibility for appointment, dismissal and transfer of civil servants, determining and enforcing salaries and benefits and, broadly, the modernisation and professionalisation of the civil service through a Code of Conduct, training and innovation. The Act also prohibits civil servants to be actively involved in political activities.

The Parliament has passed a Civil Service Act in 2007 to establish an independent CSC with the following functions.

Appointment of Chairman and Members

The Maldivian CSC has ushered in a new era in civil service in Maldives. The creation of an independent civil service and other reforms introduced by the Act of Parliament and the new Constitution subscribed to the following major changes:

1. The administration of employment service of the government organisations be removed from the President's Office
2. A distinction is made for the first time between civil service and political service
3. Permanent secretaries and all the other staff members to deliver government policies are to be appointed by the CSC
4. That there will be no minister or cabinet secretary responsible or to oversee Maldivian Civil Service

The CSC consists of five members appointed by the president. From among the members, a chairman and a vice chairman are appointed by the Parliament.

The Functions of CSC

1. To appoint, dismiss, determine the salaries and benefits and to execute everything to implement thereof to serve the people on behalf of the State of the Maldives
2. To prepare the employees of the Maldivian Civil Service to be competent in serving the government which is lawful and the People's Majlis Fairly, apolitically by respecting the laws and regulations
3. To protect the rights of the employees of the Maldivian Civil Service and to establish a fair work place
4. To formulate the responsibilities, rights, powers and duties of the employees of Maldivian Civil Service
5. To assess whether government offices value the prerequisites of the Maldivian Civil Service

6. To formulate the Regulation and the Code of Conduct of the Maldivian Civil Service

7. To monitor whether the systems established at the main offices of the government to enforce the Regulation, the Code of Conduct of the Maldivian Civil Service as per Subsection18(f) and the prerequisites of the Maldivian Civil Service are reasonable

8. To take actions upon evaluation of the complaints lodged to the commission as per Section 31

9. To submit reports on matters regarding the Maldivian Civil Service to the People's Majlis as per Sections 24 and 25

10. To implement this Act, the Regulation and the Code of Conduct of the Maldivian Civil Service

11. To investigate and take actions on complaints lodged regarding the breach of this Act and the Code of Conduct by the senior officers of the main government offices and the employees of the Maldivian Civil Service

12. To shape the Maldivian Civil Service as a career-based service or a service which has opportunities in the field

13. To create leadership role among the employees of the Maldivian Civil Service, to train and to attempt to make them able for the work

14. Provide advice and instructions to the government regarding the Maldivian Civil Service

15. To formulate guidelines to create and repeal positions of the Maldivian Civil Service and to execute them as per the guidelines

Conclusions

It is found from the above data that there exists a PSC in each country under study. The foundation of these commissions was according to their constitutions/Acts framed. The PSCs were established by the respective constitutions of the country. The PSC of Bangladesh and Sri Lanka were established on the lines of the British system and the Nepal PSC was established on the lines of India. Afghanistan is helped by international organisations to improve its administrative capacities with some innovations of its own. The powers and functions of these PSCs are different for each country. It is found from the study that the governments which are in power intend to make reforms in their bureaucratic system for rendering effective services to its society and people in general.

Some committees were formed to study the existing policy and for making suggestions. However, the suggestions given by expert committees were not implemented properly as there is no cooperation from the opposition parties to the government in power.

The study has brought out that each country is following a system of recruitment under the aegis of a service commission. But the objectives and the methods vary depending upon the nature of governance in the country. The influence of international agencies and some of their ideas, such as NPM, are found to be high in countries which are politically under the guidance of an external agency.

Bibliography

Administrative Reform Committee. 1987. *Administrative Reforms: An Agenda for Action*. Colombo: Department of Government Printing, Report No. 1.

———. 1987. *Administrative Reforms: An Agenda for Action*. Colombo: Department of government Printing, Report No. 2.

Ali, A.M.M. Shawkat. 2007. *Civil Service Management in Bangladesh: An Agenda for Policy Reform*. Dhaka: The University Press Limited.

Asian Development Bank. 2001. *Report and Recommendation of the President to the Board of Directors on a Proposed Loan to the Kingdom of Nepal for the Governance Reform Programme*. ADB: Manila.

Bratton, John and Jeffrey Gold. 1994. *Human Resource Management Theory and Practice*. London: Macmillan.

Central Bank of Sri Lanka. 1997. *Annual Report for the Year 1996*. Colombo: Central Bank of Sri Lanka.

Chaudhury, Muzaffar Ahmed. 1969. *The Civil Service in Pakistan* (2nd edition). Dhaka: National Institute of Public Administration.

Corkery, Joan. 1991. 'Civil Service Reforms: Hurdles and Helps', in Donald Curtis (ed.), *Beyond Government: Organisations for Common Benefit*. London, Macmillan Education, 1995.

Economic Commission for Africa. 2003. *Public Sector Management Reforms in Africa: Lessons Learned*. Addis Ababa, Ethiopia: Development Policy Management Division (DPMD)—Economic Commission for Africa Experience, paper presented in EROPA 43rd Executive Council Meeting and Seminar, Hanoi-Vietnam.

Flippo, Edwin B. 1984. *Personnel Management*. Singapore: Mc GrawHill.

Ghimire, Chandra. 2008. 'Transformation of New Public Management: Shaping a Hybrid in Nepal?' Thesis Submitted to the Department of Administration and Organisation Theory in Partial Fulfillment for Award of Master of Philosophy in Public Administration, Tribhuvan University.

Government of Bangladesh. 1972. *Interim Recruitment Rules*. Dhaka: Government of Bangladesh.

———. 1981. *Bangladesh Civil Service Rules*. Dhaka: Government of Bangladesh.

Government of Nepal. 2008. *Economic Survey: Fiscal Year 2007/08*. Kathmandu: Government of Nepal.

Government of Sri Lanka. 2002. *Regaining Sri Lanka: Vision and Strategy for Accelerated Development*. Colombo: Prime Minister's Office.

Hague, Rod and Martin Harrop. 2001. *Comparative Government and Politics: An Introduction*. Basingstoke: Palgrave.

Hood, Christopher. 1991. 'A Public Management for All Seasons?' *Public Administration*, 69 (1): 3–19.

Jayawardana, L. 1997. 'Sri Lanka: Reforming Public Administration', the Report on Governance: Promoting Sound Development Management, Fukuoka, Asian Development Bank.

Kearney, R.C. and S.W. Hays. 1998. 'Reinventing Government: The NPM and Civil Service Systems in International Perspective', *Review of Public Personnel Administration*, 18 (4): 38–54.

Khan, Akbar Ali and Kazi Rakibuddin Ahmad March. 2008. 'Quota System for Civil Service Recruitment in Bangladesh: An Exploratory Analysis'. Available online at http://www.bpsc,gov.bd/documents/news/25906news.doc (accessed 24 March 2014).

Lan, Z. and D.H. Rosenblom. 1992. 'Editorial: Public Administration in Transition?', *Public Administration Review*, 52 (6): 535-37.

Mahat, Ram Sharan. 2005. *In Defence of Democracy: Dynamics and Fault Lines of Nepal's Political Economy*. Nepal: Adroit Publishers.

McCourt, W. 1998. 'The New Public Selection? Competing Approaches to the Development of the Public Service Commission of Nepal'. Available online at www.man.ac.uk/idpm/ppm.wp8.html/ (accessed 25 March 2014).

Moily, M. Veerappa. 2007. 'Administrative Reform in India', *The Indian Journal of Public Administration*, LIII (3), July–September: 340–44.

Olsen, Johan P. 1997. 'Civil Service in Transition: Dilemmas and Lessons Learned', ARENA, Working Paper No. 15, July, Oslo.

Osborne, D. and T. Gaebler. 1992. *Reinventing Government: How the Entrepreneurial Spirit Is Transforming the Public Sector*. Reading: Addison–Wesley.

Pant, Sushil Kumar and Sapna Shahi. 2009. 'Public Administrations' Preparedness in Carrying out Human Rights Functions', *Nepalese Journal of Public Policy and Governance*, XXIV (1): 27.

Perry, Amanda. 2001. *Legal Systems as a Determinant of FDI: Lesson from Sri Lanka.* London: Kluwer Law International.

Pollitt, C. 1993. *Managerialism and the Public Services: Cult or Cultural Change in the 1990s?* second edition. Oxford: Blackwell Publishers.

Rasheed, Aistah. 2010. 'Government and the Civil Services Commission in Maldives', Draft paper submitted at SAARC conference in Delhi.

Rodinelli, Dennis A. 2007. 'Governments Serving People: The Changing Roles of Public Administration in Democratic Governance', in *Public Administration and Democratic Governance*, United Nations.

Somasundram, M. 1997. 'Sri Lanka Administrative Service', in M. Somasundram (ed.), *The Third Wave, Governance and Public Administration in Sri Lank.* Colombo: International Centre for Ethnic Studies.

Stahl, O. Glenn. 1962. *Public Personnel Administration*, 5th edition. New York: Harper & Row Publishers.

Thilakaratne, S. 1989. 'Some Aspects of Local Social Development in Sri Lanka', *Regional Development Dialogue.*

Tiwari, Madhu Nidhi. 1996. 'Government Cadres in Transition: The Nepalese Experience', paper presented in EROPA 43rd Executive Council Meeting and Seminar, Hanoi.

———. 1999. 'Productivity in Government', in Dinesh Pant et al. (eds), *Current Issue on Productivity.* Kathmandu: National Productivity and Economic Development Centre.

———. 2009. 'Governance Reform in Political Transition: The Case of Nepal's Civil Service Reforms', *Nepalese Journal of Public Policy and Governance*, XXIV (1).

UNDP. 1992. *Human Development Report.* New Delhi: Oxford University Press.

———. 2007–08. *Human Development Report, 2007–08.* New York: Palgrave Macmillan.

Unite Nations. 2005. 'Unlocking the Human Potential for Public Sector Performance', World Public Sector Report, Department of Economic and Social Affairs. Available online at http://unpan1.un.org/intradoc/groups/public/documents/un/unpan021616.pdf (accessed 20 February 2014).

———. 2008. 'People Matters Civic Engagement in Public Governance', World Public Sector Report. Available online at http://unpan1.un.org/intradoc/groups/public/documents/UN/UNPAN028608.pdf (accessed 20 February 2014).

Wahhab, A.M. 2009. 'Civil Service Recruitment Policy in Bangladesh: A Critical Analysis', Department of Public Administration, University of Chittgong, paper submitted at NAPSPAG conference at University of Utara, Malaysia (pp. 11–13).

Wahhab, M.A. 2006. 'Problems of Governance and the Need for Political Decentralization in Bangladesh', paper presented at NAPSIPAG Conference on Innovation, Policy Transfer and Governance: How They Can Best Contribute to Social and Human Development, University of Sydney, 4–5 December.

Wahhab, M.A. 2008. 'Status of Women in Education and Governance: The Case of Bangladesh', paper presented at the International Conference on Strengthening Governance to Combat Corruption in Asia-Pacific, New Delhi, 5–7 December.

Wanasinghe, Shelton. 1994. 'Activating the Administrative Reform Process in Sri Lanka'. Colombo: Institute of Policy Studies, Governance Series No. 1.

World Bank Legal Department. 1995. 'The World Bank and Legal Technical Assistance: Initial Lessons', Policy Research Working Paper Series No. 1414, Washington, D.C.: Word Bank.

IV

Case Studies

We have provided here some important case studies to illustrate how the civil service system in the region is functioning from the experiences narrated by those who were deeply involved in the system as heads of service commissions and senior civil servants of India.

Civil servants in India are endowed with wide knowledge through their broad experience achieved working at different levels and conditions. Thus, they are distinctly different from some of their counterparts in other countries. There are officers who are committed and creative in their approach to implement new ideas in their job. Some of them have recorded their experiences in relation to such experiments and a few have shared their familiarity with the system with us. As mentioned in the text, we have 58 categories of services at group A level and all of them are recruited through UPSC on the basis of merit. There is some bitterness in the system among some officers who are not from the general service category (that is the IAS) and from services like IRS, not given opportunity to reach the highest level in government—cabinet secretary/secretary—due to prejudices and nepotism. There is no Affirmative Action in favour of women in India, though it is implemented in support of certain social categories as per the constitutional provisions. Therefore, the lady officers who have achieved excellence and reached the highest positions in government by sheer hard work feel that the system is not open and responsive yet to fair sex.

It would be illuminating to get the feedback from the officers as to how the civil service system is working in the country with reference to some important departments of the government. It is considered that the

Right to Good Governance is to be treated as a fundamental right. The functioning of the departments of health and education in the government can be taken as a case study to find out how this right is actually put in to practice. The insights given by a veteran bureaucrat who had once occupied the highest position in Government of India as cabinet secretary and member, Planning Commission, are recorded here. He along with his assistant have conducted an empirical study to prove how the quality of life of people has been enhanced through the parameters of good governance in the area of education and health, the two important parameters of human development in India.

The Department of Customs and Central Excise is one of the oldest units of the revenue administration in India. There are several developments and changes in the department starting from the 1878 Sea Customs Act that kept on modifying from 1962 to Audit 2000 and so on to incorporate the advancements in technology and diversity of trade so as to bring more revenue to the government. The working conditions in the department are really a challenge, particularly for a women officer. However, the author laments that despite the odds that one faces on the job, including challenges of smugglers, bootleggers and the corrupt, the senior officers of the department were never promoted beyond additional secretary. It is pointed out that the officers from general administration who work mostly at the state level are promoted and brought to the Centre without much exposure of the issues of the union government. This should be changed so as to provide incentives like opportunity to occupy the position of secretary, Revenue, for those hard-working and sincere officers of the Revenue Service. It is gratifying to see that women officers in the Revenue Service are as good and effective as anyone else as testified by one of the authors. This may be taken as a case by the policy makers in personnel administration to bring fresh initiatives.

The Indian Postal Service is one of the oldest and the largest service in the world. The experience of a lady officer who got in to the service through Group A is an interesting story. The case study of the department that has the largest network of 1.55 lacs post offices narrated by a serving officer with around four decades of service to the nation is really fascinating. The study reveals how effective the civil is service in meeting the needs of communication in the remote areas of the country that are generally inaccessible. The postal service has been functioning with the sole motto of service to the people. This is one institution that unites the whole country with its presence of the central government in every village/habitation. The postal system has been diversified and is now providing, banking, insurance, savings and helping to reach the poor, needy and deprived sections of society through a host of innovative services. The department has grown from strength to strength in the age of competition from private sector. The credibility of the system is amplified with the humble postman as a symbol of public service. The postal service vindicates the need for continuation of civil service in India in an era of globalisation.

The three chapters by the heads or members of service commissions in the region narrate how the systems were evolved over a period of time and how they are serving the countries' needs and aspirations of the people.

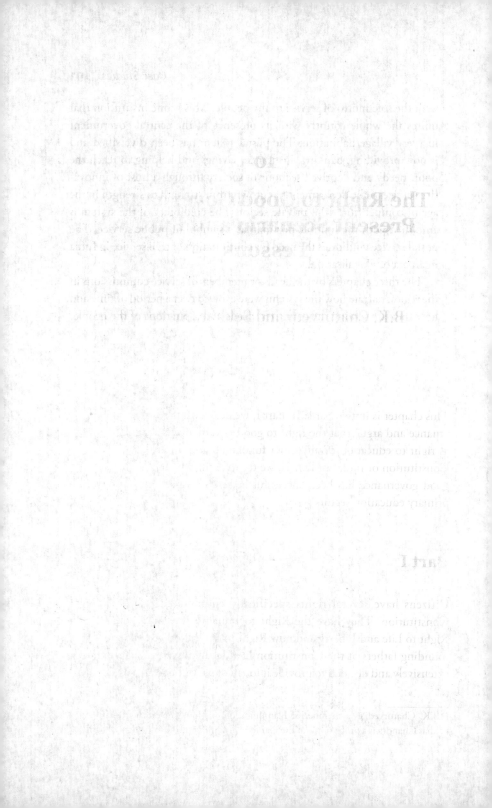

10

The Right to Good Governance: Present Scenario and Future Lessons

B.K. Chaturvedi and Sekhar Chandra*

This chapter is in two parts: In Part I, we deal with the concept of governance and argue that the right to good governance is as fundamental as right to education or any other fundamental right enshrined in the Constitution of India. In Part II, we try to identify the extent to which good governance has been successful in certain aspects of health and primary education sectors.

Part I

Citizens have several rights specifically enumerated in the Indian Constitution. They have the Right to Equality, Freedom of Speech, Right to Life and Liberty and now Right to Education of children. The founding fathers of the Constitution had debated over these questions extensively and decided to provide it for all of us. But one area which did

* B.K. Chaturvedi is a member of Planning Commission, Government of India.
Sekhar Chandra is a professional at the Planning Commission, Government of India.

not receive the attention was the citizen's right to 'Good Governance'. Effective implementation of constitutional rights is vital to provide meaning and substance to the written words and vision of our Constitution makers. Let us examine the reasons why it was not considered essential six decades back.

Before going into the background of this, let us dwell on the various implications of governance itself, as understood in international parlance. According to the World Bank, governance is 'the manner in which power is exercised in the management of a country's economic and social resources for development' (UNDP, 2006). In this definition, the concept of governance is directly associated with the management of the development process, involving both the public and private sectors. It encompasses the functioning and capability of the public sector, as well as the rules and institutions that create the framework for the conduct of both public and private business, including accountability for economic and financial performance, and regulatory frameworks relating to companies, corporations and partnerships.

The UNDP, interpreting it in a broader meaning, mentions governance as 'the exercise of economic, political and administrative authority to manage a country's affairs at all levels. It involves mechanisms, processes and institutions, through which citizens and groups articulate their interests, exercise their legal rights, meet their obligations and mediate their differences' (UNDP, 2006).

The ARC of India emphasised governance as more proactive function of the state and observed governance as 'means to achieve a proactive, responsive, accountable, sustainable and efficient administration for the country at all levels of the government' (UNDP, 2006).

The 13th Finance Commission (TFC) was extremely concerned about outcomes. It underscored a series of governance reforms. Quoting Public Distribution System (PDS), it noted that

> identifying and reaching the genuinely eligible persons in any subsidy regime is a major challenge in governance. Either the eligible are excluded or the non-eligible are included. More often, it is the voiceless poor who are crowded out in this scramble to board the gravy train. (UNDP, 2006)

The 11th Plan specifically targetted good governance and defined it so as to 'cover all aspects of the interface between individuals and businesses on the one hand and government on the other' (UNDP, 2006). Its vision of inclusive growth, reducing poverty and bridging the various divides that continue to fragment our society can only be achieved if there is a significant improvement in the quality of governance.

Thus, good governance is broadly understood as basic to achieve inclusive growth. It covers all natures of rights of citizens. In the above context, let us examine why good governance was not specifically mentioned as a fundamental right of citizen in the Constitution by the founding fathers.

When the Indian nation was born, the civil service had several key responsibilities. All these centred round the state and its core functions. Maintenance of law and order, security of the nation and collection of revenue were the main functions of the administrative system. Citizen's right to good governance and the state's obligation to provide it, as understood now, was not a part of the initial agenda. The concept of welfare of citizens and providing a certain basic quality of life, as measured by HDI, was evolved by UNDP only in 1990s. It was not central to the governance structure in the 1950s. It was at a distant periphery. The idea simply had not evolved, though Directive Principles of State Policy did cover it partially. All this has changed with recognition of need for a better life which is centre stage in governance. Infant mortality and mother's health, unacceptably high maternal mortality, absence of children from schools, mid-day meal and child nutrition, female foeticide and infanticide, good infrastructure, law and order, are questions central to governance today. Efficient running of civic services—water, sewerage and health—are citizen's rights which he can demand from the government of the day. Employment, minimum wages and new job opportunities are areas of priority for states. The citizen is now much more 'central' to the governance structure and more empowered. A new right has gradually evolved—the right to good governance, without which quality of life cannot improve.

In a country of one billion population, 'empowerment' has no meaning unless it touches the economically and socially weak segments of population, and absence of good governance is often cited as primary hurdle to achieve socio-economic empowerment of the people.

Evolution of this concept of a state committed to providing a basic quality of life to all its citizens has required change in civil services too. The civil service has been, in past, an integral part of the story of Indian development—fully involved in policy formulation, advising on alternatives and implementing it. Many of these problems of development have no precedence and innovative solutions have to be found to address them. Skills of the highest order are required of this group of civil servants. Some of the most talented and brilliant minds have been working as its members. Engineers from IITs, doctors, economists, students from the nation's best institutions, are all a part of it today. A federal polity required an administrative system in which civil servants could contribute effectively working with Union and state governments. The experience of working in the state provided the much needed local perspective while the Government of India contributed a broader vision and a national identity. This provided the unifying structure and kept a check on fissiparous tendencies during the initial years of the nation's life. In our civil service, we have an invaluable resource for bringing about change and growth in our country. It is this resource and structure which need reforms to meet these new requirements.

Civil service reforms have to be in the context of policy evolving on questions of quality of life. There is a need to empower the society both economically and socially. A series of legislations and changes in government policies and affirmative action, including reservation in education and jobs, have led to a framework for better provision of education, health and employment for weaker segments of the society and deprived sections. More than one fourth of them, however, still do not have adequate income for two square meals for the family, a proper home and essential clothing. Recently, the Tendulkar Committee has assessed the BPL numbers as about 37.6 per cent of the total population. Unless their income levels go up, the objective of our development plans cannot be said to have been achieved fully. While 8–9 per cent growth in GDP over a sustained period will certainly lead to larger employment and more income to some of these families, we need more direct measures, such as the Rural Employment Guarantee Act which is aimed at providing direct employment in various labour intensive development projects and help generate additional incomes to the marginalised and vulnerable groups close to where they live.

Empowerment of society cannot be truly meaningful without minimum standards in quality of education, basic health services and child nutrition, a reduction of the unacceptably high levels of infant mortality—52 per 1,000 births—and extremely high levels of maternal mortality—230 per 100,000 births—as per 2008 UNICEF Statistics. Nearly one crore children of a total of more than 20 crore children are not in schools. An extremely small number completes 10 years of education. Of these, girls constitute a disproportionately small proportion. It is essential that the large dropout of young children is curtailed if education has to be meaningful. Sarva Shiksha Abhiyan is a significant step in this direction. The provision of mid-day meals in all primary schools of the country has helped in two ways—by promoting nutrition and reduction in dropout rates. The National Rural Health Mission will further help in achieving better access of health services and lower maternal and infant mortality rates (IMR).

There have been efforts for improvement in governance structure in many states through e-governance to meet above objectives. They have realised the contribution of technology to achieving good governance by bringing the citizen to the centre of service delivery. E-governance has, in many cases, restored the choice to the citizen as to the quality and adequacy of services he is entitled to expect from public organisations. Citizen-centric governance means government is for the people and the services are tailored to meet their requirements. The Citizens' Charter initiative already requires that government departments should lay down the standard of service which is delivered to citizens by each government organisation. It is simply a statement and an assurance of what a citizen can expect of the organisation and the remedial measures if the promise is not fulfilled. An assured quality of service delivery is vital to all service delivery mechanisms. Citizens, in rural areas, where infrastructure facilities are minimal, must have access to their land ownership rights, details of common land provided in the land records and correct maps of their holdings. They should be able to transfer land with ease and without being harassed. Today, in Karnataka, Andhra Pradesh, Tamil Nadu, parts of Uttar Pradesh and several other states, land records have been computerised and, hence, made available with greater ease. In Maharashtra, registration of land transfers can be done with ease by citizens due to application of information technology and simplified procedures. Farmers can get information of agricultural prices in their *mandis* (markets) on a computer near their houses under the e-Chaupal programme in Madhya Pradesh and earn a remunerative price for their crops. In Andhra Pradesh, the one-stop facility through kiosks with arrangement for payment of taxes, lodging of complaints, application for getting municipal facilities, payment of some taxes, etc., has helped the citizens in accessing government services easily and with minimum harassment. The department issuing passports now assures time limits for renewal and issue of new passports. With the implementation of Ministry of Company Affairs (MCA) 21 computerisation project in the Department of Company Affairs, starting business is becoming much more business friendly. A new company could be started and registered in a few hours and returns filed online sitting in one's office. All this implies a paradigm shift in the way government is perceived and functions.

Good governance also implies a corruption-free bureaucracy. Citizens must be able to access all services such as registration of cases and their effective investigation, getting an electricity connection, municipal service, etc., without having to part with 'extra charges'.

Civil service reforms are at core of government's agenda reforms based on ARC. The measures which are proposed to be introduced or are already underway aim at ensuring a reasonable tenure of officers, holding them accountable for results and ensuring a more objective evaluation of performance. It aims to promote professionalism in the civil service keeping in view the increasing complexity of governance issues and the need for informed decision making. Civil service needs to be re-established as an important and exciting career for young men and women of the country. The reforms, which are now proposed, will contribute significantly towards this end. An efficient civil service can empower the citizens of the country to access the facilities and services provided by public organisations without harassment and with ease. It can make dealing with government agencies much more comfortable and productive than at present. One can then judge the efforts of governance from the point of view of how they impact on the citizen. The citizen has a right to expect value for money from the government and the basic requirements for a healthy and fruitful life.

The three parallel developments—civil service reforms, increasing investments in policies for improving the quality of life and emphasis on governance—have to converge gradually. The limited role of the state have now gone into a complete metamorphosis. A decent quality of life is expected of the state apparatus. In fact, this flows from the constitutional right under Article 21 which relates to Right to Life. The Article says: 'Protection of Life and Personal Liberty—No person shall be deprived of his life or personal liberty except according to procedure established by law.' The interpretation of this Article has been undertaken by the Supreme Court on numerous occasions. In 1993, in the case of Unni Krishnan, J.P. and Others vs State of Andhra Pradesh and Others, it held: 'Article 21 acts as a shield against deprivation of life or personal liberty since personal liberty and life have to hold that life which means to live with dignity takes within it education as well.'[1] The dignity of life which is a constituent of worthwhile living has now an expanded meaning. The quality of range of services expected from the state are now much higher. At that time, the Court had held the Right to Education as Fundamental Right of the citizen and mentioned as follows:

> The fundamental purpose of Education is the same at all times and in all places. It is to transfigure the human personality into a pattern of perfection through a synthetic process of the development of the body, the enrichment of the mind, the sublimation of the motions and the illumination of the spirit. Education is a preparation for a living and for life, when and hereafter. In the context of a democratic form of government which depends for its sustenance upon the enlightenment of the populace education is at once a social and political necessity. Education is enlightenment if the one that leads dignity to a man.[2]

The courts have on other occasions held right to healthy environment, emergency medical aid, right to health, right to shelter, right to privacy, right to livelihood as basic human rights.

The exercise of these rights is feasible if the governance of the state is good in itself. In its absence, they all lose their meaning. Good governance is clearly inherent in the exercises of all these rights. It is appropriate to recognise this. The good governance is a Fundamental Right, which should be so recognised in the Constitution and made justiciable.

Part II

In this part, we study the performance of states in identified areas of health and education on two counts: (a) from the perspective of the citizens of the state, which means whether facilities are leading to good outcomes and (b) from the perspective of efficiency of personnel, which means efficiency in available human resource utilisation by the states.

Health Sector

In the health sector, we have used IMR data to assess quality of services rendered by the states. Kerala performed very well on this count with an IMR of 13 against the national average of 51 per 1,000 births. We have treated Kerala as an outlier and omitted it from our analysis to understand the relative performances of the rest of the States. After Kerala, four top quality service-providing states comprise Maharashtra (32), Tamil Nadu (35), West Bengal (37) and Punjab (43) while bottom four comprise Madhya Pradesh (72), Odisha (71), Uttar Pradesh (69) and Rajasthan (67). For details, see Table 10.1.

To assess the efficiency of personnel in the health sector, we have used human resource utilisation by different states as the potential indicator. It indicates IMR per health worker available; higher the ratio, lower the efficiency and vice versa. After Kerala, the best performing state is Punjab. We have measured other states against this benchmark. Haryana (79.3 per cent), Jharkhand (60.6 per cent), West Bengal (53.1 per cent) and Chhattisgarh (46.4 per cent) are using their health resources efficiently. However, Uttar Pradesh (12.6 per cent), Andhra Pradesh (20 per cent), Rajasthan (21 per cent) and Maharashtra (22 per cent) are not using their health resources efficiently.

Further to get insight into the relative performance of states on quality of services and usage of health resources efficiently, we have divided all states in four categories: Category-I comprises states having low IMR and using health resources efficiently; Category-II comprises states having low IMR but not using health resources efficiently; Category-III comprises states having high IMR but using health resources efficiently and Category-IV comprises states having high IMR and not using available health resources efficiently (see Table 10.2).

The states of Kerala, Punjab, Jharkhand, West Bengal, Tamil Nadu and Karnataka are providing quality services to citizens and utilising available health resources efficiently while states of Andhra Pradesh,

Table 10.1
Governance Issues in States in Health Sector

	Nos. of Female Health Workers	Nos. of Male Health Workers	Total Nos. of Health Workers	Health Workers Availability Index	IMR per 1,000 Births Based on 2005–07 Data	Infant Mortality Index	Health Service Index HIS (Infant Mortality Index/Health Workers Availablity Index)	Resource Utilisation in Per cent of Different States Against the 100 Per cent of the State with Max HSI4
Andhra Pradesh	12,541	6,127	18,668	0.81	52.0	0.630	0.780	20.0
Bihar	9,127	1,074	10,201	0.84	58.0	0.586	1.329	34.1
Chhattisgarh	4,850	2,514	7,364	0.32	59.0	0.576	1.809	46.4
Gujarat	4,060	4,456	11,516	0.50	52.0	0.654	1.313	33.7
Haryana	2,592	2,031	4,623	0.20	55.0	0.618	3.092	79.3
Jharkhand	2,011	1,922	6,933	0.30	48.0	0.708	2.362	60.6
Karnataka	8,028	3,762	11,790	0.51	47.0	0.723	1.419	36.4
Kerala	5,320	2,654	7,974	0.34	13.0	Kerala has performed very well, omitted from present calculation		
Madhya Pradesh	8,718	4,030	12,748	0.55	72.0	0.472	0.856	22.0
Maharashtra	12,027	9,956	21,983	0.95	34.0	1.000	1.052	27.0
Odisha	6,768	3,392	10,160	0.44	71.0	0.479	1.090	27.9
Punjab	2,706	983	4,689	0.20	43.0	0.791	3.899	100.0
Rajasthan	12,271	2,528	14,799	0.64	65.0	0.523	0.187	21.0
Tamil Nadu	10,343	3,278	1,3621	0.59	35.0	0.971	1.649	42.3
Uttar Pradesh	21,024	2,097	23,121	1.00	69.0	0.493	0.493	12.6
West Bengal	6,051	4,215	1,0266	0.44	37.0	0.919	2.070	53.1

Source: Authors.

Table 10. 2

Performance of States in Health Sector

Category-I	Category-II
Kerala, Punjab, Jharkhand, West Bengal, Tamil Nadu and Karnataka	Maharashtra and Gujarat
Category-III	**Category-IV**
Chhattisgarh and Haryana	Andhra Pradesh, Madhya Pradesh, Bihar, Rajasthan, Odisha and Uttar Pradesh

Source: Authors.

Madhya Pradesh, Bihar, Rajasthan, Odisha and Uttar Pradesh are not performing well on both accounts. The states of Maharashtra and Gujarat are providing quality services but their resource utilisation is poor, while states of Chhattisgarh and Haryana are not providing quality services but are utilising their resources efficiently (Table 10.2). Two interesting facts are coming out of the analysis of the health sector: (a) IMRs in Jharkhand and Chhattisgarh are comparatively better. It may be noted that both Jharkhand and Chhattisgarh are tribal states. Thus, besides personnel, pattern of living and traditions also influence IMRs. (b) Andhra Pradesh is generally considered as a well-governed state but we found it having unusually high number of health workers. Its data on health workers might include *anganwadi* workers, too. This needs to be looked into.

This assessment provides a good overview of governance issues across states in health sector but has some limitations, because we have used only one indicator for the analysis. Other potential indicators are nutritional services, prevention of diseases, life expectancy, maternal mortality, etc. Because of lack of reliable data, we have refrained. Secondly, infant mortality is governed by historical factors and may not reflect recent efforts in this direction. For example, in 1961, IMR in Kerala was 51 per 1,000 births and in Madhya Pradesh was 150 per 1,000 births against national average of 115 per 1,000 births. In 2007, Kerala has 13 per 1,000 births; Madhya Pradesh has 72 per 1,000 births against national average of 55 per 1,000 births. The state of Kerala was thus to begin with in a much better position.

Education Sector

In the field of Primary Education Sector, we have used level of learning to assess quality of services rendered by the states. On this account, against the national average of 58.21 per cent, four top performing states are Kerala (74.83 per cent), Madhya Pradesh (74.57 per cent), Maharashtra (71.08 per cent) and Andhra Pradesh (68.28 per cent) while bottom four comprise Tamil Nadu (37.08 per cent), Uttar Pradesh (41.62 per cent), Rajasthan (44.29 per cent) and Karnataka (48.08 per cent) (Table 10.3). The general impression is that Tamil Nadu is a well-governed state but its inclusion in the bottom four is surprising. We have rechecked levels of learning from both Annual Status of Education Report (ASER), 2007, and National Council of Educational Research and Training (NCERT), 2007, data and it turns out that level of learning in Tamil Nadu are indeed poor (see Table 10.3).

Efficiency of personnel in the primary education sector is estimated in terms of resource utilisation by different states. It indicates level of learning per teacher available; higher the ratio, higher the efficiency and vice versa. The best performing state in this case is West Bengal. We have measured other states with respect to this benchmark. Punjab (86.83 per cent), Haryana (86.1 per cent), Bihar (78.57 per cent) and Kerala (68.32 per cent) are using their resources efficiently. However, Tamil Nadu (30.28 per cent), Karnataka (30.27 per cent), Rajasthan (34.02 per cent) and Gujarat (39.2 per cent) are not using available educational resources efficiently.

In order to get further insight into the relative performance of states on quality of services and usage of available educational resources, we have divided all states in four categories: Category-I comprises states having high level of learning and using educational resources efficiently; Category-II comprises states having high level of learning but not using educational resources efficiently; Category-III comprises states having low level of learning but using educational resources efficiently; and Category-IV comprises states having low level of learning and not using available educational resources efficiently (see Table 10.4).

The states of West Bengal, Bihar, Punjab, Maharashtra, Madhya Pradesh, Kerala and Haryana are providing quality services to citizens and

Table 10.3
Governance Issues in States in Primary Education Sector

	Teachers per 100 Children (I–VIII)	Teachers per 100 Children (I–VIII)	Level of Learning ASER 2007 Per cent Std V Children Who Can Answer Questions Based on Std II Questioned Orally	Level of Learning Index	Educational Service Index ESP (Level of Learning Index Teachers Availability Index)	Resources Utilisation in Per cent of Different States against the 100 Per cent of the State with Max ESI
Andhra Pradesh	2.54	0.838	68.28	0.912	1.088	52.03
Bihar	1.58	0.521	64.14	0.857	1.644	78.57
Chhattisgarh	2.43	0.802	54.15	0.724	0.902	43.13
Gujarat	2.57	0.848	52.05	0.696	0.820	39.20
Haryana	1.43	0.472	63.61	0.850	1.801	86.10
Jharkhand	1.98	0.653	53.52	0.715	1.095	52.32
Karnataka	3.03	1.000	48.08	0.643	0.643	30.71
Kerala	2.12	0.700	74.83	1.000	1.429	68.32
Madhya Pradesh	2.60	0.858	74.57	0.997	1.161	55.51
Maharashtra	2.52	0.832	71.08	0.950	1.142	54.59
Odisha	2.30	0.759	55.34	0.740	0.974	46.57
Punjab	1.50	0.495	67.29	0.899	1.816	86.83
Rajasthan	2.52	0.832	44.29	0.592	0.712	34.02
Tamil Nadu	2.37	0.782	37.08	0.496	0.634	30.28
Uttar Pradesh	1.19	0.393	41.62	0.556	1.416	67.70
West Bengal	1.19	0.393	61.48	0.822	2.092	100.00

Source: Authors.

Table 10.4

Performance of States in Education Sector

Category-I	Category-II
West Bengal, Bihar, Punjab, Maharashtra, Madhya Pradesh, Kerala and Haryana	Andhra Pradesh
Category-III	**Category-IV**
Uttar Pradesh	Chhattisgarh, Gujarat, Jharkhand, Karnataka, Odisha, Rajasthan and Tamil Nadu

Source: Author.

are utilising available resources efficiently while states of Chhattisgarh, Gujarat, Jharkhand, Karnataka, Odisha, Rajasthan and Tamil Nadu are not doing good on both accounts (Table 10.4). The states of Andhra Pradesh is providing quality services but not utilising its educational resources efficiently while Uttar Pradesh is not providing quality services but is using available educational resources efficiently.

Although, we have used only one indicator—level of learning—for this analysis, but we have found that other potential indicators, for example dropouts at different stages, children going for secondary or higher secondary education, etc., are closely related with the level of learning at the primary stage. Thus, it provides a good overview of governance challenges in the field of primary education.

Summary

Broadly, the states of Kerala, Punjab and West Bengal have done well on accounts of services provided to citizens as well as efficiency of personnel in the field of health and education, while the states of Odisha and Rajasthan have not done well both in providing services to citizens and effectively using available resources in both the sectors. Some of the states (Tables 10.3 and 10.4) are either not providing quality services or are not using available resources efficiently, which calls for appropriate governance measures.

Gujarat is generally regarded as well governed but we found that in the health sector, although it has low IMR, its resource utilisation is poor. Similarly, in the field of education sector, both quality of service and efficiency of resource utilisation are poor. This runs counter to the normal perception about governance in other sectors in Gujarat. Another interesting case is the state of Bihar. In education sector, Bihar is not only providing quality services but its resource utilisation is also efficient.

Notes

1. Unni Krishnan, J.P. And Others v. State of Andhra Pradesh and Others on 4 February 1993. Equivalent citations: 1993 AIR 2178, 1993 SCR (1) 594.
2. Ibid.

Reference

UNDP. 2006. *Governance for the Future: Democracy and Development in the Least Developed Countries.* New York: UNDP.

11

Indian Revenue Service: Reflections of a Woman Bureaucrat

Parveen Talha*

It is the IAS which comes to most minds when the civil services of India are talked about or written about, although there are about 23 Central Services, the officers for which are recruited through the same prestigious Civil Services Examination. Many candidates keep repeating for the examination; not only those who fail to qualify for any service, but even those who do get a Class I service or even the IPS, but fail to make it to the IAS. The ultimate aim of any civil service aspirant is to qualify for the IAS for it is the IAS which will get them the most power and authority, the most respect and social acceptability. It is the IAS which well take them to the highest rung of bureaucracy, to the best foreign postings and, finally, to the highest post-retirement positions.

It was the IRS which fell in my share and, which, over the years, got to be considered 'the next best thing'. I don't quite remember whether this service was allotted to me on merit or whether I had opted for it. As I said, a civil service aspirant fills the first option carefully, but gives his options about the Central Services with a kind of disinterest. No wonder I have forgotten my other options, although 43 years ago, when I filled

* Former Member, UPSC, and Ex-DG, Customs and Central Excise, Government of India.

up my forms, the IFS had a greater charm for a large number of the examinees. I was the family loving type who feared crossing the borders of homeland. My choice was obviously the IAS.

It was Customs and Central Excise Service which was allotted to me, and I am thankful to God that it was. Not even once did I feel that I could have done better had I entered the IAS. The postings which this uniformed service (wearing of uniforms is not mandatory for officers above the rank of deputy commissioners) offers to the officers are in the Department of Customs, Central Excise, Narcotics and now Service Tax. An officer in this service can never be bored with his job, for each department offers novel experiences and incredible variety. After a term in customs, you could find yourself walking out of the gates of a Custom House in Chenna or Mumbai, or, for that matter, Tuticorin to poppy fields in Zamania *tehsil* in Ghazipur, or, supervising superintendents in a Weighment Centre where licensed cultivators of poppy come with their opium in *tasla*s (pans) to sell to the government after *parakh* (check) and weighing. This is an unusual market where the government makes immediate payments in cash. In one charge you may be rummaging a ship, and in another raiding a warehouse stored with unmanufactured tobacco. Today you may be seizing gold biscuits from the suitcase of a blonde beauty on an international airport, tomorrow recovering heroin from the hollow of a blind man's walking stick on Satrik Chauraha near Barabanki. With some seniority you could be working in the premier intelligence agency the DRI or in the Enforcement Directorate (ED). You could have become a dreaded name for smugglers and drug traffickers because you are in the Smugglers and Foreign Exchange Manipulators (Forfeiture of Property) Act (SAFEMFOPA) office attaching their illegally acquired property.

There will also be a colourful variety in the large number of people you meet. In one charge you come across super rich industrialists, film stars and manufacturers of air conditioners, refrigerators and even aircrafts. In the next, you may have a lot to do with poor cultivators of poppy or tobacco. But all have one thought in common, to earn a little more at the expense of the law laid down for them.

Functions of Officers

The officers of this service are entrusted mainly with the Collection of Customs and Central Excise Duties. They enforce various restrictions and prohibitions in respect of import/export of goods. They control the movement of vessels and aircrafts and ensure that baggage rules are not violated by the passengers of international flights. When posted in Narcotics—Central Bureau of Narcotics (CBN) they exercise total supervision over cultivation, from sowing to lancing, to extraction of opium and its weighing and purchase by the government. The opium is finally sent to the opium factories at Ghazipur/Neemuch for manufacturing. Cultivators are licensed by the Department to grow poppy for extracting opium in notified areas of Rajasthan, Madhya Pradesh and Uttar Pradesh. Even the two factories of opium are managed by officers of the IRS.

The IRS officers perform both administrative and executive functions for which they are trained at the National Academy of Customs, Central Excise and Narcotics (NACEN). They are taught all they need to know about the tax they are collecting. These are the officers who are implementing the fiscal policy as formulated by the government. They have to be up-to-date with the changes introduced from time to time. At a senior level they have to have some idea about the canons of public finance which determine and regulate fiscal changes.

IRS officers are initially posted in the field but their services are also used, after some time, in the various directorates and directorates general and in the board and the finance ministry. In the board they do analytical and research work when in the Tax Research Unit, which handles and supplies all inputs for the annual budget. Clarifications regarding Customs, Central Excise and Service Tax and Narcotics Law are sought by field organisations which have also to be handled by the officers posted in the board/Ssecretariat. There are not many of them in positions higher than that of joint secretary.

It is the Central Board of Excise and Customs (CBEC) under the, Department of Revenue, Ministry of Finance, which administers the tax laws through its field formations that is, the Central Excise Commissionerates and Customs Houses. For Central Excise purposes, for instance, the country is divided into 10 zones. Next come the divisions and ranges, headed by deputy/assistant commissioners and superintendent of Central Excise and Customs. Inspectors are the junior most executive officers who have the maximum interaction with the assesses. Apart from the above, there are 13 DGs for Training, Revenue Intelligence, Inspection, Vigilance, Service Tax, Audit, Export Promotion, Valuation, Systems, Safeguards and Human Resource Development (HRD). There are five directorates, too, looking after Data Management, Logistics, Legal Affairs, Central Revenue Control Laboratory and Publicity and Public Relations.

Unless an officer is transferred on administrative grounds, or on his request due to an emergency, transfer and postings are done annually. Normally an officer remains in one charge for three to four years, sometimes for two years. The officer's history of postings is of little consequence when postings are decided. There are many numbers of officers who have never worked in a Custom House. There are many who have had no experience in Central Excise. Career designing and management was never given priority. Now that Directorate General of HRD has been created, perhaps, the board will keep an eye on the history of postings, while deciding not only postings of officers but also their need for a particular training in India or abroad. Career management of the service officers may now get the right attention. This Directorate General also handles Cadre Restructuring and Review which was never in place earlier.

There were two Cadre Reviews and three pay commissions during my 35 years of service which brought some relief to officers. Junior Administrative grade took 10 years, Senior Administrative grade another 11 years and Higher Administrative grade yet another 12 years for officers of my seniority. The Sixth Pay Commission has made the lives of most government servants more comfortable. The IRS officers are no exception. Earlier the salaries were indeed low. My first salary of ₹679, which I got in November 1969; this would have been perhaps sufficient had there been some suitable infrastructure in place for a probationer. But as things were, after the announcements of civil service results and the allotment of services, the officers were called straightaway to Calcutta or Bombay Customs House for training with no arrangements for stay. There was no transport allowance added to the salary. The probationer was left to his own devices in the vast city. Today an IRS officer begins with ₹36,000 and the NACEN too has excellent arrangements of stay, food, games, entertainment, etc.

Over the years, the service has seen many changes for the better on the welfare front. Almost everywhere there are residences. The office buildings are more comfortable and fitted with cooling/heating systems. The furniture in most offices is elegant and dignified. Much attention has been given to infrastructure and cleanliness. There is a Customs Welfare Fund from where not only class I officers but anyone from group A to D can get help for himself and his family in emergency situations. Bright children of Central Excise and Customs officials are also given scholarships till standard XII. The Customs Welfare Fund and the Education Fund are managed by the Directorate General of HRD.

There is another front where matters have improved over the years. Attitudes have definitely changed about women officers. Till the 1970s and early 1980s, women in this department were not considered competent enough to handle independent field charges. The pioneers among ladies who joined the department did suffer enormously due to the deeply entrenched anti-women attitude among most bosses. They did not feel embarrassed to tell a lady officer that she is not getting a particular charge because she is a lady, as my boss told me, in a very matter of fact way. Till the early 1970s, an officer, on completion of probation, was posted as superintendent (Tech) and then after a year or six months was posted as assistant collector. In my first posting as an assistant collector, I reported to Delhi. Here I was given the charge of Foreign Travel Tax. This charge had nothing to teach. No Custom Law was involved. Even if it was given to any other department the tax would have been collected. The first three precious years of my career were wasted doing nothing, learning nothing and above all losing confidence. After a year and a half I asked for a change. My boss was surprised at my request. He stated categorically that he is not in favour of giving field charges to girls. And he thought that was the end of the story. It was not. It was the beginning. In 1983, I took charge as the narcotics chief of Uttar Pradesh in the CBN. Today a lady of the 1979 batch is the narcotics commissioner of India for more than five years. In 2010, a lady from the 1975 batch was posted as the chief of the premier intelligence organization—the Directorate General of Intelligence (DGRI).

Corruption in the Service

I can say whatever needs to be said on this subject in just a sentence or two. There is corruption no doubt but not more or less than in any other service. But there is no feeling of brotherhood among the service mates. They are sitting and watching, ready to pounce at a colleague or boss or junior. More cases of vigilance, therefore, come to the public view than say in the IAS where service mates stand for each other. Will tax reforms and changes in procedures reduce corruption? I am doubtful. Corruption is because officers and staff are corrupt, not because procedures are easy to manipulate

Central Excise duties are levied by the union government on commodities manufactured or produced and consumed within India. It is an indirect tax which is passed on to the consumer by the manufacturer who pays the tax to the government. The levy of Central Excise duty began during the British rule in India. Salt was one of the dutiable items and was an important source of revenue for the British government. It attracted the ire of the freedom fighters. Gandhi's Dandi March, to symbolically manufacture salt from the waters of the sea, became the first defiance of the tax laws and shook the British like never before. But the tax could be abolished only after Independence.

In the year 1934 many more manufactured commodities such as sugar, matches and steel ingots were brought within the scope of Central Excise. In 1941, rubber tyres came in the net. Tobacco (both manufactured and un-manufactured) and cigars and cheroots came under the Central Excise in 1943. In 1944, the Central Excise and Salt Act was passed consolidating the various enactments on the subject. New duties on coffee and tea and betel nuts were imposed.

After Independence, cigarettes was added to the list of taxable items. With every year thereafter new items were added to the Central Excise Tariff. Ultimately in 1975, a general item—Item 68—was added to cover all other goods not elsewhere specified. The year 1986 brought the new tariff where the arrangement of chapters and headings was on the pattern of the International Harmonised Systems of Nomenclature (HSN) which provides separate headings for each type of good. Now the Central Excise Tariff has the same headings as the Customs Tariff. New headings were created to do away with items 68.

Sea Customs Act, 1878, which only incorporated laws related to sea, was comprehensively reviewed a little before 1962. There was Land Customs Act 1924 and Indian Aircraft Act 1911. All three Acts were consolidated into a comprehensive law and the Customs Act 1962 was enacted. Section 12 of the Customs Act 1962 is the charging section. Duties are charged according to the Tariff Act, 1985, by introducing the HSN. At the time of Independence, customs duties constituted the bulk of the revenue from the indirect taxes. Gradually duties on Central Excise also increased and, then, there came a time when the revenue from both Customs and Central Excise constituted the major part of India's Budget.

During the British days, the Imperial Custom Service (ICS) was created on the representation of the Bengal Chamber of Commerce in 1906 with specially trained and efficient officers. It was under the direct control of the Government of India. Earlier the Customs Department was organised on a provincial basis. Officers for the imperial Customs were drawn from the Indian Civil Service. Some were directly recruited in England. The Royal Commission on the Public Services under the Chairmanship of Mr Islington had recommended that no ICS officer was to be posted as collector of Customs unless he was fully trained in Customs procedure. He said that the emphasis should be on intellectual culture through a superior liberal education.

In 1948 the imperial Customs was redesignated as Indian Customs Service. In the year 1956 Indian Customs and Central Excise Services Class I (now Group A) was organised. These two services were merged into one service in 1959 and the Indian Customs and Central Excise Class I was reorganised as part of the IRS. The other part of the service was Indian Income Tax Service Class I. Prior to 1956 there was no organised group A (class I) service, on the Central Excise side. The group A posts (class I) in the Central Excise Department were filled by promotion of group B officers to the cadre of assistant collectors.

Changes in the Tax Collecting Procedures

It is a satisfying thought to have been in the IRS (Customs and Central Excise) in those 35 years when the service had to face the maximum changes and the most difficult challenges. In 1968, Self-Removal Procedure (SRP) was put in place. Prior to 1968 no excisable goods could be removed from the factory for clearance, without a proper officer assessing the goods and countersigning the gate pass on which the goods were cleared. The duty assessed by the proper officer was paid in cash in the treasury or adjusted in the Personal Ledger Account (PLA) of the assessee, and only then the goods were allowed to leave the factory. This was physical control which remained in vogue till 1968. Today there is physical control only on cigarettes. Thereafter, with a view to give relief to trade, self-removal procedure was introduced. This procedure did not require the Central Excise officers to remain at the factory gate. The manufacturer could himself clear the excisable goods. But this necessitated the assesses to keep detailed accounts. The penalty clauses were also made very stringent.

In 1994 the gate pass was replaced with the manufacturer's own invoice. Year 1996 saw another step in favour of the assessee—'self-assessment'. Now the assessee could himself assess his goods and decide the tax. He could do classification and valuation of his goods himself. The year 2000 brought the ultimate good news for the assessee. There was no need to pay duty before clearing the goods. He could pay duty every fortnight. Finally, in 2001 the Central Excise Rules, 1944, were replaced by new Central Excise Rules, 2001. The earlier 234 Rules were replaced by just 32 Rules. The classification, price and Cenvat declarations were dispensed with.

Tax Reforms

The tax reforms which began in June 1991 saw the Central Excise Duties reduced and rationalised, statutory records done away with and automation under Central Excise and Service Tax completed.

The automation procedure is known as Automation in Central Excise and Service Tax (ACES). Central Excise and service tax returns can now be filed electronically

Even on the customs front, the most important reforms are reduction and rationalisation of customs duties as also removal of import trade control. Automation of processes through the use of Electronic Data Interface (EDI) has brought the customs office at the doorstep of importers and exporters. This has made the customs clearance process faster simpler and transparent. There has been a major reduction in transaction costs and cargo release time. The assessment of each consignment has been changed to selective automated risk-managed assessment. All this is in line with international best practices. Today customs tariff, laws, procedures and processes in India are harmonised with global practices. These reforms were taken up to provide transparent and efficient business processes to strengthen trade and industry so that India could compete globally. It was recognised that there was need to integrate with the global economy through trade, investment and technology. An environment comparable to that in other developing economies was sought to be created for Indian entrepreneurs. Fiscal stabilisation was given the highest priority. The most radical changes were in the area of industrial policy. The system of industrial licensing was abolished. The public sector was drastically pruned and areas opened to private sector participation. India became supportive of foreign investment. Trade policy was substantially liberalised. The earlier complex import control regime was dismantled. All raw materials, inputs and capital goods were allowed to be imported. This liberalisation on imports was accompanied by gradual lowering of customs duties. On some items the duties were 200 per cent. These were brought down to 65 per cent by 1994. The duties on capital goods were also reduced. The idea was to bring the rates in line with those prevailing in other developing countries.

On the excise duty front, a large number of duties were specific. These were made ad valorem and exemptions were reduced. A system of getting credit on taxes paid on inputs called Modvat was in force since 1986. But Modvat was not available on excise duty paid on capital goods and on textiles and petroleum. In 1994, Modvat was extended to these goods also. For the first time service tax of 5 per cent was imposed on three services. This change in tax structure brought improvement in tax administration.

We have seen the radical changes which India's economy encountered from the dawn of Independence till today. India woke up to freedom as a totally protectionist economy. The economic boundaries were jealously guarded for industry to flourish and the BoP position to improve in India's favour. The IRS officer was the one who stood guarding the protectionist economy. Later he stood at that strategic point from where the procedural changes were implemented. Later still it was he who was at the centre of fiscal changes which ushered in liberalisation.

The IRS officer who had presided over the much dreaded physical control, licensing control and high duty era, smoothly got into his new shoes and implemented, with grace, the liberalisation programmes of the government. The procedures of tax collection had changed unrecognisably over the years. From physical control to SRP, to production-based control and then to liberalisation was a long journey which was bound to usher in a revolutionary change. The change imposed a total trust on the assessee erasing any interface with the customs and central excise man. These landmarks may appear to have reduced the role of the tax man. On the contrary, the fact is that the role of the service has widened. No government can do away with tax, but the system of collection can be made easier, more people friendly, more at par with the other countries of the world. This is exactly what India did, when the time was ripe to do so. In the interest of economic growth and development, India had to compete with world economies; it could not carry on with procedures and processes which were different.

Therefore, a number of changes and reorientations in the form of Audit 2000, Goods and Services Tax (GST), etc., have taken place after the economic reforms. The idea is to optimise efficiency and equity, to integrate India into a single common market and enhance cooperative fiscal federalism as envisaged in the constitution of India. The New GST Policy proposes imposition of dual levy of consumption-based GST in the form of Central GST (CGST) and State GST (SGST) on all goods and services, except those exempted. The new GST Policy shall bring about complete overhaul of the indirect taxation system in India. It is expected to broaden the tax base, remove the distortions which the cascading nature of taxation brings. GST is expected to instill growth in GDP, reduce price of goods, create more employment opportunities, simplify tax collection mechanism and increase relative income of all sections of society. This major reform too will be implemented by the customs, central excise and service tax officers who have proved over the years their technical strength and adaptability to changes in the environment. Today the total strength of the IRS is 2,290.

Yet, so far the rare experiences of these officers have not been used at any senior level. We do not find many officers of this service on deputation in other ministries, definitely not in positions above that of joint secretary. The posts of secretaries to the Government of India have multiplied over the years but the IRS was never given a share. Most of them are held by the IAS or IFS who have a big chunk of the share. The posts of DGPs are all of secretary rank. The other central services also have some secretary-level posts assigned to them. It should go without saying that at least in the secretary revenue's post the experiences of an IRS officer should be used for more practical handling of the challenges. The tax administrator is the man who gaurds the economic frontiers of the country. In today's global environment no territorial frontier can stand unless the men on the economic frontier are strong. Their valuable experience should not be frittered away; their confidence should not be taken for granted.

12

Indian Postal Service:
A Rewarding 'Social Service'

Humera Ahmed*

While filling the forms for the civil services examination one also has to give the choice of service. I had to do this with very little knowledge of the different services, except the IAS. Hence, while putting down my options for the services; I had put Postal Services quite high in my priority list. Why had I done it? I was not very keen on the other services, except perhaps the Audit Service. The audit figured in my parent's conversation, whenever the audit party visited their office. I had also seen the power of the CAG reports in the newspapers. I was awed by the all pervasive nature of audit. The other service which had this phenomenal presence was the post office. The ubiquitous red post box, where we posted letters to any place in the country and world, the regular and gentle postman in khaki who brought our letters and occasional parcels and money orders—these had been familiar since childhood. Its presence was also palpable in the imposing buildings such as the General Post Office in Mumbai; so was one in my vicinity where it was located in a hundred-year-old double-storeyed structure with a red Mangalore tiled roof under a gulmohur tree. Surely I thought the men and women who controlled and administered such an organisation must be very good and able.

* Postmaster General, Kolkata, West Bengal.

But on reaching the LBSNAA, Mussorie, I realised with dismay that the Postal Services were not rated high; actually they were in many cases the last option for those who could not make it to the Revenue Services such as customs or income tax. I felt very foolish, but it seemed too late to change the options. Hence when the allotment came, many laughed at me. What are you going to do in the post office? They asked. Deface stamps? Actually the words in Hindi were: '*Thappa lagao ge?*' Some were a little patronising: 'You will get importance as people will come to you for issue of stamps.' More knowledgeable ones assuaged my feelings with 'It's a small cadre and there are good houses, close to the office.'

Hence it was with great trepidation and misgivings that I reported on a cold wintry morning at Postal Staff College which at that time was located on the ninth floor of Sanchar Bhavan in Delhi. The orientation pep talk by the faculty projecting us as managers and administrators did not boost our morale but the idea that it touched the lives of every citizen through its services and the universal nature of the service did.

Over the years, I have seen the impact on the Postal Services as a result of dramatic changes in communication technology. The spread of telephony, Internet and modernised banking services have threatened the monopolistic nature of the post, as also the rising expectations of customers. How did and how will the department cope with these demands? How will it retain the trust and support of the customers and continue to be socially relevant in the present competitive environment? These are some of questions which assail and which challenge the officers who man the Postal Service. The officer who joined the Postal Service thinking it a cushy government job was in for a shock. He soon became aware of the multidimensional nature of their job and the challenges of operating a huge network in a competitive environment.

But the fact that despite the communication revolution the department has survived speaks volumes of the role played by the officers at the cutting edge, the executive and the policy level. To know and understand how this was achieved, we need to go back to the formal setting of the organisation, the incorporation of Indian Postal Service as an all India Service to man the postal network which was a legacy we inherited from the British, and its journey through the decades to become an essential component of India's development programme and policy as well as provide services to its customers on value—for money basis.

History of Postal Services in India

Though communication is as old as civilisation and various forms of conveyance of messages and *dak* existed in India, the institution as we know it was established with the Act of 1854 with the issue of a postage stamp and appointment of its first DG. The organisation was then controlled by the Department of Home, Government of India, and, therefore, perceived as an instrument of imperial expansion and consolidation. The core activity was dealing with mails that included letters, registered post, parcel and their transmission and delivery. It gradually introduced new products such as money order, insurance and postal orders and Value Payable Post (VPP) services.

As the network grew, the government started utilising it to for resource mobilisation through small savings which were introduced as an agency function in May 1883, soon followed in 1884 with Postal Life Insurance for government servants. The service continued to grow with its field formations and the setting up of the Army postal service. With the expansion of telegraph and railway lines, conveyance and transmission improved. The Act of 1898 provided it with a legislative framework. Air mail provided a rare fillip to transmission of international mail in addition to sea mail and led to the establishment of foreign mail offices.

At the time of Independence the number of post offices was about 23,344. These did not include offices in the postal systems operating under some of the princely states. During the British rule, the management of the Postal Service was under the DG and postmaster generals who were from the ICS; officers at the middle level were from the provincial group B services. With the amalgamation of the Postal Services of the Indian state and with the deliberate policy of expanding the postal network in the rural and remote areas so as to provide social connectivity as part of the social responsibility, it became essential to provide a special cadre of dedicated officers as an All India service and the Indian Postal Service was set up as a group A service in 1948.

Governance Structure

Today, this cadre manages a network of 1.55 lakh post offices, the largest in the world. It has a work force of 292,672 full-time or departmental employees and 309,915, extra-departmental employees or Gram Dak Sevak (GDS) as they are mainly in rural areas, a feature unique to this department. The regular employees man the departmental post offices whereas the GDS mans the branch post offices which are generally located in the rural areas.

The organisation is headed by a secretary to the Government of India who is also the DG of the department and chairman of the Postal Services board whose strength has been recently increased from three to six members. Below this apex body are 22 circles coterminous in most cases with states and headed by a chief postmaster general in the Higher Administrative Grade (HAG). Below him in the Senior Administrative Grade (SAG) are regional postmaster generals who have officers designated as directors in the junior administrative grade to assist them. Each region is subdivided into a number of divisions, equivalent to a revenue district headed by a superintendent or senior superintendent of post offices.

The cadre has at present 550 officers and at a given time at least 10 per cent officers are on deputation either in the central staffing scheme or in the Army Postal Service; approximately 450 group A officers have to manage a vast labour force. The Army Postal Service which is under the base circle is headed by an Indian postal officer designated as additional director general in the rank of a major general in the army. Every year at least 30 officers are on deputation to the Army Postal Service.

Besides the field formation, the department has a number of training institutions. The premier one is Postal Staff College which is responsible for in-service training of gazetted officers and is headed by a director of HAG rank. For the clerical staff, there are five postal training centres, viz., Vadodara, Mysore, Sarhanpur, Madurai, Guwahati and Darbangha headed by director-level officers. Mysore which also houses the software development centre is under an SAG officer.

Postal Staff College which during my probation, that is, in the year 1979, was located on the 9th and 11th floors of Sanchar Bhavan is now in a sprawling campus with lush greenery and landscaped gardens in Ghaziabad. Training here is in two modules. In the first, it is induction in departmental rules and administration and familiarisation with various functions of organisation. This is followed by field attachments and on-job training in various subordinate key posts, such as inspector and postmaster and also (which was not in my time) as marketing managers. In module two, personnel management, leadership and communication development along with case studies were emphasised to prepare us to undertake the onerous responsibility of managing on first appointment a strongly unionised work force of between 1,500 to 2,000 and ensuring the maintenance and upkeep of a large network of post offices mainly in the rural areas. With technology induction in the post offices and the remarkable transformation in communication, training in technology management and business development is also imparted and Staff College has a well-equipped computer lab and a visiting faculty of management experts.

Scope and Challenges

Though the training gave us the necessary knowledge it is the actual job experience which makes one realise the opportunities, potential, challenges and pitfalls of a post. My tenure as senior superintendent I considered as one of the most memorable as it is at this stage that one is at the actual implementing level where it is possible to monitor the delivery of services. While interacting with the branch postmasters in the villages, I realised the potential of the post office to become the mechanism of social change for in many places the branch postmaster who is drawn from the local community is the only central government functionary. The post office reach can, therefore, be utilised to deliver products and services as well as a dissemination of knowledge on various government programmes.

To oversee the operations in the post offices and assist the superintendent in the discharge of duties, there are sub-divisional inspector and assistant superintendent of post offices who are selected through a departmental exam from the postal assistants cadre. During the earlier period of the service, the calibre of this cadre was instrumental in enabling the divisional heads in efficiently managing the system. Over the years, many of them did not adapt to the new environment of computerisation and innovative methods of management and, therefore, became stagnant and frustrated. However with new and ingenious methods of training at the postal training centres this cadre is again being invigorated.

The job of the divisional superintendents today has more variety and challenge than it did in my time though the quantum of mails handled has drastically decreased with increase in use of mobile and email services. An unregulated courier market has also considerably eroded the document and express segment of the department. But despite this the work load of the superintendent has increased manifold with a change in the policy from expansion to consolidation and optimisation of resources with focus on self-sufficiency. In my time, we were given targets for opening new post offices, creating new posts and acquiring land for postal facilities and staff quarters. Today, the targets are on relocation of post offices and on energising and upgrading the network so that its outreach benefits the largest number of people including those in the remotest areas. The focus is on increasing business through marketing activities and on selling insurance and facilitating members of low income groups to invest in small savings.

The challenge continues as you climb the ladder. In a year and half one is in a senior timescale post which are located in large cities and at the circle headquarters where as assistant postmaster general one can have a purview of the circle functioning. As assistant postmaster general, I was able to control and monitor the saving bank and Postal Life Insurance in Maharashtra. During this tenure I realised the capacity and reach of the post office to reach the common man and provide a platform to collect information for assessing the needs for delivery of social security schemes. I became acutely aware of this aspect when I was posted as assistant director general in the Directorate in charge of plan monitoring which gave me an idea of the huge network in the rural areas. If this network could be galvanised through training, it is possible to leverage it for development of village economies. This potential was realised by the department and a post of Decentralised Distributed Generation (DDG) rural business was created in 2008.

With 9 to 10 years of service one is a director assisting the postmaster general of a region (which post one acquires after 20 years or so) in the regions management. As director of Mumbai region, which included besides Mumbai, the districts of Thane and Raigarh and also Navi Mumbai, I had 10 divisional superintendents reporting to me. The stint enabled me to oversee a gamut of operations in the city and in the rural and tribal areas of Raigarh and Thane. I was able to see the Mahila Samrudhi Yojana (MSY) a scheme of the Ministry of Women And Child Development to provide financial benefit to women, in operation in the villages; so was the marketing of Rural Postal Life Insurance which was started in 1995 by organising rural *mela*s (fairs) with the branch postmaster and sarpanch.

As far as management of high quantum of city mail was concerned (Mumbai received nearly 24 to 25 lakh mail on an average per day), I also got an opportunity to start two new schemes for processing mail with economy and speed by segmentation of traditional and business mail and by setting up mass mailing centres where pre-mailing activity and processing of business mail was outsourced.

After Mumbai, I went on deputation under the Central Staffing Scheme as director in Department of Culture where I looked after libraries, archives and museums for nearly five years. As director of libraries I was associated with the Rural Library Scheme and I strongly felt that the network of the post office could be leveraged to provide the rural population access to reading material in coordination with the district libraries department.

I returned to the department as postmaster general of Pune region. The department was trying to computerise its network so as to enable electronic transfer of money orders and letters and entered in partnership with Western Money Union for inward transfer of money. I started the Post Forums in Pune and also a philately magazine for philately enthusiasts. I found philately promotion and exhibitions a highly creative and enjoyable activity.

After Pune, I was postmaster general of Mumbai and also looked after the charge of Nagpur before being promoted with 30 years of service as chief postmaster general with a posting in Himachal Pradesh. This is my career progression as also that of most of the IPS officers and it's only a few lucky ones who are promoted as members. But most officers would agree that the job content of a chief post master general (CPMG) as head of a circle (an administrative unit) is more enriching than a member's, more so after delegation of powers to enter in MOU with private and governmental agencies for special business packages, the underlined objective of which is increasing revenue. Under such packages, a number of post offices started selling various products ranging from mutual funds to Darjeeling tea and Swami Ramdeo's products, Ganga *jal*, saris and handicrafts. The post offices in Hyderabad went so far as delivering the local specialty Haleem to houses during Ramzan.

However, these local initiatives did not contribute much to the all-India revenue and the deficit continued to increase, specially with the postal service being badly impacted by the competition from couriers, mobile operators and an increasingly customer-oriented banking service. It became acutely aware of the constraints of its legacy of a rigid culture and public perception of poor service. Piecemeal efforts to improve the financial viability and operations by rationalising the mail network and introducing air freighter service to North East did not yield the desired results.

Transformation Strategy—Road Ahead

Then in mid 2008 the department launched Project Arrow which succeeded in a dramatic makeover. The project envisaged making the department a vibrant and responsive organisation with a distinct identity and a new logo. For the first time a brand image of the post office was outlined. The new logo was unfurled and a new slogan announced: '*Dak Seva—Jan Seva*'. Key performance indicators were fixed for its core services and monitored on a regular basis by the board and secretary post. A comprehensive programme to computerise all departmental offices—hitherto limited to 300 offices— and bring them online was started. By the end of 2011, we would have all the 25,000 departmental post offices computerised.

With total computerisation of its departmental outlets, India Post is well on its way of launching core banking services in the near future in nearly 5,000 post offices across the country. It is also improving the transmission and delivery of its mail services through mechanisation and computerisation of its operations and upgrading of its monitoring mechanism. By introducing track and trace system for Speed Registered and parcel post and by improvements in electronic money transfer it has been trying to regain lost ground.

But the main challenge before the department still remains: how to be financially self-sufficient while providing the universal service obligation in the rural areas. With the opening of the economy and globalisation, rural India's huge potential is being recognised. Many mutual fund and insurance companies want to tap the rural market and are keen to use the outreach of the postal network which had enabled the government to reach the rural population in fulfilling its objective of financial inclusion by leveraging its network for payment of wages under Mahatma Gandhi National Rural Employment Guarantee Scheme (MGNREGS), old age pension and other welfare doles. Data for cost price index for rural areas is also collected through the post offices. National Bank for Agriculture and Rural Development (NABARD)–post office linkage that is providing micro credit to self-help groups is also to be implemented through the post offices as a pilot scheme.

Hence, in the past 20 years, the department has been innovating, modernising and diversifying in order to optimally utilise its last mile delivery advantage, especially in the rural and hilly areas, to enable the department to be socially relevant and economically viable. Its vision statement for the 12th Plan is quite ambitious. It is: 'India Post's products and services will be the customer's first choice.' A vision is kept with the new challenges of the economy and the impact of globalisation on the country.

The potential of the huge network in the social and economic development of the communities it serves can be utilised if the post office is mainstreamed in the activities of the communities it serves and technology inducted. The rural Information and Communication Technologies (ICT) programme of the department has identified 25 per cent of the branch offices for induction in 2012. The department together with other stakeholders is drawing up a road map to explore engagement of the rural network towards development of village economies and also increase its own revenue. The roadmap also envisages the rural entrepreneurship training for rural personnel for increasing the capacity of the network. Once the rural post office effectively integrates with village life, the benefits will be immense.

Conclusion

While fulfilling the vision and upgrading the network is a huge challenge to officers and staff of the department as a whole, the rewards of being a member of this department are many. First and foremost to me it is an opportunity of performing a useful public service—a service to the common man. It is, I think, a highly paid social service if performed with the right spirit. Then as far as other facilities are concerned, such as housing and welfare, the level of satisfaction is quite high. Many of the official quarters are in the same premises as the post office. This location has considerably benefited lady officers who have been able to look after their families more conveniently than their counterparts in other services.

Further it is easier to undertake any welfare activity as the huge network enables mobilisation of resources. Many of the circles have a voluntary contribution fund from which financial assistance on death and health grounds is given. During draughts and earthquakes considerable amounts are collected for the victims and their families. Proactive and socially committed officers utilise this staff strength for conducting blood donation camps and tree plantation. For some the sports and cultural activities have provided an effective platform. But the biggest opportunity is the training and experience it provides to its officers in human resource management and logistics which are required in operating the largest post office network in the world.

13

Functioning of Union Public Service Commission of India

K.S. Chalam

The creation of UPSC after Independence was one of the first moves by the government to create a culture of autonomy for the executive. Though some of the structures created by the British India government were retained, it was largely through the efforts of the chairmen, who were meticulously chosen both by Jawahar Lal Nehru and Sardar Patel, that the stature and prestige of the institution is maintained that stands intact till this day. Though India could boast of the civil service system prevailing during the time of Kautilya in the 4th century BC, the present system has, however, evolved over a period of time during the modern period.

The first PSC in India came in to existence in the month of October 1926 as part of Section 96(c) of the Government of India Act, 1919. Later when constitutional reforms were attempted by the British India government, the needs of the civil services were considered as part of the Government of India Act, 1935. Officers of the civil service were recruited through the British Civil Service Commission and examinations were held in England. It was only after 1922, examinations were held in India under the auspices of the British Civil Service Commission. The functions of the commission were entrusted to the PSC (India). The same functions that were performed by the British Civil Service Commission established in 1855 were assigned to it to avoid patronage in recruitment. Before Independence, a combined examination was held in India for the

Indian Audit and Accounts Service, Imperial Custom Service, Indian Railways and Accounts Service, Military Accounts Service, Postal Services (class II), Commercial Department of the Superior Revenue Establishment of State Railways along with a separate examination for IPS.

The FPSC was renamed as UPSC in 1950 after the Constitution coming in to operation. A number of changes have been brought about to bring uniformity in the system of recruitment including the examination pattern, number of attempts, age of entry, etc. R.N. Banerjee, the second chairman of UPSC after Independence, has narrated how the changes were affected as follows:

[In] mid-1948 a high powered committee of Secretaries, presided over by the late Sri Girija Shankar Bajpai (then holding the newly created post of Secretary General in the External Affairs) examined the vacuum caused in the services and government decided that a Special Recruitment Board should be constituted immediately to recruit overage personnel (with some administrative experience and background from the 'open market', that is to say, commercial business institutions, industries, provincial services, universities, bar, Etc.) after a brief training such personnel could perhaps plug the gaps created in the Services. The then Chairman of the FPSC a retired member of the ICS, was in bad health and had to remain on long leave and the commission was left only with three or four members, the senior-most member having to shoulder and also the administrative responsibility of the Chairman intermittently. So this work was beyond the capacity of the commission. The Commission readily agreed to this new work of recruitment being entrusted to the Special Recruitment Board. I was appointed Chairman of the Board and two members of the Commission and one non-official of standing were made members. While interviewing candidates in each state, the Chief Secretary and Inspector General of the Police of the State were also to be members of the Board. This was about August 1948 and the Board started work almost immediately. While we took a week off after prolonged periods of interviews conducted in the south, I got a message one day at Madurai from the local collector to attend to a trunk call from Delhi. Mr. R.A. Gopalaswami, ICS, then acting as Joint Secretary in the Ministry of Home Affairs, told me that Sardar Patel as Home Minister had taken a final decision to appoint me as Chairman of the FPSC (in addition to my duties as Chairman of Special Recruitment Board) as the ailing Chairman had resigned and the vacancy had to be filled immediately. In view of the ban on post-retirement re-employment in Government services he naturally wanted my previous concurrence in the decision. I took 24 hours for a reply and accepted the offer. This was about December, 1948. I returned to Delhi for a few days to take over charge and make interim arrangements for coordination of my work as Chairman both of the FPSC and the Special

Recruitment Board. It was a tremendous responsibility with hard work ahead. Fortunately, the SRB had been provided with a competent Secretary (a senior ICS Deputy Secretary of the Home Ministry) and a Secretariat with ancillary staff and office out-fit. There was no interruption in the smooth working of the Board but for such work as the FPSC had to do only one senior member and one or two temporary members were available. (Banerjee, 1976)

Structure of Examination

Though there were several attempts to tinker with the recruitment procedures, it was during 1976 a comprehensive attempt was made to bring a new scheme of civil services examination through a committee on Recruitment Policy and Selection Methods. The committee was chaired by D.S. Kothari, Ex-chairman, University Grants Commission (UGC). The Kothari Committee has recommended three stages to screen the large number of candidates. They are: (a) preliminary examination (objective type) for selecting candidates to take up the main examination, (b) main examination (written examination followed by an interview) for selecting candidates for entry in to the services, and (c) post-training test at the end of the foundation course at the Academy, including an interview by a board constituted by the UPSC. The government did not accept the third test and the remaining parts were introduced in 1979. At the end of every 10 years, the examination system was reviewed and new patterns suggested. Therefore, Satish Chandra, ex-chairman, UGC, was appointed as chairman of the committee in 1989. He recommended the continuation of the Kothari Committee recommendations with introduction of a compulsory essay paper in the main examination. The Civil Services Examination Review Committee under the chairmanship of Yogender Alagh was appointed in 2001. The Committee has made far-reaching recommendations in devising a new structure of syllabus without specifying any particular discipline as the knowledge base on which tests are to be organised. The government did not accept the recommendations in the way the structure was recommended by Alagh Committee. A review committee under the chairmanship of Arun Nigvekar, former chairman, UGC, was appointed by UPSC. The existing system of examination and the structure of syllabus were examined by the Nigvekar Committee and have broadly agreed with the Alagh Committee on the subjects to be examined for the mains.

The Alagh Committee has in fact examined several issues related to civil services. The second ARC in its 10th Report cited Alagh to say:

> It is shown by research that there is a positive correlation between a higher level of education and performance in Examination. Besides, considering the magnitude and importance of this examination, the graduate requirement seems to discharge the non-serious candidates who may apply in large number without any serious preparation and understanding for purpose of trial and may ultimately clog the system. In view of this, it is essential to prescribe graduation as the minimum educational qualification as the candidates are expected to reach a certain level of, maturity by that time. In this way, it will work as a filter. However, the committee recommends that the candidates may continue to be permitted to take the Preliminary Examination while studying for their degree, as at present. (Government of India, 2008)

The ARC has also made recommendations on this subject and wanted that the preliminary examination should consist of an objective type test having one or two papers on general studies, including the Constitution of India, the Indian legal system, Indian economy, polity, history and culture. There should be no optional subjects (Government of India, 2008).

After several rounds of academic and administrative exercises, the UPSC has now ended up with a structure of examination both for preliminary and main examinations from the year 2013. However, there was uproar among the candidates and civil society organisations when the notification was issued in April 2013. The Parliament was stalled and there were street agitations against the decision of making English and Hindi as the medium of examination and the eligibility condition of a pass in the relevant language to take up language as an optional paper. There was also criticism against the UPSC/government for the alleged bias against rural and weaker sections in the formulation of the recommendations by the elite committees. In fact, the Kothari Commission recommendations have made civil services a dream job to every eligible citizen, irrespective of their social and economic background. This according to some critiques is shattered when the preliminary examination in the form of CSAT (designed in the mode of Common Admission Tests [CAT] for institutes of management) was introduced.

The present system of examination for the year 2013 consists of two stages. The first phase relating to CSAT consists of two papers with objective questions related to comprehension and general studies each with 200 marks. The main examination consists of Part I in written examination which involves English comprehension and essay (at standard X level). There are four General Studies papers comprising all disciplinary knowledge and everyday science and technology divided into four broad areas, including a separate paper on ethics and civil service aptitude. There is provision for only one optional paper (with a choice of 25 subjects) and the languages instead of two earlier. The total marks in written test is 1800 and for personality test (PT) is 275, which make it 2075 in total. It is reported that those who qualified and finally made a grade in the civil services in 2012 have scored less than 50 per cent in written test. The consequences of the present changes that are brought in now would be known only after a year in 2014.

Personality Test

The PT is a unique measure to test the aptitude, temper, alertness and empathy for the stakeholders of the candidates in an interactive session. Each PT board is chaired by one member of the UPSC and assisted by four advisers. However, the present system of PT has undergone several variations. There is no minimum per cent of marks to be obtained in PT now. But it was not like this in the beginning as revealed by R.N. Banerjee. He said that a minimum pass mark was laid down as compulsory for the PTs. As a result, quite a number of cases occurred where candidates scored very high marks in the written test but failed to qualify because of not obtaining the minimum in the PT. The practice evoked a great deal of criticism from the public and Parliament. The ministers and departments of government were, however, insistent that a compulsory minimum standard at the PT must be retained. After carefully considering the matter year after year the Commission came to the conclusion that an interview board of the kind constituted can be expected to size up the trend of the personal qualities of young people even after a conversation of 15/20 minutes. Some credit or debit in respect of this test was, therefore, not unfair. But it was a sound step that a compulsory minimal performance was abolished after I left the Commission. The British Civil Service Commission introduced PT first for the ICS examination in 1922 but a minimum standard was not made compulsory. Even with low marks in the PT candidates having scored high marks in the written test, therefore, used to be successful. Incidentally, in the spirit of the judicial dictum that justice should not only be done but must be seen to be done we insisted that even though a candidate at any interview—for all kinds of recruitment—appeared to be definitely below the mark even from the very outset, he should be given the impression that he was disposed of quite summarily.

The set-up and procedure for conducting the written examinations were also overhauled. Even before he joined as a regular member I could obtain the advice of the late Mr Nirmal Kumar Sidhanta to advise us in regard to possible improvements. He devised a procedure by which the largest practicable measure of uniformity was secured in the evaluation of written papers. The moderator, head examiner and all examiners sat together scrutinising and comparing one another's marking of sample answer papers and thus evolving a common standard.

The Commission's primary responsibility is recruitment; the responsibility for the training of these recruits rests with the ministries and/or departments of the government. We felt that improved facilities for proper training of recruits were still called for. The late Mr K.M. Panikkar who represented the External Affairs Ministry in the annual interviews and took a very active part in conducting them left a note with the Commission and the Ministry recording this view.

Women began to be taken into the IAS and other services in my time. Gossips was afloat that the government was rather diffident about admitting women to the services but a threat by Rajkumari Amrit Kaur to resign her seat on the cabinet prevented the government from going any further. The best justification for admitting women came in the reply which our second or third women candidate gave to our question (at the interview) whether in view of the unemployment amongst boys it was wise to admit women to the services. She replied quietly, 'Sir, I understand that you are selecting only boys of A-1 class. All the boys are not of A-1 class while many girls are of A-1 class!' This lady has been an ambassador for some years now and the soundness of her reply has been more than amply borne out by the large number of women who have been flooding our lists of successful candidates and outshining the boys. The four or five who joined the services in my time are doing very well; one has already become an ambassador and one an additional secretary. I have met, and heard of, a Punjabi lady who even from her early career showed executive and administrative capacity of a very high order (Banerjee, 1976).

There are occasions when the unsuccessful candidates have approached the apex court claiming that they were not given fair chance or alleged bias in the PT conducted by various service commissions, including the UPSC. Now the proportion of marks allocated for the PT has been reduced to less than 15 per cent of the total marks. Therefore, 275 marks for PT in the current system that is recommended is less than 15 per cent of 2075, which is within the prescribed limit. In fact, the Commission briefs every adviser who serves on the interview boards. Each board is informed that the interview is not intended to be a test of either special-ised or general knowledge of the candidates which would have already been tested in the written examination. It should never be in the nature of cross-examination. Keeping the diversity of the candidates and the controversies involved, UPSC has done away with the minimum marks criterion in PT for selection in the civil services examination. The marks obtained by the candidates in the written test are a guarded secret not even revealed to the chairmen of the boards so that the boards are not prejudiced while interviewing the candidates.

Disciplinary Proceedings

Among the different functions of the Commission, disciplinary proceed-ings related to officers of not only All India Services but also every public servant under the Government of India go to the UPSC for final advice under Article 320(3)(c) of the Constitution. It is reported that there were about 60 cases in the 1950s and the number has reached the maximum of 854 in 2006–07 and 850 in 2009–10. There are different categories of cases ranging from minor penalty of censure to major penalty of dismissal from service of officials of different services including group D. Though

UPSC does not have the appellate authority like some European commissions, the Commission, however, functions as the disciplinary wing of the president of India. Therefore, if any of the recommendations are not acceptable to the concerned ministry, the fact has to be processed through the PM and the point of not accepting the advice of the UPSC needs to be reported to the Parliament.

The UPSC being a constitutional body is entrusted with another important function of conducting Departmental Promotion Committee (DPC) meetings. DPC in the popular parlance is a routine exercise wherein the concerned department sends the requisition to conduct the DPC for promotion of their officers up to the level of DG/secretary in government. After a careful examination of the records the date is intimated to the department concerned and the officer/officers from the department depending upon the grade meet under the chairmanship of a member in UPSC and finalise the names on the basis of ACRs as per norms prescribed. However, some departments have taken exemption from consultation provided under the Constitution on the plea that it would be delayed to process the proceedings under UPSC and other such pretexts. It seems the UPSC is consulting the government to get back all the posts once again in to their purview claiming that they have enough strength and expertise now to take up the function.

Integrity and Accountability

The structure of the UPSC, its functions, powers and obligations are laid down in the Constitution. Unlike in other countries, the status of the Commission and its members are guarded and equated with other constitutional bodies, such as the Supreme Court and Election Commission. The tenure of the member is fixed as six years without any provision for renewal. The member once appointed is not allowed to accept any job under the government after retirement. This condition was made intentionally to maintain the integrity of the incumbent who after accepting the assignment should under no circumstances be obliged to the executive or others under the promise of a post-retirement assignment. However, it has created some difficulties to those who entered the Commission at a young age and are prohibited to make use of their services for the good of the nation after retirement. R.N. Banerjee has voiced this in the beginning saying,

> Much is made of the ban on a Member's reappointment in Government Service after retirement as a guarantee for ensuring that they discharge their duties without fear or favour. This is rather an illusory notion. The personal character and moral standard of the Chairman and members must obviously be the best guarantee against any deviation from the highest standard of impartiality and objectivity which must be maintained in the discharge of their duties. As head of the institution, the Chairman's position is rather delicate. I have referred above to my having to enforce full time attendance in office. I had also unofficial hints passed on to me by the Home Ministers that one or two of our members were reported to listening to gossip from parties interested in cases pending before the Commission. As I felt that I must function, I used to mention such communication at our weekly meetings and end up with an appeal that we must not give any ground for such gossip. Apart from a limited number of cases of personal approach from officers of my status, I had no case of any official or member of the Government seeking to influence me in any case. (Banerjee, 1976)

The main function of the UPSC must obviously be to replenish and maintain in full strength the superior Central Service. This work the Commission has been doing very successfully. They have been able to obtain the best personnel available. I have been a resident of Delhi for the last 21 years after retirement and have a fair amount of contact with the members of the new services. A few years ago I had the occasion to meet one (a deputy secretary) of them on behalf of an organisation interested in the sale of a special type of aircraft. The deputy secretary explained to my satisfaction that my offer could not be entertained. Before I left, I passed on to him how deeply I was impressed with the clarity and cogency of his argument. The officer said, 'Sir, you have forgotten that you recruited me 14 years ago!' That was so, although I did not remember it at that time. This officer is now holding one of the most responsible offices under the central government (Banerjee, 1976).

The integrity and trustworthiness of the Commission is never questioned except in the form of protests when some reforms or modifications are made. The fact that the candidates who are qualified in the 20 group A and 5 group B civil services examination have come from different socio-economic and regional backgrounds representing the mosaic of India is a testimony of the good work and the reputation of the organisation. The accountability of the Commission is ensured through the annual report, consisting of various activities during a period of one year, which is kept before the Parliament for scrutiny.

India has chosen the path of parliamentary form of democracy with secularism and socialism as its constitutional ideals. It is necessary to select and train a cadre of competent and dedicated young people to take up the responsibilities of translating the above ideals into a reality through administrative action. The Department of Personnel, Grievances and Pensions came in to existence as a separate wing under the direct control of the PM to provide administrative support to the UPSC and other autonomous bodies. The UPSC, however, has to go a long way in its journey of bringing democracy, secularism and socialism as the mantras of governance in its search for the best among the candidates.

India as a developing country has undergone several modifications in the process of governance and in the economic policy formulation over a period of time. The country chose a path that was distinct from its original trajectory in 1991. The role of the civil service is redefined to take up a proactive role in the formulation of policies in the private sector. The public sector that was enjoying commanding heights of the economy was given a tepid treatment with the message for the young civil servant to facilitate private sector development. This change in emphasis in the role of the civil servant places a different HR requirement for the governance of the country. The UPSC needs to change its attitude and procedures in recruiting people who would possess such qualities. The country is still based on a democratic structure guided by a constitutional morality. There were amendments in the Constitution to affect democratic decentralisation through traditional institutions, such as the panchayat, nagar panchayat, etc. It seems the power that is concentrated in certain pockets of social groups and urban areas and political cliques do pose challenges to a pluralistic society. As Abid Hussain puts it,

[I]n the absence of dispersal of power, political liberty, so essential for the working of democracy, cannot be fostered. In the absence of devolution of power and separation of powers, the dominant political and bureaucratic classes monopolise power and are inclined to act undemocratically, placing emphasis on authority and obedience undermining the independence of institutions....

Democracy is just not for the survival of fittest. It is to achieve a life of dignity for the largest number of people. A high quality of democratic life cannot be achieved by society unless the society itself, its organs of governance, its civic institutions are permeated with a high moral sense which results in sense of justice towards all its members irrespective of their different identities.... A democratic state should provide incentives and motivations for such a life, for without it, democracy could become an empty soulless shell. (Hussain, 2001, pp. 33–43)

Keeping the objectives of a modern democratic society and the challenges of globalisation and the pressures, the civil servant is made to function under great strain. Therefore, recruitment of suitable HR to manage the economy and society is a formidable task. The UPSC that has contributed eight decades of unique service to the nation would definitely take the challenges ahead and remain as one of the premier constitutional institutions of South Asia.

References

Banerjee, R.N. 1976. 'My Chairmanship of Union Public Service Commission', in *Golden Jubilee Souvenir 1926–76*. New Delhi: UPSC.

Hussain, Abid. 2001. 'Democracy—The defining Feature of our Time,' in *Platinum Jubilee Souvenir 1926–01*. New Delhi: UPSC.

Government of India. 2008. *Second Administrative Reforms Commission: Refurbishing of Personnel Administration—Scaling New Heights*. New Delhi: Government of India.

14

Pakistan: Federal Public Service Commission and Its Functions

Rana Bhagwandas*

Civil services are institutions of a state,[1] irrespective of the system or form of governments pursued. The expression 'civil services' cover different branches of administration manned by permanent government servants.[2] It is but logical that inductions into or removals from the permanent offices be regulated by fair and transparent personnel management systems, leaving no cause for dissatisfaction for any stakeholders, dully enforced and overseen by a body free of any kind of influence. The directors of East India Company that ruled India before its formal transfer to British Crown were expected to swear an oath that they would shun 'jobbery and nepotism' in matters of recruitments.[3]

Conscious of the inherent benefits of entrusting selections of personnel for the newly independent dominion of Pakistan, in 1947, our founding fathers expanded functional domain of Pakistan's newly constituted PSC, entrusted with additional functions[4] as compared to erstwhile Indian Public Service Commission (IPSC).[5] The 24-member Basic Principles Committee mandated by the First Constituent Assembly in 1950 to draft proposals for the permanent Constitution recommended continuation of the Commission's role and status[6] determined in 1947 and retained till 13 August 1973 in successive Constitutions.[7] However, the 1973

* Chairman, Pakistan Public Service Commission.

Constitution made a significant departure to redefine its parameters. The Federal Public Service Commission Act, 1973,[8] was enacted in pursuance of Article 242 of the 1973 Constitution whereby its functions were reduced. The Federal Service Commission Ordinance, 1977,[9] replaced the 1973 Act, with a self-evident charter and features enshrined in it. Before we go through various developments leading to the functions assigned to present FPSC in 1977, let us briefly walk through the historical developments, having a direct bearing on its work and status.

Historical Perspective

Husain (1992) reports that the origins of the PSCs in the South Asian subcontinent may be traced back to the Government of India Act, 1858, under which power of regulating appointments to the ICS was vested in the secretary of state who was to act on the advice and assistance of Her Majesty's civil service commissioners.[10] By then, the British Crown had resumed the governmental functions from the East India Company, relieved to the extent of recruitments to Crown Services in India. However, despite Queen Victoria's declaration that Indians would be freely admitted into the Crown Services, only a few candidates offered to serve the colonial government. In 1886, a PSC was constituted with Sir C.U. Atchison as its chairman, which recommended that, among others, the cadre of covenanted civil services should be reduced to an elite cadre, limiting its number to only the important administrative appointments for the ICS of India; other posts were transferred to indigenous Provincial Civil Service. Recruitment to the ICS was made through annual examinations held in Britain (Husain, 1992). However, responding to demands for 'Indianisation' of the civil services, as also advised to the Royal Civil Service Commission by the late Quaid-e-Azam Mohammad Ali Jinnah,[11] candidates were allowed to appear in the examination held in India as well. The Islington Commission (1912–17) recommended that civil services should be put into four categories, namely Imperial, Central, Provincial and Subordinate services. The ICS, with a limited cadre, maintained its singular superiority among the services, though some modifications were made with respect to place of postings of its officers.

After these reforms, a larger proportion of Indians were inducted into the civil services, without excluding induction of British officers. These measures contributed to the establishment of a responsible indigenous public service in India, sensitive to public service needs (Husain, 1992).

The next set of reforms initiated consequent to the Montague-Chelmsford Report incorporated specific proportions of representations for Indians and Europeans in the ICS which was to increase progressively in favour of the Indians, every year. These provided protection to civil servants against dismissals or removals, except upon holding of a proper inquiry against them, under due process of law. These safeguards were incorporated in the Government of India Act, 1919 (Husain, 1992).

The 1919 Act provided for establishment of a PSC at the Centre, entrusted with the task of recruitments to the higher echelons in civil services, with requisite independence and security against unhealthy personal and political considerations. The 1923 Lee Commission recommended division of All India Services into three groups and its following recommendations were later incorporated in Government of India Act, 1935:

1. First group comprising the ICS, Indian Police, Indian Service for Engineers (Irrigation Branch), Customs and the Indian Forest Service to be controlled by the secretary of state
2. The second group comprising such services as the higher education, agriculture, roads and buildings, etc., to go to the provinces
3. The third group compromising Railways and Post and Telegraph to be shared between the secretary of state and the Government of India

With the commencement of the Statutory Commission Act in 1927, the PSC was established with five members, including a chairman who held office for five years' renewable term; the chairman, on vacation of office, was not eligible to hold any other office in India, under the Crown, though members were eligible for chairmanship.[12] With the introduction of federal system of government on enforcement of the Government of India Act, 1935, constitutional safeguards were provided to enable the IPSC to discharge functions as a specialised body to assist the executive branch for recruitment of professionally qualified persons to public services and posts under federal responsibility besides a set of other rule-making or advisory functions with respect to the career progression and discipline of crown employees and departmental recruitments. Its independence from all extraneous influences or pressures was secured by reaffirming security of specified tenures for the chairman and members, otherwise barred from any other appointment under the Crown without permission of the governor general. The Commission's uninterrupted funding and secretariat support was assured by basic law. In pursuance of the above charter, the IPSC was designated to conduct open competitive examinations for initial recruitments for all superior services, except the ICS, under the control of governor general, besides many other functions including adjudication of grievances, etc. At the relevant time, in addition to services of the federation and civil posts under the federation, selections for specified All India Services, a service common between Centre and provinces/states created as a legal fiction, was assigned to the IPSC. With respect to appointments to the ICS, Royal Civil Service commissioners continued to formulate recommendations for secretary of state for India, after open examinations followed by endorsement by the Central Legislative Council with two-third majority vote within one year.[13]

The governor general, at his discretion, was competent to make appointments for the IPSC's chairman and members against fixed tenures, with a condition that at least 50 per cent members were to be drawn from amongst persons with 10 years minimum service under the Crown; provincial governors would do likewise, for respective provincial commissions. The 1935 Act listed below mentioned functions for the IPSC:

To conduct tests and examinations for appointments to superior services/civil posts under the Government.
To advise the Government:-
  On all matters relating to methods of and qualifications for appointments to civil services and posts, including those earmarked for recruitment by departmental authorities;
  On the principles to be followed in making appointments, to civil services and posts and in making promotions and transfers from one service to another and on suitability of candidates for such appointments, promotions and transfers;
  On all disciplinary matters affecting a person serving His Majesty in civil capacity in India including memorials or petitions relating to such matters;

On any claim by or in respect of a person who is serving or has served His Majesty in India that any costs incurred by him in defending legal proceedings instituted against him in respect of acts done or purporting to be done in the execution of his duty should be paid out of the revenues of the Federation or, as the case may be, the Province;

On any claim for the award of a pension in respect of injuries sustained by a person while serving His Majesty in a civil capacity in India, and any question as to the amount of any such award;

Appointments and allocation of posts between various communities or subordinate ranks of the Police; and

To discharge additional functions assigned to the Commission; and any other matter referred by the Governor General or, as the case may be, by the Governor in case of State Commissions.[14]

Out of these functions, those listed against serial number (vii) and (viii) had an added significance in the context of newly demarcated 'Division of Legislative and Executive Powers' amongst the federating units, with implications for dispute resolution mechanism prescribed on the one hand for inter-personal grievances of the Crown employees and complaints by federating units regarding transgression into the assigned mandate, on the other. The above cited provisions had authorised assignment of matters relating to All India Services to the IPSC, except the ICS.

In the backdrop of massive population movement between the two newly created dominions of India and Pakistan that generated considerable strains on the newly established state of Pakistan, it was a formidable task to settle over 6 million refugees without previous experience or international assistance. Therefore, new services like 'Pakistan Foreign Services' were constituted by executive orders along with pre-existing service institutions strengthened, through an assignment of oversight responsibility to the Commission.[15]

With respect to legislative framework, pending drafting of a permanent constitution, days before independence on 12 August 1947, the Provisional Constitution[16] was adopted by the directly elected constituent assembly to govern the country in accordance with the 1935 Act after specified adaptations. It had laid constitutional foundations for the establishment of PSC with an expanded role in the management of public service institutions. The basic law not only sanctified existing provisions regarding the Commission's composition and structure, tenure for its members, assured funding and Secretariat support and functions with operational autonomy, it incorporated significant additions to its functions as listed below:

1. Discretionary structures and powers of the governor general were wiped off from the basic law in its entirety as per dictates of the parliamentary system; appointments of the chairman and members of the Commission were subjected to advice of the PM.
2. At the federal level, Pakistan Public Service Commission as successor to IPSC was made the sole constitutional institution responsible for recruitment to all superior services and federal posts, including the selections for service earlier assigned to the royal commissioners; the latter function with respect to All-Pakistan Services constituted the Commission's additional responsibilities in terms of sub-para (vii and viii) in para 7 above, since retained by Provisional Constitution, in 1947.[17]
3. Number of All-Pakistan Services, common between Federation and Provinces placed under Federal management responsibility, was reduced to two that is, Pakistan Administrative Service (PAS) the short-lived successor to the ICS, and the PPS.

The 1935 Act, as amended in 1947, endorsed provisions for entrustment of additional functions to the Commission, beyond what were vested in its predecessor institution during 1935–47.[18] Over time, at the federal level, despite repeated changes in its nomenclature, Pakistan Public Service Commission (1947–56), Federal Public Service Commission (1956–62), Central Public Service Commission (1962–72) and Federal Public Service Commission with effect from 1972 onwards, the Commission continued to discharge and perform the functions entrusted to it by its founding fathers until 14 August 1973.

However, what two disruptions in the constitutional rule during October 1958–June 1962 and March 1969–April 1972 did not do was achieved by the Ordinance[19] promulgated on 15 August 1973, in pursuance relevant constitutional provisions.[20] The Ordinance, later converted into an Act of Parliament, reduced the Commission's functions from 8 to 2. It contemplated the following:

1. Appointment of the chairman and members by the federal government empowered to determine their tenures and terms of service.

2. Its advisory function was limited to initial appointments and matters relating to promotion and transfer and disciplinary matters were excluded from its purview.

3. Appointments to 'Services of the Federation' were excluded from FPSC purview, but it continued to conduct annual examinations for Basic Pay Scale (BPS) which had 17 posts in these services; simultaneously, the executive initiated lateral inductions at every level, in every office by invoking office memorandum (OM)–based management practices[21] of questionable vires; in due course, these had far-reaching implications for the administrative structures of the state in general and administrative relations of the federating units, in particular.

4. Appointments in the state enterprises and corporations were added to the FPSC charter but in practice, the FPSC did not undertake this function.

5. After the 1977 Martial Law, the FPSC Act 1973 was repealed and replaced in December 1977, by the FPSC Ordinance[22] which harmonised its non-confirming practice since August 1973 with the law by following legislative changes:

   - Initial appointments in 'Services of the Federation' were brought back to the FPSC purview.
   - 'State Enterprises and Corporate sector' stood excluded from the FPSC charter.
   - In 1980, inductions against quota earmarked for Armed Forces were subjected to Defence Officers Services Board based mechanisms after validating appointments made without the FPSC recommendations during 1977–80.[23]
   - In 1985, by a constitutional amendment, appointment of the chairman was subjected to President's discretion;[24] but the 18th Constitutional amendment restored primacy of the PM's advice,[25] as was the case in 1947.

In 2000, the FPSC Ordinance was further amended:

1. To grant five-years non-renewable statutory tenure to the chairman and the members; but this was reversed by an ordinance, in 2005, with immediate effect to summarily relieve the chairman and a few members.
2. Removal of the chairman and members was subjected to Supreme Judicial Council framework, to provide security of service at par with Judges of the Superior Courts; this safeguard was practically nullified in 2005.
3. Consultation for determination of principles of transfers from one service to another were restored as per pre-1973 framework enshrined in Constitutional rules enforced in 1966 for FPSC examination-based conditional transfers; however, in purported exercise of powers from the newly inserted 'proviso' to sub-Section (1) of Section 9 of the Civil Servants Act 1973, Federal Government, continued inter-services reallocation and reshuffling, without the FPSC's obligatory inputs.[26]
4. By a parallel amendment in the Civil Servants Act 1973, the FPSC chairman was designated as Central Silk Board (CSB) Chairperson for promotions from BPS 19 to BPS 20 and from BPS 20 to BPS 21;[27] this decision was later reversed by two Ordinances issued in 2009 and 2010[28] but the practice was resumed on expiry of the second Ordinance in 2010.

The above adumbration provides a bird's eye view of two distinct phases through which the FPSC's constitutional (1947–73) and statutory functions (1973–to date) evolved after independence, in 1947. Its grievances redressal function was devolved to Federal Service Tribunals, established in pursuance of Article 212 of the Constitution (relieving it of other functions, for example, guarantees/protections) by way of reimbursement of legitimate litigation expenses. They were ensured even in colonial period. In the wake of extra-ordinary generation of intra and inter-services tensions amongst regular civil servants, the morale of public service members was impacted in general. The individual employees were/ are obliged to seek professional legal assistance at own costs, even if the cause of grievance be for reasons beyond their control. Proliferation of service litigation for redressal of grievances amply testifies the dimensions of this observation. The FPSC's role to contain and arrest consequential erosion in quality of public service to be rendered to the citizen needs a revision of the role of FPSC. Specific details which are relevant to constitutional and statutory provisions under which the present FPSC functions and the framework under which it conducts annual examinations for superior services are contained in Annex 14.1. Annex 14.2 provides brief resume on prescribed procedures for holding Annual Competitive Examination for Superior Services.

As noted above, the constitutional scheme in operation till 14 August 1973, there has been a reduction in the number of functions assigned to FPSC from 8 to 2 as listed in para 4. Here it is also relevant to flag that the following functions were assigned to the neutral FPSC on behalf of federating units, in pursuance of the political consensus and agreements of 27 December 1949 sanctified by successive Constitutions[29] to-date:

1. to advise with respect to methods of and qualifications for initial appointments to two All-Pakistan Services assigned to the federal government for management
2. to conduct test and examinations for appointments on domicile-based merit in two All-Pakistan Services
3. to conduct post-Academy examinations prescribed for termination of obligated probations and for determination of inter-se seniority of the officers of two All-Pakistan Services

While (1) and (2) above were further reaffirmed by the FPSC Ordinance/Act 1973, in practice these were disregarded in material particulars to marginalise the FPSC's additional role, of a neutral trustee to operationalise two inter-provincial agreements. In addition to Article 212 dispensation for redressal of inter-personal grievances, these 'agency functions' impinged on dispute resolution mechanism enshrined in Article 184(1) of the Constitution, pursuant to two subsisting inter-provincial agreements re functioning of the two All-Pakistan Services recognised and sanctified by the Constitution; these obligations could not have been disregarded.[30]

Since All-Pakistan Services extended their operation into provincial domains, expressly delineated by the Provisional Constitution of 1947 it may be instructive to provide a brief overview of the background of functions of the FPSC as custodian of the inter-provincial trust since independence. On inception, the Pakistan Administrative Service (PAS) was composed as successor to the ICS as the newest All-Pakistan Services was composed of officers drawn from former ICS, various federal/Provincial Services, General Administrative Reserve (GAR), Indian Political Service and War Inductees. PPS was likewise beefed up with additional elements from Provincial Police Service officers and War Inductees, excluding those reverted to the provinces. Without engaging the nascent Pakistan Public Service Commission (PPSC), a committee headed by the secretary general, Government of Pakistan, recommended these selections as one-time expedient dispensed with rigours of the Royal Commissioners/IPSC practice of open competition. As stated earlier, after independence, the two service institutions, known as the Steel Framework, were retained and managed as All-Pakistan Services; the political consensus developed at Provincial Premiers' Conference, chaired by the late Prime Minister on 27 December 1949, endorsed that decision. Later, the new regulatory frameworks for these two services were determined after extensive consultations with the approval of the Federal Cabinet.

Legal instruments were notified, containing procedural details and principles on management of services, in terms of relevant constitutional agreements and provisions. These were cited as the CSP (Composition and Cadre) Rules 1954 and the PPS (Composition, Cadre and Seniority) Rules 1969; Acts XXI of 1965 and XVI of 1967 were enacted to regulate unique functional requirements of the CSP and dully sanctified the nomenclature of the service besides determination of post-sharing formulae; of these, the 1965 Act was framed on the recommendations of the High Courts, the Supreme Court and the federating units. The substantive covenants of the inter-provincial agreements were added to avoid inter-provincial complaints with additional and specific substantive functions to the FPSC.

1. The number of posts and their nomenclatures were determined; the description of posts reflected the regulatory functions assignable to the service members under various provincial and federal laws.
2. The posts for appointments through initial recruitments, promotions and transfers were specified and delineated in addition to

posts reserved for deputation, training and leave; these were not to be varied, to avoid ad hocism or patronage.

3. Provincial representation was made proportionate to the number of posts on respective provincial cadres.

4. The Pakistan Public Service Commission was designated as the sole/neutral agency to make recommendations for appointments after country-wide open competition for initial recruitment, holding examinations before termination of probations, determination of principles for promotion and appointments by transfer from the Bar, PCS or Armed Forces and in disciplinary matters. Appointments from the Provincial Services, encadrement of officers from Provincial Service Commission (PCS) (Executive) and PCS (Judicial) Branches, Provincial Police and selections from the Bar on the recommendation of the High Courts for appointments against specified posts and inductions from the Armed Forces, all required the Commission's positive endorsement for approval of appointments by the president. Successive constitutions—1956, 1962, 1972 and 1973—sustained and sanctified these agreements.[31]

In this regard, special note may be taken of the decisions unfolded by self-regulatory organisations (SROs) issued by the federal government on 21 August 1973. Through these SROs the Commission's contractual consultations were dispensed with, without consulting the contracting federating units, with respect to initial appointments to CSP, an All-Pakistan Service, at every level by substituting Rule 3 of the 1954 agreement by aforementioned SROs dated 21 August and 15 September 1973 under Section 25 of the Civil Servants Act 1973, irrelevant ab initio, with respect to structure of a constitutionally sanctified service institution. Creation, abolition or merger of All-Pakistan Services or changes in nomenclature through OM-based instruments have disregarded substantive inter-provincial covenants. Therefore, the FPSC Ordinance 1973 has incorporated statutory duties as an obligatory management practice. These also disregarded President's Order IV of 1975 which adapted Act XXI of 1965 besides Act XVI of 1967 (later repealed in 1980) which sanctified the nomenclature of the CSP and regulated covenants regarding sharing of federal and provincial posts amongst various services and sources.

In due course, constitutional and statutory distinction between 'All-Pakistan Service' institutions, 'Services of the Federation' and 'Provincial Services' disappeared in practice, notwithstanding distinct legal sanctions for management of those service institutions.

Leaving aside the legal safeguards, the FPSC has continued to enjoy unqualified public trust and confidence in its transparent and professional contributions throughout its existence, by way of merit-based recommendations for initial appointments in public service and posts. Due regard was given to representation of federating units, and with respect to matters regarding promotions and principles of transfers from one service to another, disciplinary matters and payment of litigation expenses. The Commission continued its advisory inputs for formulating departmental rules/regulations for all departmental posts, from lowest to the top management cadres by methods of and qualifications for appointments from various sources specified by it. These were intended to strengthen good governance. Thus conceived and nurtured, the Commission's advice was valued by the executive in all matters impinging on the personnel management, having bearing on substantive and procedural aspects of public service in general. As a neutral forum, it contributed to fair compliance in enforcing the terms and conditions of public servants, as guaranteed by the successive constitutions of 1956, 1962 and 1972.

The Commission was neither designed nor perceived as a mere apolitical recruitment agency, or limited to work as an advisory body; it had a substantial role to perform for quality consideration with respect to elements that composed various streams of public service, at every stage of career progression of the individual employee, as a team player. As stakeholder, assured job security for permanent members of public service institutions may not be sufficient per se for many, but it was a necessary precondition for own health of the state, especially as wages did not strictly match the needs and aspirations of its employees. While independence of the Commission, as a constitutional organ, had to be and was indeed meticulously preserved, maintained and sustained by men of integrity and character who were assigned to it from time to time, as its custodians for all seasons and all reasons, those who designed its statutory charters, from 1973 onwards or varied as expedient, did not comprehend these dimensions of good governance, in their entirety.

Annex 14.1

Constitution of the Islamic Republic of Pakistan, 1973
(As amended till 31 January 2011)

Article 242, Public Service Commission: (1) Majlis-e-Shoora (Parliament) in relation to the affairs of the Federation, and the Provincial Assembly of a Province in relation to the affairs of the Province, may, by law, provide for the establishment and constitution of a Public Service Commission.

(1A) The Chairman of the Public service commission constituted in relation to the affairs of the Federation shall be appointed by the President on the advice of the Prime Minister

(1B) The Chairman of the Public service commission constituted in relation to the affairs of a Province shall be appointed by the Governor on the advice of the Chief Minister

(2) Public Service Commission shall perform such Functions as may be prescribed by law'
Federal Public Service Commission Ordinance 1977 (Ordinance XLV of 1977)

Note: As amended till 2007 and the terms of office of chairman and members are now modified as per this amendment.

Annex 14.2

Recruitment Procedures for Selections in Superior Services

Recruitment to the Superior Services in Pakistan is made through an *'Open Competitive Examination'* held for following Occupational Groups and Services, subject to availability of vacancies in BPS 17 conveyed by the Government:

1. Commerce and Trade Group
2. Customs and Excise Group
3. District Management Group
4. Foreign Service of Pakistan

5. Inland Revenue Service
6. Information Group
7. Military Lands and Cantonment Group
8. Office Management Group
9. Pakistan Audit and Accounts Service
10. Police Service of Pakistan
11. Postal Group
12. Railways (Commercial and Transportation) Group

The competitive examination is open and fair and carries credibility for domicile based-merit selections by Federal Public Service Commission (FPSC) known as an impartial apolitical agency.

Regional Quotas

The vacancies are distributed among various regions according to the following quota reservations

No.		Percentage
1.	Merit	7.5
2.	Punjab (including Federal area of Islamabad)	50.0
3.	Sindh	19.0
	The share of Sindh is further divided in the following ratio:	
	a) Urban Areas (Karachi, Hyderabad, Sukkur) 40.0	7.6
	b) Rural Areas 60.0	11.4
4.	Khyber Pakhtunkhwa (Formerly NWFP)	11.5
5.	Balochistan	6.0
6.	Gilgit-Baltistan and Federally Administered Tribal Areas	4.0
7.	Azad Jammu and Kashmir	2.0
	Total	100

10 per cent and 5 per cent vacancies for **women** and **minorities** are reserved on merit respectively in each service/group in addition to their participation in open competition against overall provincial/regional quota.

Annual Competitive Examination

The Examination comprises four parts:

1. Written Examination
2. Medical Test
3. Psychological Assessment
4. Viva Voce/Interview

The written examination carries 1200 marks—600 for compulsory subject and 600 for optional subjects. Compulsory subjects in which every candidate has to appear include Essay in English (100), English Précis and Composition (100), three papers of General Knowledge—Everyday Science (100), Current Affairs (100) and Pakistan Affairs (100)—and Islamiyat (100). A non-Muslim has the option to appear in Islamiyat. If he does not want to take up Islamiyat, his Pakistan Affairs paper is treated as carrying 200 marks and half the marks secured in that paper are counted in lieu of Islamiyat.

There are forty optional subjects carrying 100 or 200 marks each. These subjects are arranged in nine groups. A candidate has to select three or more subjects carrying a total of 600 marks in such a way that those selected from any one group do not carry more than 200 marks.

There are restrictions on combining Business Administration with Public Administration, International Law with International Relation and Urdu with any Regional Language (Sindhi, Pashto, Punjabi and Balochi). Question papers in optional subjects are set at a minimum standard of an Honours Degree of a university in Pakistan. The language for the examination is English. However, papers of Urdu, regional languages, Arabic and Persian can be written in Urdu/English or the respective language. Islamiyat paper can be attempted in Urdu or English.

A candidate who:

Fails to secure 40 per cent marks in any compulsory subject or 50 per cent marks in aggregate fails to qualify; less than 33 per cent marks in any optional subject are given no credit for that subject.

Qualifies the written examination are required to appear before a Medical Board for medical examination to ensure that they, except the disabled candidates, are free from any physical or mental disability likely to interfere with the performance of their job; and

Pass the written examination are called for a psychological test comprising a paper and pencil test, group tasks and an interview with a psychologist except those who were earlier allocated to another group and wish to reappear. The objective of the psychological test is assessment of candidate's 'abilities, attitudes and personality characteristics with special regard to his aptitude' for civil service. Psychological test does not carry any marks but a report on each candidate is written by the psychologist which is placed before panels of Commission's Members for final interview.

After the psychological test, the candidates are interviewed by a panel of FPSC Chairman and Members to assess their suitability for various civil services. In doing so, the panel avowedly attaches 'particular importance to the moral and ethical qualities of the candidate, his/her intelligence and mental alertness, his/her vigour and strength of character and his/her potential qualities of leadership'. Extra curricular activities such as sports, debates, hobbies, Etc. are taken into account. The interview carries 300 marks; anyone securing less than 100 marks fails and renders himself ineligible for selection.

A merit list is finally prepared on the basis of aggregate marks secured by each candidate in the written examination and viva voce. FPSC allocates successful candidates to various services/groups on the basis of the candidate's position on the merit list, keeping in view his preferences and provincial/regional quotas. The recommendations are sent to the Establishment Division for appointments by respective appointing authorities.

Source: Curriculum and Research Wing, FPSC Secretariat, Islamabad.

Notes

1. PLD 1992 SC 646 Re: Kh. Tariq Rahim.
2. The Constitution Commission Report, Rawalpindi: 1960: Chapter XI.
3. The East India Company Acts 1780 and 1797 (211 Geo 3, c. 70 and 37 Geo 3, c. 142).
4. Governor General's Order 22 of 1947.
5. Government of India Act 1935 (26 Geo 5, c. 2).
6. The Basic Principles Committee Report submitted to the Constituent Assembly of Pakistan on 12 March 1949: Chapter II in part IX.
7. Constitutions of Islamic Republic of Pakistan:
   (a) 1956: Part X, Chapter II Articles 184–90 read with Articles 127 and 224.
   (b) 1962: Part VIII, Chapter 2, Articles 180–90 read with Articles 4, 143 and 225.
   (c) 1972: Part IX, Chapter 2, Articles 223–33 read with Articles 3, 147 and 280.
   (d) 1973: Part XII, Chapter 1, Article 242 read with articles 4, 146 and 268.
8. The Federal Public Service Commission Act, 1973.
9. Constitution of the Islamic Republic of Pakistan 1973: Article 242.
10. Government of India Act 1935 (26 Geo 5, c. 2).
11. Jinnah's Evidence before the Islington Commission: Minutes of Evidences in Parliamentary papers 1914, India Office Record vol. 22 col. 7294

quoted as Appendix III in Riaz Ahmed's 'Quaid-e-Azam as Magistrate', Islamabad (1984).

12. The Government of India (Statutory Commissions) Act 1927 (17 and 18 Geo 5, c. 24).
13. Government of India Act 1935 (26 Geo 5, c. 2): Clause (3) of Section 266 (3).
14. Ibid., Sections 266 and 267.
15. Governor General's Order 22 of 1947.
16. Ibid.
17. The FPSC (Amendment) Ordinance 2005.
18. Governor General's Order 22 of 1947.
19. The Federal Public Service Commission Act, 1973.
20. Constitution of the Islamic Republic of Pakistan 1973: Article 242.
21. ESTACODE Establishment Division, Edition 2007: Volume II, Chapter 8 (pp. 599–674).
22. The FPSC Ordinance (No. XLV of 1977) 1977.
23. The FPSC (Amendment) Ordinance 1980.
24. Revival of Constitution (P.O. 14 of 1985): Clause (1A) inserted in Article 242.
25. The Constitution (18th Amendment) Act 2010: Substituted clause (1B) in Article 242.
26. The Civil Servants (Amendment) Ordinance 2001: Insertions/additions in Section 9 of Ordinance No. XXXII of 2002.
27. Ibid.
28. The FPSC Ordinances 2009 and 2010, since lapsed.
29. The Constitutions of Islamic Republic of Pakistan: 1947, 1956, 1962, 1972 and 1973.
30. Ibid.; 1973 Constitution: Articles 4, 146, 240 (Explanation), 241, 260 and 268, Act XXI of 1965 adapted by PO 4 of 1975 and Act XVI of 1967 since repealed in 1980.
31. (a) Cabinet Secretariat (Establishment Division) Notification No. F.25/12/5 I-SEI dated 21 June 1954: Civil Service of Pakistan (Composition and Cadre) Rules 1954 notified under Section 241 of the 1935 Act. These rules were amended in 1966 with consensus of federating units vide SRO 546(k)/66 dated 8 June 1966, and later without consensus in 1973 by SRO No. 1237 (I) dated 21 August 1973, ESTACODE: 2007 Edition, Volume I (pp. 584–85); and
    (b) Ministry of Interior, Home Division, letter no. 10/1/50-Police dated 11 March 1950 that gave effect to December 1949 Inter-Provincial Agreement and Federal Cabinet Resolution of January 1950; in 1962, the service management was assigned to Establishment Division that notified Police Service of Pakistan (Composition, Cadre and Seniority) Rules 1969 under Provisional Constitution of 1969 since repealed by Police Service of Pakistan (Composition and Cadre) Rules 1985 notified under Section 25 of the Civil Servants Act 1973 read with That Division's OM No. 3/2/75/-ARC dated 31 May 1975.

Reference

Husain, Agha Iftikhar. 1992. *Civil Service in Pakistan.* Islamabad: Pakistan Public Administrative Research Centre.

15

Functioning of Royal Bhutan Service Commission

Pirthiman Pradhan*

Introduction

Bhutan launched its 1st Five Year Plan in 1961, abandoning its age old policy of self-imposed isolation. Since then the country has seen unprecedented achievements in socio-economic development. Bhutan entered into a democratic constitutional monarchical form of government from 2008. The Parliament, consisting of the king, National Council and National Assembly, is the highest law-making body. The king is the head of state and the government is represented by Lhengye Zhungtshog (Cabinet), headed by the PM.

Bhutan's development is guided by the philosophy of Gross National Happiness (GNH) which is based on four key pillars: (a) sustainable and equitable socio-economic development, (b) conservation of natural environment, (c) preservation and promotion of culture and spiritual heritage and (d) good governance.

Pursuing the GNH pathway, particularly its fourth pillar of good governance, HR development has been always accorded high priority by the Royal Government with the full conviction that human capital is crucial in materialising and sustaining the socio-economic development goals.

---

* Member, Royal Civil Service Commission, Royal Government of Bhutan.

'Bhutan 2020: A Vision for Peace, Prosperity and Happiness' believes in developing the latent potential of every individual to meaningfully participate in the development of the nation. The vision also envisages developing a long-term HRD perspective plan, providing enabling environment to achieve full and innate potential for all its citizens, strengthening existing institutions and creating new ones, effective integration of moral and ethical values in the learning process and development of required knowledge and skills for the emerging economy.

The 10th Five Year (2008–13) Civil Service Human Resource Master Plan aims to effectively integrate and align human resources of the country to the emerging development needs of the country with focus on to enhance productivity and professionalism, improving quality and coverage of education and training, and creation of employment opportunities.

The Royal Civil Service Commission (RCSC), along with the Royal Audit Authority (RAA), Anti-corruption Commission (ACC) and Election Commission of Bhutan (ECB), is a constitutional body entrusted with planning and implementation of all HR activities for the civil service agencies. The Commission was established in 1982 under the Royal Charter as an independent personnel agency of the government. Since then, the RCSC has been responsible for the HR plan for the civil service agencies, along with personnel policies and administration as entrusted under the Royal Charter 1982.

The Civil Service of Bhutan has evolved over the last 50 years. It has grown over the period in terms of strength as well as professional competence. The civil service management began truly with the personnel administration principles and practices. Today the modern principles and practices are increasingly adopted for managing the civil service of the country. The necessity has arisen from the cognizance that without a competent civil service, the country would find it difficult in formulating policies and strategies and successfully implementing programmes and projects, and above all in sustaining growth and development. In these contexts, improving the efficiency of the civil service has always been the most important governance issue.

The challenges have become more complex with changing environments and challenges which needs dynamic response. For these reasons, the reforms in the civil service of Bhutan have been a continuous process.

History of the Commission

At that time when Bhutan launched its 1st Five Year Plan in 1961, the respective agencies had the authority to recruit, place and promote its employees. In 1973, the Department of Manpower was established under the Ministry of Development responsible for civil service personnel administration across the government.

As the civil service personnel administration became more complex, the Royal Government recognised the need to have a strong central personnel agency with clear mandate. Thus, under the Royal Charter, the RCSC was established in June 1982. The Royal Charter mandated the RCSC to ensure uniformity of personnel actions in the civil service throughout the kingdom as the central personnel agency of the Royal Government of Bhutan (RGoB). Accordingly, the then Department of Manpower was upgraded to the RCSC Secretariat headed by a secretary. The Royal Charter required that the chairman of the Commission submits annual report of the Commission to His Majesty the King.

The Royal Charter of the RCSC indeed marked the beginning of a planned and coordinated approach in addressing human resource management and development needs of the country. The Royal Charter formed the fundamental legal framework for the RCSC in managing and framing rules of the civil service.

In July 1982, a 16-member commission was instituted, chaired by the representative of His Majesty the King to the Ministry of Development. The members of the commission were the government ministers, including the chief of the Royal Bhutan Army, chief of judiciary, chairman and members of the Royal Advisory Council, and secretary of RCSC Secretariat as member secretary.

In April 1991, the commission was reconstituted. The commission had nine members, including all government ministers, chairman of the Royal Advisory Council, auditor general and secretary of RCSC Secretariat as member secretary. The chairmanship was to be rotated among six government ministers in every six months.

In October 1996, the commission was reconstituted for the second time with 15 members. This time, four government secretaries were included in the composition alongside eight government ministers, chairman of the Royal Advisory Council, auditor general and secretary of RCSC Secretariat as member secretary. In August 1998, the commission was reconstituted for the third time with exclusion of government secretaries from the composition of the commission.

In October 2003, the National Assembly resolved that the RCSC be reconstituted and strengthened to protect politicisation of the bureaucracy. It was resolved that the RCSC should represent all the three branches of the government under a chairman to be appointed by His Majesty the King. Accordingly, all government ministers relinquished from the membership of the RCSC. A new seven member commission was then reconstituted with government secretaries and senior civil servants at executive positions as members and the secretary of the RCSC Secretariat as member secretary.

On 18 July 2008, the Constitution of the Kingdom of Bhutan was adopted. Section 2 of Article 26 of the Constitution says:

> The Commission shall consist of a Chairperson and four members appointed by the Druk Gyalpo from among eminent persons having such qualifications and experience as would enhance the performance of the Commission, from the list of names recommended jointly by the Prime Minister, the Chief Justice of Bhutan, the Speaker, the Chairperson of the National Council and the Leader of the Opposition Party.

As per the provisions of the Constitution, a full-time commission with a chairperson and four Commissioners was appointed by His Majesty the King in January 2009.

Roles and Functions of the Commission

The Royal Charter 1982, Chapter 5, Section 5.01 says; 'The Commission shall have the powers to formulate, review and ensure implementation of all personnel policies, rules and regulations and actions of the Civil Services as provided in this Charter.' Accordingly, policy-making functions and responsibilities, rule-making functions and responsibilities, and executive functions and responsibilities were elaborated in chapters seven, eight and nine of the Charter, respectively.

Bound by the prescribed functions and responsibilities, the RCSC continued to exercise as truly central personnel agencies of the government, which determined the HR strength of agencies, executed training of civil servants and remained responsible for recruitments, promotion, separation and disciplinary action. On this ground RCSC has been unique in its feature as every facet of civil service was centralised at RCSC.

The ground rule for governance of the Civil Service of Bhutan is provided by the Bhutan Civil Service Rules and Regulations (BCSR). Guided by the Royal Charter 1982, the RCSC initiated the process of amending the existing rules and regulations and enunciation of new ones wherever required in the year 1987. The process culminated with the publication of the first edition of BCSR in 1990. Subsequently, the BCSR was revised in the year 2002, 2006 and 2010. The BCSR 2010 was the first edition of the BCSR in post-Constitution era of Bhutan.

The RCSC initiated the process of decentralisation of civil service management in the year 2006. In 2007, the recruitment in the operational position category and in 2008 the recruitment in supervisory and support position category, and promotion up to second highest position of professional and management position category were decentralised.

Also in 2008, the authority to approve and execute the short-term training defined as six months and below, both formal and informal, were decentralised. In 2010, the promotion to the top position of the professional and management position category earlier retained with RCSC was also decentralised.

For effective management of decentralised HR actions, HR committees are instituted at each agency level, as a shadow organisation, to ensure all decentralised HR actions are taken as per the BCSR to eliminate all forms of nepotism.

The Constitution of the Kingdom of Bhutan, adopted in 2008, restated the roles and functions of the RCSC. Article 26, Section 1 states: 'There shall be a Royal Civil Service Commission, which shall promote and ensure an independent and apolitical civil service that shall discharge its public duties in an efficient, transparent and accountable manner.'

While Section 8 states: 'The Commission shall meet regularly and shall be supported by a permanent Secretariat, which shall function as the central personnel agency of the Government.' These two provisions of the Constitution largely define the roles and functions of the RCSC.

The provisions of the Constitution have been reinforced in the Civil Service Bill of Bhutan 2010, passed by the two houses of the Parliament, which says; 'The Commission shall be independent in the exercise of its power and duties under this act and shall exercise such powers and duties without fear, favour or prejudice in the interest of ensuring effective and efficient administration of the Civil Service.' As per the Bill some of the specific functions of the Commission are:

1. Prescribe, amend and enforce rules and regulations
2. Promulgate policies, standards and guidelines for the civil service and adopt plans and programmes in consultation with the agencies
3. Formulate, administer and evaluate programmes pertaining to the development and retention of qualified and competent work force in the civil service
4. Promote and maintain the highest level of prestige, morale and well-being of the civil service
5. Conduct periodic HR auditing across all agencies and special investigation on HR actions, where necessary
6. Ensure establishment of a HR committee in each agency with standard functions and responsibilities to ensure proper personnel administration and HR development and monitor their functions
7. Manage civil service selection examination
8. Maintain up-to-date personnel information as prescribed in the BCSR
9. With the decentralisation of a number of HR management functions, there has been a major shift in the roles and responsibilities of the RCSC. Prior to the reform process initiated in 2005, the Civil Service of Bhutan was among some of the absolute centralised systems. Today the Civil Service of Bhutan is largely a decentralised system. The RCSC, however, requires all decentralised HR actions be taken in accordance to the Civil Service Bill and BCSR.

The Constitution requires the Commission submits annual report on its policies and performances to His Majesty the King and the PM.

The Structure of the Commission

The organisational structure of the RCSC in its current state is as presented in Figure 15.1.

The Commission is supported by a permanent Secretariat as per the provision of the Constitution. The architect of the structure has been determined keeping in view the national policy of having 'small, compact and efficient' civil service, which is being exercised in determining the growth in civil service.

The Structure of the Civil Service

The structure of the Civil Service of Bhutan currently has a hierarchy of four discrete position categories: the operational, supervisory and support, professional and management, and executive and specialist position categories (Figure 15.2). Within each position category there is a hierarchy of position levels.

Composition of the Civil Service

The strength of civil service as on 31 December 2010 was 22,512, comprising 21,639 regular civil servants and 873 on contract. During the 10th Five Year Plan (July 2008 to June 2013), based on the figures as at 1 July 2008 and 31 December 2010, there was a growth of 15.35 per cent.

Since the year 2000, there has been a near linear growth in the civil service strength (Figure 15.3). As of 31 December 2010, there were 54.64 per cent civil servants under the Dzongkhag (district) Administration and Thromde (local governments) while the rests were with central ministries and agencies.

The civil service constitutes 3.24 per cent of the total population of the country and 6.78 per cent of the economically active labour force.

Figure 15.1
Organisation Structure of the RCSC

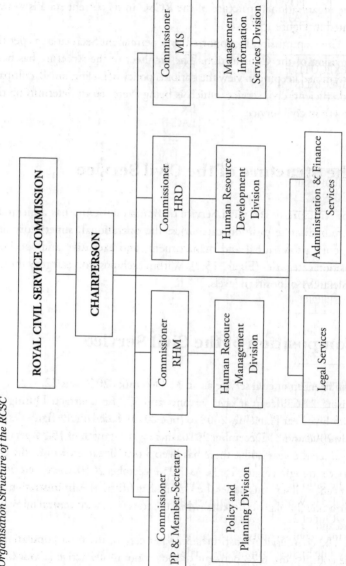

Source: Author.

Figure 15.2

Civil Service Structure

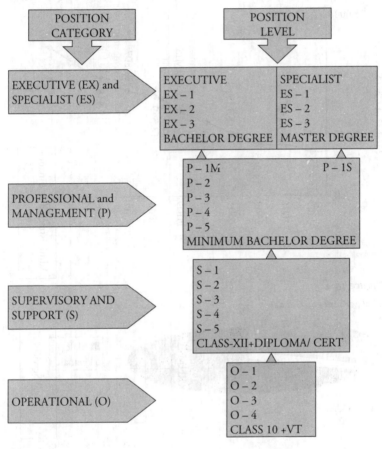

Source: Author.

The ratio of civil servants strength to total population stands at a ratio of 1:31. Women constitute 31.36 per cent of the civil service strength.

Out of 22,512 civil servants as of 31 December 2010, there were 7,059 female civil servants constituting 31.36 per cent (Figure 15.4).

The highest number of female civil servants was in the Education and Training Services and it was followed by the General Administration and

Figure 15.3

Civil Service Staffing Trend

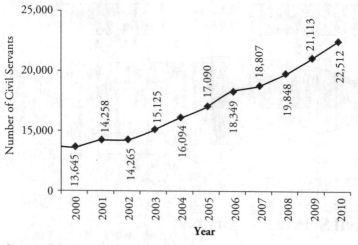

Figure 15.4

Civil Servants by Gender

Support Services, and Medical Services. The statistics indicate that it will take some time to have relatively equal number of male and female civil servants, as there is still a significant gap at the entry levels.

As of 31 December 2010, the Professional and Management Position Category constituted 49.33 per cent of the total civil service strength, followed by Supervisory and Support Position Category with 40.40 per cent, Operational Position Category with 9.08 per cent, Executive Position Category with 0.81 per cent and Specialist Position Category with 0.39 (Figure 15.5).

Figure 15.5

Civil Servants by Position Category

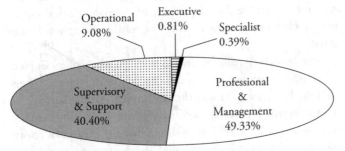

Source: Author.

Civil Service Reforms

In 1989, the RCSC adopted the cadre system and classified the civil service occupations into eight cadres with a hierarchy of 17 grades, and defined the entry qualification and entry grade for each cadre.

The reform initiated in 1980s focused 'cutting-down-to size', primarily through job reduction and retrenchment of non-performing civil servants. This was followed by the next phase in early 1990s with a broader range of reforms aimed at having merit-based civil service governed by BCSR.

In 1999, the government undertook a good governance initiative. The specific recommendations of the initiative to the RCSC were to reinforce merit-based career progression and expedite job classification. This recommendation was reinforced by the good governance plus initiative in 2005. On this line, the RCSC initiated a major reform in 2005 and replaced the cadre system introduced in the year 1989 with the position-based system. However, the civil service continues to be a 'closed system' as there is no lateral entry as in case of typical position-based system.

The reform was driven by the need to have a more responsive, efficient, ethical and apolitical civil services for a democratic Bhutan. The ultimate goal of the reform was to have a 'merit-based civil service' that dissociates from politicisation and provide desired stability and continuity across governments of different political philosophies.

The reform brought multiple changes in a short period of time which was found insufficient for communicating and convincing the agencies about the reform. Because the adaptability of the system could not be ascertained in advance a long process of fine tuning and review had to be expedited.

The reform strongly signalled the needs to affirm adaptability and sensitivity of the reform in advance. The stakeholders must own the change process and the full concurrence of the government, particularly on the financial implications, is necessary before the reform is actually launched.

The lessons learnt from reforms indicate that the process of reform have to be simple and progressive although the desire to adopt the most advance innovations in civil service management, devised by the developed countries, is natural.

The Royal Civil Service

The high government investment in civil service personnel has necessitated the Civil Service of Bhutan to remain competent and relevant. The civil service is expected to have the capacity to foresee the emerging challenges and address them effectively and efficiently.

With the democratic system of governance embraced in 2008, it became necessary to have a non-partisan civil service to protect the civil service from leaning to any of the political parties or from garnering patronage over its independence. The change in governance required to further strengthen the merit-based civil service system with strong values and code of ethics.

Recruitment

All recruitments are based on merit through open competition. The RCSC initiated the process of decentralisation of civil service recruitment in the year 2006. In 2007, the recruitment to operational position category was decentralised up Dzongkhag (district) and autonomous agency level, while in 2008, the recruitment up to supervisory and support position category was decentralised up to ministries and central government agencies.

In 2010, the in-service recruitment to the top position of the professional and management category too was decentralised to the ministries and central government agencies. Now the ministries and agencies can recruit for the positions in compliance with the BCSR.

For all fresh recruitments, the RCSC allocates the employment ID number without which the employment is illegal. By doing so, the RCSC ensures that the recruitment is within the approved staff strength.

As on date the RCSC recruits university graduates in professional and management position category through BCSE and it remains a major task. Also the in-service recruitment in the executive position category through open competition continues to be the primary responsibility of the RCSC.

The process of in-service recruitment in the executive position and top position of professional and management position categories involves written examination, panel interview, performance rating for last three years, and feedback from the immediate subordinates on leadership attributes.

At the agency level, the HR committees have the delegated authorities to conduct decentralised recruitments while at RCSC, the Commission members, including the head of the agency for which the executive candidate is being selected, makes the quorum of the selection panel. The HR committees at the agency level has also have the delegated authority to act as disciplinary committee.

Classification of Civil Service Occupation

To date the Civil Service of Bhutan has 19 major occupational groups and 94 subgroups. For example, the medical service is a major occupational group and it is further divided into eight occupational subgroups along the disciplinary lines.

The 'Civil Service Position Directory' of the BCSR defines the position category for each of the 94 occupational sub-groups. Also the position directory defines the entry level and entry qualification, and also the scope of career progression with the entry qualification within the 'broad banded positions' in every position category.

This new system of classifying the civil service occupation has enabled RCSC to have a better means to plan and manage the civil Service. It has become easier to have occupational standards, competency framework, career progression and succession plan, training need analysis and development at the smallest occupational unit and civil service establishment control with higher level of precision.

Selection of Senior Executives

To be in the executive position category one has to come through three successive stages of selection over a span of one's career. In the old cadre system, a civil servant, as experience is gained, continued to progress in the career path and occupy senior executive positions in the government. The seniority used to play a dominant role in career progression.

In today's scenario, the university graduates join the civil service at professional and management position category through BCSE. The graduates, besides technical graduates, are required to undergo a one year pre-service training before joining the civil service.

These civil servants as they progress in their career path are required to compete for top managerial position of professional and management position category through open competition. The candidates are selected through written examination and panel interview. Their performance ratings are credited as part of panel interview.

In the third stage, the candidates for executive positions are selected from those civil servants who have gained sufficient experience in the top position of the professional and management position category. The candidates are again selected through open competition and are required to appear for written examination and panel interview. Their performance ratings and also the feedback from fellow colleagues are credited in the process of selection.

It is also viewed important to credit specific in-service professional training in the process of in-service recruitment to the executive positions.

The RCSC feels this unique successive selection procedure crediting their performance rating, professional training, experience and confirmation of leadership qualities is a sound practice and working well in Bhutan.

Appraisal System

With the BCSR 2002, the RCSC introduced the rating scale method of appraisal using the scale of 1 to 5. The scope of appraisal was categorised into job performance attributes with scoring weightage of 60 per cent and job behavioural attributes with 40 per cent. The important advantage of it was easy to use and understand.

In 2005, the RCSC further molded the appraisal system with much rigour using the scale of 0 to 4 with biannual appraisal cycle. However, the BCSR 2010 reinstated the annual appraisal cycle from pragmatic point of view.

In the current appraisal system, provision has been made for the immediate supervisor and manager to comment on performance and core competencies. Thus the subjective method has been integrated to the empirical method of appraisal.

Also the BCSR 2010 requires the HR committee to review the ratings of the supervisor and managers to rule out both positive and negative link between the appraisers and appraisee. Further the feedback from the immediate subordinates made mandatory for top position holders of professional and management position category and executive position holders has added the essence to the performance appraisal system.

HR Development

During 9th Five Year Plan (2004–08), Bhutan spent 1.736 per cent of the plan outlay on HR development. For 10th Five Year Plan (2008–13), budget allocation for HR development in the civil service is 2.95 per cent of the plan out lay.

The RCSC has categorised HR development into pre-service and in-service training. For non-technical graduates selected through BCSE for professional and management position category, the one year pre-service training is mandatory. The pre-service training leads postgraduate diploma in the fields of Public Administration, Financial Management, Education, and National Law. This is made mandatory to ensure that new recruits are properly inducted into the civil service with appropriate professional knowledge, skills and competence.

Increasingly there has been a quest to have specific pre-service training for occupational groups such as procurement and similar others which are vulnerable to corruption including internal audit justified by the competency requirement of those specific occupational groups.

The in-service training is guided by the gap in competence as reflected in the 10th Five Year Plan (2008–13) HR Master Plan and selection is done through open competition exercising the merit principle. The in-service training provides opportunity to meet the minimum qualification requirement identified in the civil service position directory necessary for career progression.

In 2008, the authority to approve and execute the short term training was decentralised to the agencies. The RCSC remains responsible for planning and executing long-term training. The long-term training continues to be the primary mandate of the RCSC. However, for sound HR development, having the competency framework for each occupational group supported by career progression and succession plans continues to be a challenge.

Efficiency

The answer for efficiency is often exclusively sought within the boundary of HR management, while the answer lies on something else. The efficiency in the dynamic environment is also determined by the structural architect of the organisation. However, re-structuring and right sizing the civil service through organisation development exercise is rarely considered important.

Responding to the calls for greater accountability and efficiency, the RGoB used the instrument of programme agreement in the 9th Five Year Plan, for accomplishing the set targets as a public sector management tool. In the 10th Five Year Plan, the RGoB applied 'performance agreements' in full scale across the government agencies. These instruments are expected to provide desired autonomy and authority as practicable to the managers nearest to where result is produced thus the efficiency at the system level would be realised.

Often doing too many things by civil servants also has been highlighted as the cause of inefficiency. The RCSC has been making its effort for outsourcing plausible development functions. This would let civil service for providing platform for private sector for public service delivery and concentrate on executing specific government functions that cannot be outsourced or privatised, and for provision of regulatory services.

Ethics and Integrity

In managing ethics and integrity in the civil service, the Civil Service Code of Conducts and Ethics comes in the forefront requiring compliance with laws, rules and procedures and the need for upholding integrity at individual level.

The Civil Service Bill of Bhutan 2010 defines the conflict of interest and BCSR 2010 attempts to foster public confidence in the integrity of civil servants through

1. prohibition on engaging in trade and commercial activities which have conflict of interest,
2. asset declaration,
3. non-acceptance of gifts,
4. restriction on holding dual jobs while serving as civil servant,
5. not passing public information to private interest group, and
6. maintaining confidence of information and action potentially leading to favouritism and nepotism.

Across all notions, the RCSC is of the view that there should be strong internal control and compliance services within the civil service to ensure (a) the reliability and integrity of financial information, (b) the compliance with the laws, rules and regulations, (c) the public assets are appropriately recorded and accounted and (d) a sound control environment through effective communication promoting control consciousness among civil servants.

Motivation and Moral

The motivation and morale of civil servants emanate from the reciprocal relationship between opportunity for career progression, performance and reward. However, there is no straight jacket that fits all profession and position hierarchy. In reality, the things that are required to boost morale are the human factors that develop pride among individuals being what they are.

In Bhutan, civil service is still the major job provider. Everyone dreams to be a civil servant for it provides opportunities to upgrade both academic and professional qualifications, a career progression opportunity and, most importantly, the job security. The fledgling private sector industries are yet to convince the youths of Bhutan in the aspect of job security.

Conclusion

To be successful in managing civil service, the Civil Service Act in consonance with the Constitution, and well-laid civil service rules and regulations are the imperatives. However, the rigidity in control function has its limits beyond which greater role will have to be played by modern management practices.

The RCSC gained immense insight and experience in aligning HR strategies with the strategies of the agencies through the successive process of decentralisation. Although with decentralisation, there has emerged the challenge of monitoring and evaluation, having accurate records and information and in ensuring all HR actions are taken in compliance to the BCSR, the greater benefits have been foreseen by taking HR action at the site where actual development is taking place.

The new classification of civil service occupation has provided much easier means to plan and control the civil service establishment, identify competency gap and execute planned HR development. Since it provides a complete map of the civil service, it is easier to develop succession plan.

Much insight and experiences have been gained in recruitment procedures though open competition and in the conduct of BCSE. The process with which the senior executives are being recruited has been yielding positive impacts. The process involving three successive stages would go a long way creating impact in the Bhutan civil service system. The improvement brought in the appraisal system too is notable.

Bibliography

Aberbach J.D., R.D. Putman and B.A. Rockham. 1981. *Bureaucrats and Politicians in Western Democracies*. Massachusetts: Harvard University Press.

Adam, J. 1997. *Dilemmas of Administrative Behaviour*. Englewood Cliffs: Prentice Hall.

Albrow, Martin. 1970. *Bureaucracy*. New York: Praeger Publishers.

Appleby, Paul H. 1957. *Policy in Administration*. Alabama: University of Alabama.

Armstrong, Johns A. 1973. *The European Administrative Elite*. Princeton: Princeton University Press.

Arora, Ramesh K. (ed.). 1974. *Administrative Change in India*. Jaipur: Aalkeh Publishers.

Avasthi, A. and Ramesh K. Arora (eds). 1978. *Bureaucracy and Development: Indian Perspectives*. New Delhi: Associated Publishing House.

Banks, J.A. 1996. *The Elite in the Welfare State*. London: Faber & Faber.

Bekke, A.J.G.M., J.L. Perry and Th.A.J. Toonen (eds). 1996. *Civil Service Systems in Comprehensive Perspective*. Bloomington: Indiana University Press.

Bensman, Joseph and Bernard Rosenderg. 1963. *Mass, Class and Bureaucracy*. New Jersey: Prentice Hall.

Benz, A. and K.H. Goetz (ed.). *A New German Public Sector? Reform,Adaptation and Stability*. Dartmouth: Adershot.

Bhambhri, C.P. 1971. *Bureaucracy and Politics in India*. New Delhi: Vikas.

———. 1972. *Administrators in a Changing Society*. New Delhi: National Publishing House.

Bhattachaya, Mohit. 1979. *Bureaucracy and Development Administration*. New Delhi: Uppal.

Blan, P. 1955. *The Dynamics of Bureaucracy*. Chicago: University of Chicago Press.

Blau, Peter M. 1955. *The Dynamics of Bureaus of Bureaucracy: A Study of Interpersonal in Two Government Agencies Relations*. Chicago: University of Chicago Press.

Bonarjee, N.B. 1970. *Under Two Masters*. Calcutta: Oxford University Press.

Braibanti, Ralph (ed.). 1966. *Asian Bureaucratic Systems: Emergent from the British Imperial Tradition*. Durham: Duke University Press.

Carl, J. Friederich. 1966. *Constitutional Government and Democracy*. New Delhi: Oxford and IBH Publishing Co.

Chalam, K.S. 2010. *Deconstructing Higher Education Reforms in India*. New Delhi: Gyan Publishing House.

———. 2011. *Economic Reforms and social Exclusion*. New Delhi: SAGE Publications.

Chalam, K.S. 2011. 'Report on the Official Visit to Australian Public Service Commission', UPSC, New Delhi.

Chester, Sir D.N. 1981. *The English Administrative System 1780–1870*. Oxford: Clarendon Press.

Chaturvedi, T.N. 1979. 'Role of Administrators in Democracy', in Navinchandra Joshi (ed.), *Democracy and Human Values*. New Delhi: Sterling.

———. 1985. *Administrative Accountability*. New Delhi: Indian Institute of Public Administration.

Chettur, S.K. 1962. *The Steel Frame and I*. Bombay: Asia Publishing House.

Crozier, Michael. 1964. *The Bureaucratic Phenomena*. Chicago: University of Chicago Press.

David, T. Stanley. 1964. *The Higher Civil Service: An Evaluation of Federal Personnel Practices*. Washington, D.C.: The Brooking Institution.

Denhardt, K. 1988. *The Ethics of Public service*. Westport: Greenwood Press.

Deshmukh, C.K. 1974. *The Course of My Life*. New Delhi: Orient Longman.

Dharamvira. 1975. *Memoirs of a civil Servant*. New Delhi: Vikas.

Dimock, Marshall E. 1959. *Administrative Vitality: The Conflict with Bureaucracy*. New York: Harper & Row Publishers.

Douglas, M. 1986. *How Institutions Think*. Syracuse: Syracuse University Press.

Dube, S.C. (ed.). 1979. *Public Service and Social Responsibility*. New Delhi: Vikas.

Eldersveld, S.J., V. Jagannadham and A.P. Baraabas. 1968. *The Citizen and the Administrator in a Developing Democracy*. New Delhi: IIPA.

Francis, Francel. 2006. *India's Political Economy 1947-2004*. New Delhi: Oxford University Press.

Frazmand, A. (ed.). 1997. *Modern Systems of Government: Exploring the Role of Bureaucracy*. Thousand Oaks: SAGE Publications.

Fry, G.K. 1985. *The Changing Civil Service*. London: Allen and Unwin.

———. 1993. *Reforming the Civil Service: The Fulton Committee on the British Home Civil Service*. Edinburgh: Edinburgh University Press.

Galdden, E.N. 1956. *Civil Service or Bureaucracy*. London: Staples Press.

Getth, H.H. and Mills C.W. (eds). 1948. *From Max Weber: Essays in Sociology*. New York: Oxford University Press.

Gladden, E.N. 1945. *The Civil Service: Its Problems and Future*. London: Staples Press.

Gowala, A.D. 1952. *The Role of the Administrator: Past, Present and Future*. Pune: Goghale Institute of Politics and Economics.

Gowala, A.H. 1951. *Report on Public Administration*. New Delhi: Planning Commission.

Habermas, Jurgen. 1970. *Towards a Trditional Society*. Boston: Beacon Books.

Henry, Nicholas. 1980. *Public Administration and Public Affairs*. Englewood Cliffs: Prentice Hall.

Hummel, P. Ralph. 1977. *Bureaucratic Experience*. New York: St. Martins Press.

Jha, L.K. 1987. *Mr Red Tape*. Ahmedabed: Allied Publishers.

Kapoor, Devesh and Pratap Bhanu Mehta. 2007. *Public Institutions in India*. New Delhi: Oxford University Press.

Kast, Fremont E. and James E. Rosentweig. 1970. *Organisation and Management: A Systems Approach*. New York: McGraw Hill.

Kelsall, R.K. 1955. *Higher Civil servants in Britain*. London: Routledge.

Khanna, K.K. 1984. *Bureaucratic Blunder World: A Behavioural Profile of the Indian Bureaucracy*. New Delhi: National Publishing House.

Laski, Harold J. 1928. *Parliamentary Government in England*. London: Allen & Unwin.

Lipsky, Michael. 1980. *Street Level Bureaucracy*. New York: Russell Sage.

Maheswari, S.R. 1992. *Administrative Reform in India: Past, Present and Future Prospects*. New Delhi: Centre for policy Research.

———. 2006. *Public Administration in India*. New Delhi: Oxford University Press.

Mamnmhie, Evan. 1926. *Life in the Indian Civil Service*. London: Chapman & Hall.

Mathur, Kuldeep. 1972. *Bureaucratic Response to Development: A Study of Block Development Officers in Rajasthan*. New Delhi: National Publishing House.

Mehta, Prayag. 1989. *Bureaucracy Organizational Behavior and Development*. New Delhi: SAGE Publications.

———. 1989. *Bureaucracy as Instrument of Development*. New Delhi: SAGE Publications.

Mishra, S.N. 1986. *Panchayat Raj Bureaucracy and Rural Development*. New Delhi: Indian Institute of Public Administration.

Misra, B.B. 1970. *Administrative History of India, 1834.1974: General Administration*. London: Oxford University Press.

———. 1977. *The Bureaucracy in India Analysis of Historical Development up to 1947*. New Delhi: Oxford University Press.

———. 1986. *Government and Bureaucracy in India, 1947–76*. New Delhi: Oxford University Press.

Muthayya, B.C. and Gnanakannan I. (eds). 1973. *Developmental Personnel: A Psycho-Social Study across Three States in India*. Hyderabad: National Institute of Community Development.

Nehru, Jawaharalal. 1964. 'The Role of the Civil Servant', Jawaharlal Nehru's Speeches. New Delh: Publications Division.

North, D.C. 1990. *Institutional Change and Economic Performance*. New York: Cambridge University Press.

O'Malley, L.S.S. 1965. *The Indian Civil Service*. London: Frank Cass & Company.

Panjabi, Kewal L. (ed.). 1965. *Civil Servant in India*. Bombay: Bharatiya Vidya Bhavan.

Peters, Guy B. 1995. *The Unfinished Agenda of Civil Service Reform: Implications of the Grace Commission Report*. Washington, D.C.: The Brookings Institute.

Rai, Haridwar and S.P. Singh. 1979. *Current Ideas and Issues in Indian Administration— A Developmental Perspective*. New Delhi: Uppal Publishing House.

Rajagopalachari, C. 1955. *The Good Administrator*. New Delhi: Publications Division.

Ram, N.V.R. 1978. *Games Bureaucrats Play*. New Delhi: Vikas.

Rao, P.V.R. 1970. *Red Tape and White Cap*. New Delhi: Orient Longman.

———. 1975. *Public Servant in Modem India*. Mysore: Administmtion Training Institute.

Ray, Jayant Kumar. 1981. *Administrators in a Mixed Polity.* New Delhi: Macmillan.

Ray, Syamal Mumar. 1979. *Indian Bureaucracy at the Crossroads.* New Delhi: Sterling.

Reinhard, Bedix. 1949. *Higher Civil Servants in American Society.* Boulder: University of Colorado Press.

Rigs, Gred W. 1964. *Administration in Developing Countries.* Boston: Houghton MiMins.

Rigs, R. 1984. *Understanding Big Government: The Programme Approach.* London: SAGE Publications.

Robbins, Stephen P. 1978. *The Administrative Process.* New Delhi: Prentice-Hall of India Private Limited.

Salmon, Lord. 1976. 'Report of the Royal Commission on Standards in Public Life', HMSO, 6524, London.

Sapru, R.K. 1985. *Civil Service Administration in India.* New Delhi: Deep and Deep.

Simon, Herbert A. 1957. *Administrative Behaviour: A Study of Decision Making Processes in Administrative Organisations.* New York: Macmillan.

Singh, Narendra Kumar. 1974. 'Value Orientations of Bureaucrats in an Indian State: A Sociological analysis', in Ramesh K. Arora (ed.), *Administrative Change in India.* Jaipur: Aalekh publishers.

Sivararnan, B. 1970. *The Role of Civil Services in Administration of India.* New Delhi: Training Division, Department of Personnel.

Suleiman, Ezra. 1974. *The French Administrative Elite: Power, Politics and Bureaucracy.* Princeton: Princeton University Press.

Swerdlow, Irving (ed.). 1963. *Development Administration: Concepts and Problems.* Syracuse: Syracuse University Press.

Taub, Richard B. 1969. *Bureaucrats under Stress: Administrators and Administration in an Indian State.* Berkeley: University of California Press.

Therborn, Goran. 1980. *What Does the Ruling Class Do When It Rules?* London: Verso.

Tripathi, P.K. 1959. *Reminiscences of a Public Servant.* Cuttack: Orissa Mission Press.

Union Public Service Commission. 1976. *Golden Jubilee Souvenir.* New Delhi: UPSC.

———. 2001. *Diamond Jubilee Souvenir.* UPSC: New Delhi.

Upadhyaya, R.B. and K.C. Sharma. 1987. *Politicocracy, Bureaucracy and Technocracy in India.* Jaipur: Shashi.

Veerappa, Moily. 2008. *Second Administrative Reforms Commission Report, Tenth Report, Refurbishing of Personnel Administration-Scaling New Heights.* New Delhi: Government of India.

Webber, Marx. 1947. *The Theory of Social and Economic Organisation.* New York: Oxford University Press.

Weidner, W. 1970. *Development Administration in Asia.* Durham: Duke University Press.

Wilson, James Q. 2000. *Bureaucracy: What Government Agencies Do and Do It?* New York: Basic Books.

World Bank. 1997. *World Development Report-1997.* World Bank: Washington, D.C.

———. 1999. *Civil Service Reform: A Review of World Bank Assistance.* World Bank: Washington, D.C.

About the Editor and Contributors

Editor

K.S. Chalam is a well-known political economist and educationist, and a former member of the Union Public Service Commission (UPSC), New Delhi. He has been the Vice Chancellor of the Dravidian University in Andhra Pradesh and had taught in the Department of Economics, Andhra University, between 1976 and 2005. He is known as the founder of the Academic Staff College Scheme in the country and was its first director.

Dr Chalam was on the Planning Board of the Madhya Pradesh government during 2002–04. He was the recipient of the UGC Young Social Scientist Award in Economics in 1984. Author of *Caste-Based Reservations and Human Development in India* (2007, SAGE) and *Economic Reforms and Social Exclusion* (2011, SAGE), he has travelled widely and has participated in and chaired sessions at various international conferences.

Currently, Dr Chalam is associated with National Human Rights Commission, New Delhi, as a Special Rapporteur.

Contributors

Humera Ahmed is the Director General (DG) of West Bengal, Department of Posts, Government of India. Ahmed is an Indian Postal Service officer. She has earlier worked as the DG of Gujarat and Mumbai. A creative writer, she has published short stories in reputed weeklies and published papers on postal service in India.

Mohammad Hamid Ansari is the current Vice President of India. He is a former diplomat from the Indian Foreign Service. He was Vice Chancellor of Aligarh Muslim University and has been the Indian ambassador to United Arab Emirates, Afghanistan, Iran and Australia. He is a voracious reader and has published two books on Iran: *Traveling through Conflict: Essays on the Politics of West Asia* (authored, 2008) and *Iran Today: Twenty Five Years after the Islamic Revolution* (edited, 2005). He was awarded Padma Shri in 1984.

Sekhar Chandra is a young professional at the Planning Commission, Government of India. Chandra has been working under B.K. Chaturvedi on several research projects.

B.K. Chaturvedi is a Member of the Planning Commission, Government of India. He is a 1966 batch Indian Administrative Service officer and a former cabinet secretary. He has served as secretary in several important departments, such as HRD, Public Enterprises, and has published papers in the area of public service.

Justice Rana Bhagwandas, Chairman, Pakistan Public Service Commission, is former chief justice of Pakistan during the judicial crisis in 2007. After demitting office as chief justice, he was offered the chairman of Federal Pakistan Service Commission and in that capacity had visited India to participate in a SAARC meeting.

D. Francis is associated with the Department of Economics, Dr. B. R. Ambedkar University, Etcherla, Srikakulam, Andhra Pradesh, and has been teaching quantitative methods in the department. He received his PhD on Human Development in 1990, and has published papers in reputed journals.

Madhav Godbole is former Secretary Home, Government of India, during the P.V. Narasimha Rao government. Godbole handled the Ayodhya dispute of 1992. He is the author of the book *Unfinished Innings: Reflections of a Civil Servant*, published in 1996.

Bhure Lal is currently assisting the Supreme Court of India on environmental issues. A doctorate in economics, Lal is a former member of the UPSC. He investigated the Bofors scam as the chief of the Enforcement

Directorate. Lal is also known for his path-breaking initiative of introducing the cleaner CNG fuel in Delhi. He is the author of two published books and has delivered lectures at different forums.

Pirthiman Pradhan is a Member of Royal Civil Service Commission, Royal Government of Bhutan. He has participated and represented the Royal Bhutan Service Commission along with the chairman in the meeting of the Heads of Service Commissions held in New Delhi. He has published papers on public service.

T.S.N. Sastry is a Professor and Head of Department of Law at University of Pune, Maharashtra. He specialises in the area of good governance and social security, and has several research projects related to human rights and public service to his credit.

P.K. Saxena is a Professor of Public Administration, Rajasthan University, Jaipur. Saxena is an expert in the area of New Public Management. He is currently undertaking a research project on 'Power Sector Reforms in India' and has published widely in this area.

Parveen Talha taught in the Lucknow University from 1965 to 1969, before joining the Indian Revenue Service in 1969—the first ever Muslim woman to enter any Class I civil service through the civil services examination. She was the deputy narcotics commissioner of Uttar Pradesh, and remains till now the only woman officer to have worked in Central Bureau of Narcotics. She won the President's award in 2000 for distinguished record of service. She has also been a member of the UPSC. Talha is also a writer and has published short stories based on which a Hindi serial was televised.

N. Vittal is former Central Vigilance Commissioner of India from the 1960 IAS batch. He served as the chairman of Public Enterprises Selection Board and as secretary of the Department of Electronics and Information Technology, Government of India. He has published books on information technology, red tapism and Indian bureaucracy.

Index